PERFORMANCE AND POLITICS IN A DIGITAL POPULIST AGE

This book re-evaluates the role of performance in global politics in the face of populism and the digital mediatisation of political interactions. As political communications are increasingly conducted in online environments, 'post-truth' performances become evermore central to democratic processes. It is therefore essential to reconsider the political potency of performance and theatricality in order to effectively reinvigorate democracy in the 21st century. Drawing on Applied Theatre practices, this book shows that performance is inherently concerned with cooperative and collaborative encounters across difference, and performance might therefore support effective responses to digital populism. The analysis addresses the performative aspects of populist political movements in the United States and the United Kingdom. The chapters engage with aspects of performance and theatricality not commonly broached in Politics and International Relations scholarship, including interpersonal engagement, creative embodiment and interactive affect, making a case for the importance of these features to democratic engagement. This book resonates with recent debates regarding the relevance and treatment of Arts and Performance as IR subjects, methodologies and practices and will be of interest to scholars and students of global politics, international relations, performance studies, radical democracy and mass communication and culture.

Cami Rowe works across the disciplines of Theatre, Performance and International Politics. She holds research degrees in International Politics and Theatre and is currently Senior Lecturer in Applied and Socially Engaged Theatre at the Lancaster University Institute for the Contemporary Arts. Her research addresses the theatrical elements of global politics and the efficacy of performance interventions.

Interventions

The Series provides a forum for innovative and interdisciplinary work that engages with alternative critical, post-structural, feminist, postcolonial, psycho-analytic and cultural approaches to international relations and global politics. In our first 5 years, we have published 60 volumes.

We aim to advance understanding of the key areas in which scholars working within broad critical post-structural traditions have chosen to make their inter-ventions and to present innovative analyses of important topics. Titles in the series engage with critical thinkers in philosophy, sociology, politics and other disciplines and provide situated historical, empirical and textual studies in international politics.

We are very happy to discuss your ideas at any stage of the project: just contact us for advice or proposal guidelines. Proposals should be submitted directly to the Series Editors:

- Jenny Edkins (jennyedkins@hotmail.com) and
- Nick Vaughan-Williams (N.Vaughan-Williams@Warwick.ac.uk).

'As Michel Foucault has famously stated, "knowledge is not made for under-standing; it is made for cutting". In this spirit The Edkins – Vaughan-Williams Interventions series solicits cutting edge, critical works that challenge main-stream understandings in international relations. It is the best place to contribute post disciplinary works that think rather than merely recognize and affirm the world recycled in IR's traditional geopolitical imaginary'.

Michael J. Shapiro, University of Hawai'i at Manoa, USA

Edited by Jenny Edkins, Aberystwyth University
and Nick Vaughan-Williams, University of Warwick

Violence, Discourse and Politics in China's Uyghur Region
The Terroristization of Xinjiang
Pablo A. Rodríguez-Merino

Performance and International Relations in a Digital Populist Age
Imagining Resistance
Cami Rowe

For more information about this series, please visit: https://www.routledge.com/series/INT

PERFORMANCE AND POLITICS IN A DIGITAL POPULIST AGE

Imagining Alternatives

Cami Rowe

Routledge
Taylor & Francis Group

LONDON AND NEW YORK

First published 2023
by Routledge
4 Park Square, Milton Park, Abingdon, Oxon OX14 4RN

and by Routledge
605 Third Avenue, New York, NY 10158

Routledge is an imprint of the Taylor & Francis Group, an informa business

British Library Cataloguing-in-Publication Data
A catalogue record for this book is available from the British Library

ISBN: 978-0-367-42438-1 (hbk)
ISBN: 978-1-032-41958-9 (pbk)
ISBN: 978-0-367-82412-9 (ebk)

DOI: 10.4324/9780367824129

Typeset in Bembo
by KnowledgeWorks Global Ltd.

To Russell and The Girls.

CONTENTS

ACKNOWLEDGEMENTS

This book has taken shape over a number of years, comprising one part of a wider practice-based research project. As a result, there are a great many people who have inspired, influenced and supported me along the way.

First and foremost, I owe the greatest debt to my students, whose input over the years has been pivotal to the development of my thinking about populism, social media and performance. I have known for many years that I gain far more knowledge from my interactions with students than I could ever hope to impart to them. This includes everyone from first-year undergraduate students in a theatre studio to PhD students in research methodology seminars. The ideas in this book are squarely the product of conversations I've had with groups like this over the past several years. In particular, I want to thank students I taught on the Goldsmiths MA contextual module on Radical Performance; undergraduate students on the BA in Performance, Politics and Society at Goldsmiths; Lancaster University undergraduates studying Theatre for Social Change; and the PhD students I have had the privilege to supervise in recent years. Without these early conversations, I would never have learned so much about the unique knowledge that performance practice can bring to political contexts, nor gained such an appreciation for the robustness of theatrical practice-based inquiry.

At its core, this book is a reflection of the interdisciplinary path I have taken throughout my career. In this regard, I was privileged to work alongside colleagues at Goldsmiths College for a number of years who significantly impacted my understanding of the politics of performance. I would like to thank Osita Okagbue, Anna Furse and Göze Saner for their support, as well as Sue Mayo and Mojisola Adebayo, who collaborated with me to develop a new undergraduate curriculum that fused Applied performance and political theory. The creation of the Goldsmiths BA in Performance, Politics and Society gave me an appreciation of some of the conceptual challenges and disciplinary boundaries that complicate performance-and-politics interdisciplinarity; I continue to be inspired by the work of these colleagues and their open-hearted commitment to theatre as a tool for political change.

I am also indebted to a number of colleagues whose friendship has kept me going through a global pandemic. There are a few special women in particular who deserve mentions here for providing sympathetic ears and open arms: Thank you sincerely to my dearest Philippa Burt, Maryam Ghorbankarimi, Eleanor Kilroy and Leonie Elliot-Graves. All of you have listened more than your fair share to my sometimes unreasonably pessimistic views on the world and nudged me toward more sophisticated perspectives on media, performance and society. I am eagerly anticipating the amazing things that each of you will bring into the world in the near future.

Maryam Ghorbankirimi also played a pivotal role in the research itself, cheerfully running through the rain with a fast-decaying papier mache puppet in her arms after an anti-Trump demonstration in central London. She was one of the first volunteers to sign up for an early pilot project where the practical work was developed and evaluated. She joined Eddie Edmunds, Georgina Jackson, Patrycja Paul and Daphna Baram in generously submitting themselves to my nascent ideas and offering me vital feedback and insights early in this work.

This book would also not have been possible without the generous support from my colleagues within the Theatre Department at Lancaster University, who made it possible for me to take a research sabbatical in the midst of a global pandemic. Thank you to Tim Etchells, Karen Juers Munby, Andrew Quick and Nigel Stewart.

Finally, a personal thank you to my partner Russell. I cannot express the depth of my gratitude for the sacrifices he has made to enable this work to be completed. I am forever grateful for his support and encouragement.

INTRODUCTION

> Somewhere right now a man, woman or child is dying a violent death. Is that drama? Is death by itself a priori dramatic or do those who're dying have the responsibility, if you will, to die in an engaging way if they expect us to be moved by them. [...] The dramatic events we follow from around our country or from around the world, produced by earthquakes or wars or personal misfortune, have now become theater. Good theater. Bad theater. But theater [sic]. Our response to those events is shaped by the same principles of dramatic criticism I use when reviewing a play.
>
> *Tesich 1997, 7–8*

The quotation above from Steve Tesich's play, *Art and Leisure* illustrates the extent to which performance is implicated in digital populist, post-truth contexts; when factual realities are fervidly contested, especially in increasingly mediatised contexts, anyone seeking to highlight overlooked events or information is required to perform in an 'engaging way', so that political audiences might be effectively moved to action. This demand is only exacerbated when political interaction becomes marked by populist tendencies. Populism relies in its own way on theatrical performance, significantly more so than political interactions more generally, as it embraces a rejection of traditional political behaviours and requires an ability to appeal to unusually broad audiences. The conjunction of digital hypermediatisation and populist politics has altered the terrain of global politics, necessitating a re-evaluation of the political functions of performance.

In this vein, this book is based on an overarching belief that performance practices might provide a way of exploring encounters with others that is especially relevant for the study of global politics in the present age. This work draws on my own experience as a performance practitioner and theorist to suggest new

DOI: 10.4324/9780367824129-1

avenues of inquiry rooted in an understanding of the live, experiential elements of theatre in applied contexts. Throughout my career I have been particularly influenced by theatre practitioners whose work has been inspired by the complex and difficult intersections of political violence and performance; and populism, as I will discuss in Chapter 2, is characterised by a particular set of performance qualities which are in many ways at odds with creative practices that seek to address the roots of political conflict. Therefore, the overarching premise of this book is that we can gain insights into the operations of populist politics by reconsidering them through the practical and philosophical lenses offered by theatre practices that seek to address conflict. By holding up the performative and theatrical traits of contemporary populism against selected theatre practices, we can gain more insights into how populism operates through its unique features and deficiencies.[1]

Underpinning this agenda is my perception that the political landscape has altered significantly over the past several years, in terms of the ways that performance is implicated in political interactions – thus necessitating a reassessment of the political potential of performance. As a researcher and theatre practitioner, my career has focused primarily on the capacity for performance to challenge, disrupt and transform political debate; but given the rise of digitally mediated populist politics, I believe that the time is ripe to reinterrogate the interventionary capacities of performance, and to seek new analytical and methodological approaches that might enhance our understanding of the role of performance in global politics. The chapters within this book will investigate digital populist political interaction by interrogating its qualities of performance, including modes of participation and engagement; corporeally situated perception and relationality; and affective and aesthetic dynamics. This work focuses primarily on the political cultures of the United States and United Kingdom, both of which have experienced intense political division in recent years. I have lived and worked extensively in both of these countries, and therefore have sufficient familiarity with the particular manifestations of populism in each location. In this introductory chapter I expand on the contextual terrain of the book by examining the ways that political performance is changing in the wake of digitally mediated communications, which encourage and shape populist approaches to political interaction.

In broad terms, theatrical performance is fundamentally rooted in an encounter with difference, as audiences meet spectators and exchanges of meaning and affect are collaboratively experienced. This innate interest in exchange and negotiation might help to explain why so many influential theatre practitioners have developed their experiments in reference to their experiences of war and political violence (e.g. Augusto Boal, Bertolt Brecht, Ngugi wa Thiong'o, to name just a few). Relatedly, a wide array of scholars from multiple disciplinary backgrounds have demonstrated an interest in theatre's potential to meaningfully intervene in politics-as-usual. But it is becoming increasingly recognised that the capacity to achieve this in practice is limited by complex factors (e.g. Bishop 2012; Kershaw

1999; Rancière 2011). In earlier decades it was common for scholars to assert that virtually any performance practice has the potential to create a moment of disruptive liminality or dissensus that might lead to social transformation; however, society and politics have evolved in recent years in ways that challenge the capacity of even the most creative or radical performance to disrupt the status quo. Most pressingly, we need to give more sustained consideration to the ways that populist politics, enacted via digital media platforms, alters the role of performance in society.

The topic of populism will be covered extensively in Chapter 2; for now it is only necessary to note that recent waves of populism have emerged in the wake of financial crisis, growing wealth disparities, and the perceived failures of representative democracy. In response, populism offers an avenue for renewed political engagement by people who otherwise feel alienated or disenfranchised from the political status quo. Charismatic populist leaders – whether they emerge as sincere figureheads of grassroots political movements, or simply step forward to cynically capitalise on the sentiments of public disaffection – champion the voice of 'the people' and provide a broad umbrella under which disparate political claims can be united in opposition to elite or powerful entities. Populism can reinvigorate public participation in politics, but it can also result in confrontation and exclusion.

The challenges presented by populism have been variously articulated by scholars espousing divergent viewpoints (e.g. Canovan 2005; Gerbaudo 2017; Laclau 2005; Mouffe 2018; Mudde 2009; Müller 2016). A great deal of attention has rightfully been aimed at the global rise of right wing populism and its tendency to villainise precarious or marginal groups. However, for the purposes of this study, I am most interested in the risks that populism of all ideological stripes presents with regard to productive democratic engagement. I consider populism in relation to the broader principles of radical democracy which emphasise broadened and reinvigorated political participation by and for the people. Notably, the ability of populism to realise radical democratic goals is contested. Theorists like Chantal Mouffe call for a 'left populism' that can forge links across broad swathes of society and thus mobilise otherwise disenfranchised publics to counter the dangers of right wing populism. Others, like Cas Mudde and Jan Warner-Müller for example, are more sceptical, stressing populism's propensity to downplay important areas of internal difference and foster antagonistic attitudes toward others (Mouffe 2018; Mudde 2009; Müller 2016). I am attendant to arguments from both sides, and ultimately seek to show how performance practices might address the pitfalls of populism in order to more effectively pursue vibrant, inclusive and pluralist political engagement.

In order to make the case for this, it is essential to consider the ways that populism in the present day is frequently enacted through digitally mediated channels. When considering the potential impact of any proposed performance practice, it must first be acknowledged that it will take place within a social environment that is already saturated by theatricality and artifice. To an extent theatricality has always marked political interaction, as human society is fundamentally underpinned by our ability to present selective versions of our selves in particular contexts (Alexander et al. 2006; Goffman 1956); but it is also necessary to take a closer look at the theatrical nature of dominant modes of politics in any given context, if we are to understand the potential of alternative performance practices (Kershaw 1992). In present times, this means that we need to focus more specifically on the ways that people engage in heightened forms of theatrical presentation, driven by the central role that social media plays in politics. As political communications come to be staged online as much as or more than in person, this impacts the ways that people present themselves and experience their interactions with others.

This circumstance has not emerged suddenly; on the contrary, it is one that has been developing gradually in conjunction with the innovations of digital media throughout the 20th and 21st centuries; As the public has increasingly received political information through media that enables heightened theatrical framing (e.g. film, television and latterly, social media), their degree of cynical spectatorship has increased in parallel (Chouliaraki 2006). In many ways this is simply a continuation of the phenomenon of mediatisation described by theorists like Guy Debord and Jean Baudrillard, in reference to circumstances arising from the mid-20th century onward (Moffitt 2016). Debord, and later Baudrillard, developed their theories of the spectacle, simulacra and the hyperreal amidst advances in late-20th century technology, *viz.* the rise of colour television, 24–hour news production, infotainment, reality television, and society's increasing tendency to creatively produce and *show* simulations of itself as a chief mode of being (Baudrillard 1994; Debord 1994). These developments are often compared to the innovations of social media news sites in the present day (Sutherland 2012). However, the pervasiveness of social media as the go-to medium for political interaction poses especially troubling questions.

It is from the confluence of hypermediatisation and populism that 'digital populism' emerges (e.g. Kim 2008; Prior 2021). To some extent, this is simply an extension of the relationship between populism and mediatisation more generally; for example, it has long been recognised that the competitive market of print and television news media drives populism by highlighting unusual, disruptive or sensational content – traits that are common to populist political styles (Moffitt 2016; Prior 2021). However, populism in recent years is marked by the changing relationship between media production and consumption that digital media facilitates. In social media environments each individual is both a creator and spectator of political theatricality – we view video clips, photographs or memes, and we share them with others or make our own alternatives. Rarely have we experienced in a first-person, embodied fashion the political phenomena that inform or illustrate our opinions and that we choose to share with others. Furthermore, when we do physically participate, we often pair this participation with the production of social media content – capturing ourselves or others on handheld devices, not only with basic documentation in mind but with a conscious intent to produce affective material to be consumed by others online at a later moment. This means that much of our experience of the political is fundamentally disembodied, as our focus becomes the digital product that will be circulated *about* the experience, rather than the experience itself.

However, digital populism also has a natural affinity with political projects that seek to broaden and diversify participation in politics (Gerbaudo 2018; Margetts 2018). Because of its decentralised nature, with content generated and promoted by individuals with ostensibly equal opportunities for networking and visibility, social media platforms seem to complement radical democratic principles in their relatively horizontal structure and operation (although the veracity of such perceptions is questionable and will be addressed in later chapters). As Helder Prior describes, 'now, each individual can, by dispensing with journalistic mediation, access the public sphere, condition media agendas and topics of discussion and interact in the local and global networks of digital communication that characterize the network society' (Prior 2021, 56). Yet despite this potential, it seems that in many cases online environments exacerbate the negative tendencies of populism. The individually tailored nature of social media content, combined with the ability to remain cloaked behind the safety of a remote keyboard, means that individual users are more likely to have their existing set of values and beliefs upheld, and to communicate these beliefs confrontationally and competitively. Further insights can be gained by looking at the way that digital populism is also imbricated with the emergence of 'post-truth' politics.

As people become ever-more aware of the fact that the unseen algorithms of social media influence their perception of the world, they simultaneously increase their scepticism about others' viewpoints due to their possible basis in skewed or partial information. Thus, the digital media context of populism is enmeshed with the complications of 'post-truth' or 'post-factual' politics. Prevalent references to 'fake news', disinformation and a 'post-truth' environment have undoubtedly shaped political interactions in recent years – and it is surely no coincidence that the very term 'post-truth' was coined by a playwright, Steve Tesich, whose play was quoted at the outset of this chapter (Oxford Languages 2018; Tesich 1992, 13). Where people once spoke of 'political theatre' as a somewhat exceptional feature of political processes, it seems now to have reached a level of normalisation such that the public *expects* a certain degree of theatricality behind every political utterance or act. As a result, political communication becomes marked by heightened theatricality, accompanied by increasingly cynical spectatorship of content generated by others. Theatricality thus operates as both a covert means of gaining visibility, and a justification for suspecting or dismissing the ideas that don't conform to one's own world views. Although it would be easy to associate such tactics with the bombastic and audacious characters of particular political leaders, we should not underestimate the extent to which such attitudes pervade political interaction at all levels.

The implications of post-truth are stark when we bring performance into the frame; because information is routinely met with heightened scepticism, even when purportedly conveyed by first-person participants, the precise ways that we perform our thoughts, beliefs, and information online is paramount. To be effective in digital populist communications it is essential for individuals to convey their information through persuasive, attention-attracting means – necessitating a carefully-thought-out theatricality. This phenomenon was poignantly illustrated in Tesich's play, *Art and Leisure*. In this work, American cultural and political dilemmas are presented through the parable of main character 'Alex Chaney', a theatre critic. Chaney is unable to engage meaningfully with the world at any level – whether in personal relationships or in perceptions of global suffering – because of his overdeveloped ability to view the world for its potential to *affect* him dramatically. His skills as a theatre critic have seeped into every aspect of his existence, leaving him a detached spectator of life in search of dramatic experiences that might genuinely move him emotionally (Tesich 1997).

Although written more than two decades ago, this play resonates with our present political climate, saturated as it is with hypermediatised digital communications that compete to gain the attention of mass audiences. Here we can see the connections to our present-day, social-media-driven society: bombarded by a constant flow of mediated representations of political experience, we become less inclined to experience the political world ourselves as reality, but instead observe and critique it in the same way that a theatre critic detachedly observes the power of a performance. If sufficiently moved, we might click on a 'like' button or a sharing icon and perpetuate the flow of representations for others, and perhaps deceive ourselves that this action constitutes a genuine interaction with the world around us. This is a key component in the side-lining of genuine political engagement between individuals, promoting a team-sport approach to politics. It demonstrates just what the stakes are when we think about the role of performance in democratic politics – given the rise of populism, in conjunction with digital mediatisation, how can we make use of performance and theatricality in new and different ways in order to facilitate broad participation and reinvigorated debate, without succumbing to antagonistic conflict? This is a question that requires us to go beyond a consideration of theatre and performance as a theoretical metaphor or a logical framework, and engage more directly with its live, material and creative elements.

In the chapters that follow, I seek to interrogate the potential for performance practice to create meaningful political interventions in a digital populist context, especially by reinvigorating democratic interaction through performance practice. The chapters aim to demonstrate the notion that performance, especially when it is understood from material and experiential angles, can reawaken our attention to the circulations of power within any interaction, and thus reveal new insights about politics. I approach this task by focusing on selected aspects of political interaction, including interactive engagement, corporeal presence and modes of aesthetics and affect. These thematic areas have been selected in order to demonstrate the linkage between digital mediatisation, populism, and performance – together, they paint a picture of the ways that live, embodied performance practice might help to counterbalance some of the risks and deficiencies of digital populism.

Chapter 1 provides a discussion of recent efforts to combine Performance and Politics, especially within Politics and IR research. It establishes the political and philosophical stakes of such projects by foregrounding them against historical approaches to interdisciplinarity. This leads to an argument for greater engagement with practice-based theatre and performance epistemologies, particularly making the case for paying more attention to corporeal experience. In addition to a summary of key contributions by Politics scholars, it outlines my own experience as a researcher whose career has spanned the fields of Theatre and International Politics. The concluding section of this chapter outlines the key influences behind my own Applied Theatre practice, which will also provide the basis for the discussion of performance in the chapters to follow. These include the vocal work of Alfred Wolfsohn and the Roy Hart Theatre, seminal Applied Theatre practitioner Augusto Boal, and the activist puppetry of Peter Schumann's Bread and Puppet Theatre.

Chapter 2 discusses the broad context of populism, considering competing perspectives on its democratic merits. Positioned alongside the principles of radical democracy, populism is interrogated for its relative capacity to achieve pluralist inclusivity and productive forms of political engagement. These principles are discussed with reference to key features of populism, including the construction of a bloc called 'the people'; populist leadership; and dominant affective dispositions. Examples from populist movements in the United States and United Kingdom are drawn upon to illustrate how these features unfold in practice. The notion of 'left populism' is introduced and complicated with reference to the rise of digital populist interactions. The chapter argues that left populist aims cannot be achieved without paying attention to the ways that populist interaction unfolds in practice; this, I suggest, requires more integration of knowledge drawn from the field of Applied Theatre.

Chapter 3 continues the discussion of populism as an interactive process. The focus here is on examining the modes of engagement and interaction that populism tends to engender. The chapter gives specific consideration to calls for agonistic pluralism that stress the fundamental need for respectful engagement across difference. Agonism is explored alongside its roots in ancient Greek theatre, leading to a suggestion that more recent theatre practice might reveal further insights into practical applications of agonism in the present day. After reviewing the ways that digital mediatisation complicates the pursuit of agonistic engagement, I introduce Augusto Boal's concept of metaxis as a means of understanding how agonism might be facilitated through performance-derived practices. An examination of the central features of Boal's work reveals some key principles that underpin the sustenance of fluid, agonistic engagement in practice.

Chapter 4 turns to the topic of embodied experience, which I see as an essential element of performative and theatrical interactions, and one that is significantly altered though not entirely diminished in online environments. The chapter begins with an overview of recent scholarly treatments of embodiment, particularly those that emphasise material corporeality. It develops a case for considering the manner in which bodies retain knowledge of past experiences and the impact of this on interpersonal communication. The complications of digital media are discussed, considering the ways that the body is materially present in such contexts as well as the tendency for corporeal knowledge to be sidelined or silenced. The chapter finishes with an account of practices that might be adapted to enable participants to recentre corporeal communication in political interactions. This discussion refers especially to activities inspired by Alfred Wolfsohn's vocal techniques.

Chapter 5 continues the discussion of embodied experience by focusing on tactile and kinaesthetic encounters with the exterior world. Informed by new materialist concepts, the chapter begins by establishing the ways that material encounters with both non-human and human entities can alter an individual's perceptions and orientations toward others. I evaluate the role of haptic sensations in populist encounters and the comparative minimisation of corporeal presence when populist interactions occur online. The chapter proceeds to consider theatrical practices that foreground interactive touch and movement, demonstrating that these can inspire new understandings of the relationship between the self, the environment and the objects and people that populate that environment. I discuss the elements of movement, voice and puppetry that I use in my own Applied Theatre workshops, and consider the avenues of perception that these make available to participants when they are charged with exploring sensitive political issues.

Chapters 6 and 7 explore aesthetic and affective dimensions of collaborative performance practice. These are grouped under the themes of fear and failure on the one hand, and pleasure and beauty on the other. The chapters explore the ways that these qualities are experienced both as affective sensations and as aesthetic modes. I consider the ways that these qualities can reinforce antagonistic attitudes, especially in digitally mediated contexts, before turning to applied performance practices to understand how fear, failure, pleasure and beauty might also serve agonistic ends. Chapter 6 focuses on the ways that Theatre of the Oppressed and vocal practices can transform fear and failure into democratically productive emotions. Chapter 7 revisits Schumann's Bread and Puppet Theatre to make a case for the role of pleasure and beauty in the pursuit of agonistic engagement.

Ultimately, this book seeks to make the case that performance practices, especially those that facilitate direct engagement in embodied, interactive theatricality, might prove useful to political projects that seek to reinvigorate democracy.

PART I

Political Populism through the Lens of Performance

1

PERFORMANCE AND POLITICS

Scene 1. *A young man struggles through the mud of First World War trenches, the screams of his comrades echoing around him. Shells burst to his left and right, the night sky briefly illuminated by violent streaming stars. He throws himself to the ground, his hands clawing at the slippery earth, trying to gain purchase to move forward. 'Comrade!' 'Comrade!' Screams of pain rise up all around him. Some call clearly for help, others scream and groan in weird abstractions of the human voice. The young man looks rapidly from right to left and behind him. He hesitates, then pushes himself forward again through the mud. His attention is focused only on preserving his own life for the next few precious minutes.*

Suddenly he realises that one of the screams is his own.

Scene 2. *A small boy walks obediently beside his mother and father into the Silesian forest, away from the town that has been home to him since his birth. One hand is firmly grasped by his mother and the other clutches to his chest a small wooden puppet and a book of fairy tales. The boy drags his feet, looking down at the forest floor, glancing every now and then over his shoulder at the scene behind him. His hometown of Breslau spreads out behind him, threatened by imminent Allied bombing and approaching Soviet tanks.*

Scene 3. *A theatre director hangs by his knees from a thin wooden bar, dangling before the bemused onlookers below. But this is no theatrical feat – the Director is hanging from the infamous pau de arara torture device. His wrists and ankles are bound together, securing him helplessly to the pole. He is naked and wholly vulnerable to the blows aimed his way by the military police. They prod him verbally and physically, demanding that he admit that he has defamed Brazil through his playwriting practice.*

Abruptly, one of the Director's torturers begins to speak to him in a different tone. He momentarily drops his attitude of superiority and speculates wearily that

DOI: 10.4324/9780367824129-3

> *both he and the Director are each simply playing out theatrical roles – either could*
> *at any moment become the torturer, the other the tortured, if only their roles were*
> *somehow ordained to swap.*

Each of the scenes above illustrates the formative experiences of an individual who would later become an influential theatre practitioner. The first, Alfred Wolfsohn, drew on his post-traumatic aural hallucinations to develop vocal therapy techniques and an approach to actor training (Wise 2007). The second, Peter Schumann, discovered the simple value of myths, fairy tales and naïve puppetry and adopted these as the basis of his avant-garde communal theatre experiments (Kourilsky 1974; Pollak 2017). The last, Augusto Boal, developed radically innovative theatrical tactics that would enable ordinary people to explore social and political roles different to those they experienced in their day-to-day lives – and in the process, explore the embodiment of power as it operates in interaction with others (Boal 1998, 2008).

What, we might ask, do the experiences of war outlined above have to do with the recent resurgence of populism in global politics and its relationship to performance? In the first instance, these examples demonstrate the extent to which performance and politics innately overlap; in each case, the memories of these war experiences are couched within memories of theatricality – the theatricality of the voice in pain; the comfort provided by puppets who bring fairy tales to life; and the characterisation of torturers to tortured within the masquerades of a violent military coup. Perhaps more significantly though, each of the individuals depicted above went on to mobilise their experiences of political violence to develop dynamically new methods of performance, which in turn sought to change the nature of political interaction in their particular contexts (Boal 1998; Pollak 2017; Wise 2007). The chapters that follow in this book are underpinned by the belief that interdisciplinary Politics-and-Performance research would be enhanced by paying greater attention to theatrical practices like the ones outlined above, which, due to their connections to experiences of war and political violence, might reveal new insights about the ways that performance can impact political interaction.

In many ways, research that interrogates the role of performance in political conflict has never felt more relevant – this is, after all the age of Donald Trumps and Boris Johnsons, staging their theatricalised rallies and photo opportunities – who can forget, for example, scenes of Donald Trump mimicking a disabled reporter to the delight of his cheering audience; or images of Boris Johnson standing in front of a quintessential double-decker bus, touting the lie that the National Health Service would be £350 million better off each week after Brexit? These were not simply bombastic utterances by politicians emboldened by their maverick popularity – frequently, populist leadership involves carefully crafted characters and scripts that depart from these players' earlier personas (Wood et al. 2016). This is also an era when the performative elements of street protest have never been more vibrant or more extensively planned with social media capture and circulation in mind; 'left populist' candidates have often cemented their associations with such movements by performatively emphasising physical traits or biographical backstories that align with the dominant demographic markers of these movements – as we've seen, for example, in the campaigns of Bernie Sanders and Alexandria Ocasio-Cortez in the United States and Jeremy Corbyn in the United Kingdom (Bennister et al. 2017; Winter 2020; Zummo 2020). This is also, of course, a time when the outraged supporters of a losing presidential candidate can act out their fantasies of armed invasion by performing a militaristic insurrection on the premises of a national capitol. At the same time, as noted in this book's introduction, emerging social and cultural trends call into question the extent to which performance and theatricality can meaningfully intervene in society and effect true political change.

In order to undertake a renewed investigation of the emerging relationship between Politics and Performance, especially as it manifests within divisive and conflictual contexts, it is useful to first recall the ways that these two fields have already been brought into conversation in recent scholarship. In this chapter, I begin the task of interrogating the role of performance in present-day digital populism by reviewing the chief ways that performance has been treated in political scholarship to date. This will establish a case for the relevance of aspects of performance that are not often employed in studies of political phenomena. By reconsidering some of the key innovations that have been made by politics scholars interested in performance and theatricality, we not only acknowledge the important gains that have been achieved; we can also cast a critical eye on the field in order to identify areas that are under-explored and that might provide important knowledge that would otherwise remain overlooked.

This chapter unfolds as follows: first, I reposition Politics-and-Performance scholarship within the broader context of interdisciplinarity to establish the philosophical and political stakes of such projects. This provides a framework to appreciate the contributions made by a variety of researchers in Politics and International Relations – while it is not possible to provide a comprehensive survey of such work, the contributions mentioned below illustrate the range of ways that performance and theatricality have been applied to global politics research in recent years. Following this, I expand on two key areas which I feel need further consideration in order to move Politics-and-Performance research forward in a more dynamic and diverse fashion: these are attention to non-Western performance practices and to practice-based research. The conclusion of this chapter outlines my own practical theatre experience, highlighting the influence of Alfred Wolfsohn, Peter Schumann and Augusto Boal, whose ideas and insights will be applied to the analysis of digital populism in the chapters to come.

Interdisciplinarity: Creative Foundations

I have always identified strongly with Jack Halberstam's assertion that 'for some kooky minds, disciplines actually get in the way of answers and theorems precisely because they offer maps of thought where intuition and blind fumbling might yield better results' (Halberstam 2011, 6). But why should this be the case? Why should it still require a 'kooky' mind to resist the pressures to conform to and replicate disciplinary borders within academic research? And what are the social and political stakes of doing so? These are questions that are increasingly being asked by scholars as it becomes clear that our traditional demarcation of subjects into discipline areas is often a hindrance to the generation of new knowledge. This is not a new perspective of course, especially given the influence of Foucault's writings on power and knowledge within the academy (Ball 2012; Foucault 1975); yet disciplinary walls persist, reinforced by economic, political and cultural forces that sometimes seem impenetrably resilient.

It should be acknowledged that the ordering of scholarship and research into disciplines varies between institutions, and perhaps even more so among different national approaches to higher education. But there is a shared history that speaks to what is at stake when we either accept academic disciplines as given or attempt to destabilise them. Furthermore, this history reveals important insights about the ways that Politics-and-Performance scholarship sits alongside the politics of academia and knowledge production more generally. Because of this, it is useful to consider the broad history of interdisciplinarity in some depth before considering Politics-and-Performance projects more specifically.

Disciplines as we know them today emerged largely in the mid-1800s, including the division of fields between the natural sciences, social sciences and humanities (and later, the arts). The emergence of academic disciplines paralleled changes in society and economics, as individual workers' roles became significantly more specialised and, to an extent, divorced from the overall objective – just as a cobbler might transform into a specialist skilled at punching holes in leather rather than crafting an entire shoe, so did scholars back away from investigations of the world at large, moving toward silos of disciplinary knowledge (Jacobs 2013). There were great advantages to this ordering of scholarly labour, as it encouraged highly detailed and focused considerations of particular elements of social phenomena. As the world grew in complexity while experiences of distance and difference shrank, the ordering of knowledge into disciplinary frames enabled sufficiently narrow explorations of complex phenomena. But the change was also fuelled by increasing professionalisation, not only of academic institutions but also in the vocational pursuit of academic study itself. Universities began to think of themselves as competitors with other institutions and students as investors who would be rewarded by enhanced future career outcomes. This led to the development of more regulated structures within universities that would better lend themselves to measuring outcomes, validating knowledge production and regulating qualifications – ultimately facilitating a market-driven model of higher education (Repko et al. 2020, 30).

This scenario was not without its critics: the emerging crystallisation of academic disciplines was seen by some as evidence of a problematic but growing alignment between government, business and education (Moran 2010). By the mid-20th century, such critiques had gained stature in academic circles, and an increasing number of non-traditional institutions emerged that challenged disciplinary structures (see, e.g., Tufts University, Goddard College, Sussex University, Goldsmiths College, to name just a few) (Repko et al. 2020). 'Interdisciplinarity' was thus a reflection of the drive for educational reform, innovation and progress, with the aim of creating more inclusive and socially progressive approaches to education (Stehr and Weingart 2000). Given added impetus by Foucault's writings on discipline (1975), by the late 20th century, new academic subjects, such as Cultural Studies, Women's Studies, Environmental Studies, African-American Studies and more, emerged to challenge orthodox disciplinary frameworks.

Such trends were also reflected in changing attitudes within the mainstream of the Social Sciences, where researchers increasingly framed their work with reference to theorists and philosophers working in areas such as post-structuralist philosophy, feminist theory and postcolonial theory – consequently developing reputations as scholarly figures whose work has no concrete disciplinary 'home'. In Politics, a broadened view of political subject matter has taken hold, with greater heed paid to hitherto marginalised topics and a greater diversity of scholars taking up places within academic studies of politics – thus challenging the white, middle-class perspectives emanating primarily from Europe and North America (Jessop and Sum 2001, 90). All of this has underpinned the development of more receptive attitudes toward interdisciplinarity.

Despite this, interdisciplinary projects face a number of challenges that can limit their capacity to truly transform the traditional structuring of academic subjects. These come from multiple directions, ranging from government policies to the requirements of funding agencies. Research projects must be carefully designed if they are to robustly challenge disciplinary walls. In the first instance, interdisciplinary engagements that venture across *fields* are still comparatively rare. It is far more common to find interdisciplinarity across subjects housed within the same broad field, for example Social Sciences. Combinations of fields, for example the Social Sciences with the Arts, are harder to come by. This is perhaps due, at least in part, to the gaps that exist between the epistemological foundations of comparatively disparate fields, which can lead to discrepancies regarding perceived theoretical and methodological legitimacy. When researchers speak different languages, and when those languages are based on unfamiliar conceptual vocabularies, it can be difficult to establish genuine collaboration or integration.

In such cases, there is sometimes a tendency for projects that perceive themselves as interdisciplinary to proceed with an unequal contribution from the various disciplines in question – in other words, there tends to be a driving discipline and a secondary discipline that is added in or applied secondarily. Although this is not always the case, it necessitates taking note of what Andrew Sayer refers to as 'disciplinary imperialism' (Sayer 2018). This occurs when one discipline, in effect, visits another for the purpose of taking what is of use to their own discipline without necessarily understanding the full context of those intellectual and practical materials; these materials are then applied or interwoven with areas of concern for the driving discipline. In my experience, this seems to be a particular risk for projects that make ancillary use of the Arts, as artists and scholars of the arts are all too often drafted into projects to lend 'impact' but are given little opportunity to make meaningful contributions that would be of equal benefit to their own disciplines. Given that Arts-based subjects are almost always more precarious and more marginalised than their Social Science counterparts within cultural, political and academic spheres, this suggests that a serious interrogation of the ethics of interdisciplinary scholarship is required.

Given these potential pitfalls, it is perhaps useful to stress Julie Thompson Klein's call for 'transdisciplinarity' (2010), which aims for a full integration of methods and theories across disciplines. Crucially, the product of such projects should be substantially new, innovative and creative – something more and different than either field could or would produce on its own. This is a distinctly radical and transformative approach to the blending of disciplines. We might apply this ideal to Performance-and-Politics research by pursuing work that develops heightened insights for both disciplines. Situating this goal within the broader philosophical principles that have historically underpinned academic interdisciplinarity, we might strive for an approach that enhances knowledge generation across the Arts and Social Sciences but that furthermore embraces a radical social and political agenda: to get to the root of what is at stake when human beings interact simultaneously creatively *and* politically, with and for one another.

Theatre, Performance and International Politics

Given the philosophical and political stakes inherent to interdisciplinarity, it seems useful to briefly review the ways that Political scholarship has addressed theatre and performance in order to understand what more might be done to further the generation of creative, transformative knowledge that enhances both fields. To do so, this section reflects on my own experience as a Performance scholar-practitioner who latterly moved into the discipline of Politics. The journey from one to the other – before I eventually situated myself adamantly in between – took a sometimes bewildering path; more than a few times, I experienced confused, sceptical and (once or twice) downright worried looks when speaking about Performance at International Politics conferences. Despite groundbreaking models of interdisciplinarity established by the likes of Debbie Lisle, Michael Shapiro, Roland Bleiker, Cynthia Weber, Stephen Chan, and Christine Sylvester for example,[1] overt mentions of performance (and especially *theatre*) were not always welcomed in Politics and IR with open arms. Yet this work has also been bolstered by dynamic and insightful contributions from a small but influential number of Politics scholars who have understood and championed the value of theatre and performance and whose work I wish to highlight here. Although I am not able to provide a comprehensive account, I aim to point out what I, as a sometimes-interloper in both fields, have perceived to be illustrative of evolutions in the thinking and doing of Performance within Politics and International Relations circles.

To some extent, performance has long been present in the background of Politics research. This is especially true of research that is grounded in Sociological approaches, where we find figures such as Erving Goffman making largely metaphorical use of theatrical concepts to understand human identity and interaction; for example, examining the human capacity for selective artifice in the presentation of a particular 'self' intended to influence others (e.g. Alexander et al. 2006; Goffman 1956). For the most part, though, such approaches are illustrative of a tendency to adopt the conceptual language of performance but engage relatively little with the study or practice of actual theatre and performance. Judith Butler's concept of performativity offers another obvious route for Performance to be brought to bear on political issues, but Butler's earlier work predominantly stressed the discursive and representational role of the body in performance, taking a somewhat cautious view of creativity and theatricality (1996). Accordingly, much of the Politics scholarship dealing with performativity has not extensively considered theatrical performance until comparatively recently.

Despite the obvious existence of common ground, it is only within the past two decades that Politics researchers have begun to engage with creative theatre and performance in a sustained and direct fashion, especially by venturing into areas of creative practice and engaging in collaborations with Theatre and Performance colleagues. It is somewhat surprising that theatrical performance is a comparatively under-researched area within Politics. The very fact that Plato questioned the societal value of playwrights in the *Republic* certainly provides us with a strong clue about the political potency of theatre. Plato suggested that playwrights and poets dealing in mimesis should be exiled from his ideal society, believing them to be purveyors of imitative fictions who encourage the passions over reason (2007). Throughout history, critiques of the social function of theatre have often rested on scepticism about theatre's ability to play upon audiences' emotions at the expense of rational deliberation or useful civic participation (Stern 2014). This suggests an attitude to the performing arts that in some ways parallels the divisions between Politics and Theatre in academic spheres – Politics is considered a serious subject, traditionally explained through reference to rational behaviours or systemic orders and evidenced by concrete empirical data. Theatre, on the other hand, might encourage us to sing and dance our way into something beyond the rational, something not easily documented, measured and assessed.

Similar barriers have also been applied within Politics disciplines to cordon off and marginalise aspects of human experience; the historical neglect of the personal in Politics scholarship, as opposed to the state-centric or institutional, bears a marked similarity to the anti-theatrical prejudice that has existed in academia, and in society and politics more broadly, for centuries (Barish 1985). It is perhaps not surprising then that, as theatre and performance were historically roped off as separate and mostly irrelevant to the serious study of Politics, scholars who were interested in other long-neglected issues seemed to sense a natural affinity between Politics and Performance. As a result, some of the most fruitful early endeavours to combine Performance with Politics came from Politics researchers working in areas of feminism and postcolonial theory.

For example, one seminal contribution came from the October 2003 edition of the *Borderlands* journal – a special issue on 'Dramaturgies of Violence in International Relations'. This volume contained a provocative collection of articles, including works on Harold Pinter, Martial Arts and other direct engagements with theatricality. These articles contain accounts of international phenomena that apply an understanding of theatrical devices and their impact on spectators, using this to gain new knowledge of international issues like war and migration. For example, Christine Sylvester provided a dramaturgical analysis of political violence – one that reads the participants of international events as actors, following or departing from existing scripts, with all the theatricality expected from a gripping stage drama. While this was largely a metaphorical treatment of the theatrical, Sylvester focused on the ways that social performances relate to individual experiences of power and disempowerment, and in doing so, she touched upon the way that political performances can be understood not just for their semiotic value but also at the level of interpersonal experience (Sylvester 2003a).

This celebration of the knowledge-generating capacities of theatricality was carried on in Vivienne Jabri's contribution, where she positioned artistic practices in opposition to IR's historical preference for all-encompassing explanatory frameworks that downplay complexity and, ultimately, the political (Jabri 2003). Crucially, Jabri made the case that theatre and performance can reveal the specificities of political interaction and thus bring the political back into focus in the study of International Politics.

While the *Borderlands* issue held great promise, other scholars were finding fecund political material in the theatres of Ancient Greece. Mark Chou and Roland Bleiker turned to Athenian tragedy to glean new insights about democratic interaction (2009); Louisa Odysseos analysed the essential function of comedy within political society (2001). Such scholars delved into the specifics of ancient theatres, drawing insights from the theatrical techniques of acting and staging, the architectonics of theatre spaces and the relationship between theatrical events and political society. While such approaches might benefit from acknowledging the broader historical and geographic foundations of theatre and performance beyond that of Ancient Greece,[2] these examples are laudable for the extent to which they recognise the close relationship between theatre-making, spectatorship and democratic political processes.

Efforts to further advance the application of performance knowledge to politics were particularly bolstered by Jenny Edkins' and Adrian Kear's 2013 anthology, *International Politics and Performance* (2013). This work, comprised of chapters by both performance and politics scholars, was especially notable for its efforts to address the material and creative elements of theatre and performance, alongside semantic and hermeneutic usages. Additionally, Edkins and Kear framed this work as an effort toward 'pre-disciplinary cross-talk', which would address the complex ways that performance and politics are enfolded together and 'inter-animate' one another (2013, 8). In this way, their thinking aligns with the trans-disciplinarity advocated by Julie Thompson Klein, as it speaks to a desire to avoid prescriptive frames or systems of thought at the expense of otherwise highly productive, open-ended explorations.

Perhaps more than any other body of performance knowledge, the field of 'Performance Studies' has been especially popular among political researchers. Performance Studies is a strand of performance scholarship that was initially developed in the 1970s by Performance Artist and academic Richard Schechner in collaboration with anthropologist Victor Turner. In line with moves in avant-garde Theatre at the time which sought to reintegrate performance with real-life experience and thus become a vehicle for social transformation, Schechner developed a very broad definition of performance:

> Performance is a very inclusive notion of action; theatre is only one node on a continuum that reaches from ritualisation in animal behaviour (including humans) through performances in everyday life – greetings, displays of emotion, family scenes, and so on – to rites, ceremonies and performances: large-scale theatrical performances.
>
> *Schechner 1977, 1*

What emerged was a trend in academia that became especially popular in the 1990s and early 2000s, as theatre scholars began applying their knowledge of performance and theatricality to a broad gamut of human interaction. Among Politics researchers, Performance Studies provided a conceptual language that could be comparatively easily assimilated into Politics scholarship. In particular, Shirin Rai began to make use of Schechner's work to analyse the workings of parliaments (2010), and this influential work later inspired an interdisciplinary anthology co-edited with Theatre and Performance scholar Janelle Reinelt (Rai and Reinelt 2016). Performance Studies approaches like these have undoubtedly helped to legitimise theatre and performance within Politics spheres.

My own earliest contributions invoked Performance Studies in an effort to appeal to the existing sensibilities of Politics scholars (2009, 2010). Yet even while writing such work, I felt it to be a somewhat strategic undertaking that left out important elements of live theatre experience. Performance Studies is a diverse field, covering a broad range of epistemological and methodological approaches; at its best, Performance Studies provides new insights into the social and political impact of performed interactions by paying close attention to their heightened creative elements. But due to its foundational influences from anthropology, this sub-field can also lead scholarship to err too much toward an emphasis on structural or systematic frameworks that downplay the messy, productive uncertainties of performance.

To my mind, a key issue here is an occasional tendency in Politics-and-Performance scholarship to favour the representational aspects of performance – that is, the ways that performances appear before and are 'read' by spectators. Such approaches take account of the social and political factors that colour these acts and readings but frequently neglect the essence of theatrical experience – that is, what happens between feeling, sensing bodies when we perform publicly and politically. To achieve the latter, we need Politics scholarship that is more adventurous in terms of its engagement with live, creative *practice*. This, I feel, is a crucially under-theorised aspect of Performance among Politics scholarship – yet, as I will show in the chapters of this book, it is these interactive, experiential, embodied elements that make performance a unique form of social interaction and that lend it potent political force.

To my mind, then, the most exciting Performance-and-Politics research of recent years has been undertaken by Politics scholars who also have a grounding in performance practice. For example, researchers like Felix Rösch, Catherine Charrett and Susanna Hast, among a growing number of others, have adopted practice-based methods that make use of performance and theatricality as a methodological tool to understand political phenomena (Charrett 2019; Hast 2018; Rösch 2018, 2021). When performance is invoked not only as an object of study but simultaneously as a research method, we begin to understand the full range of insights that it can bring to the study of Politics. Research that encompasses performance *practice* – whether from the perspective of a theatre-maker, facilitator, participant or any other active role – often demonstrates the ways that representation, aesthetics and affect are intertwined and dependent on ephemerally experienced interaction and collaboration. Practice can get to the heart of the messy uncertainty that more traditional approaches overlook. With this in mind, I believe that an emphasis on political performance practice might be uniquely adept at responding to the principles that have underpinned academic interdisciplinarity as a philosophical and political movement – in part because such projects are especially useful to reveal operations of power and politics that we might not otherwise apprehend.

'Noises Off': Knowledge Waiting in the Wings

One key aspect of interdisciplinary engagement that remains underdeveloped in Politics scholarship is consideration of non-Western theatre and performance practices. While individual contributors have provided an array of studies dealing with specific non-Western contexts or issues, to date the application of performance knowledge to politics has too often reflected the historical marginalisation of non-Western and indigenous performance within the field of Theatre and Performance. While progress is undoubtedly being made in this regard, it remains the case that we might broaden our understanding of performance's implications in politics by turning our focus to non-Western contexts. For example, many researchers have attempted to refine our understanding of democratic politics by turning to ancient Greek theatre for information; the relatively concurrent emergence of classical theatre and democracy certainly lends credence to this approach – but why not also turn to the history of performance and politics in, for example, historical African and Asian contexts, where we find many examples of complex, sophisticated performance practices that go hand in hand with social and political functions? (Chattopadhyay 2020; Okagbue 2013). Indeed, one of the challenges for scholars now is that our very notion of 'theatre' is so deeply enmeshed with Western-centric definitions of performance that don't map easily onto the rich array of practices evident from diverse geographic and cultural contexts.

To overcome these limitations, we need to acknowledge and address the ways that Theatre and Performance disciplines have evolved in order to understand precisely what has been lacking. Taking Performance Studies as an example, scholars within this sub-field have, for a number of years, suggested a need to reassess its value as an activist and social justice-oriented 'anti-discipline' (Schechner 2002). Scholars like Jon McKenzie, James Harding and Virginie Magnat have asked challenging questions about the field's origins in Western-oriented perspectives, and particularly its relationship to anthropology's colonial legacies (e.g. Magnat 2016; McKenzie 2006; Reinelt 2007). However, Performance Studies scholars also recognise that diversification and decolonisation of performance theory cannot be accomplished simply through greater inclusion of under-represented communities and practices; on the contrary, such approaches risk re-centring the white, Western canon by simply inserting contributions from Black and Global Majority and indigenous scholars in a relatively empty gesture. Instead, scholars are calling for a rethink of the epistemological foundations of Performance fields in order to address the root issues that marginalise knowledge and perspectives at a foundational level. Many assert that *practice* is key to this (Fortier 2002; Hastrup 1995; Magnat 2016; Taylor 2020).

One way that performance theory can address the exclusionary blind sides it has inherited from its foundational roots is by returning to an epistemological framework that avoids linguistically dominated ways of knowing the world, which are themselves inflected by their specific cultural contexts (Magnat 2016, 142). By paying greater attention to performance as practice, we are better equipped to tap into knowledge and experiences that are not easily translated into verbal communication and are often not readily apparent to outside eyes. As Kirsten Hastrup explains, 'most cultural knowledge is stored in actions rather than words' (Hastrup, cited in Magnat 2016, 142), rendering the body a primary repository of knowledge and experience. This embodied knowledge might be mobilised through practice as a means of intervention, resistance or creative agency (Denzin et al. 2008; Taylor 2020). Most significantly, this attention to materially experienced performance has the potential to truly diversify and decolonise applications of performance theory because it opens up the frames of knowing and thinking and feeling the world beyond those that have been constructed and sustained by those with power. For Politics researchers, this suggests a need for greater emphasis on the ways that performance is experienced interactively between people; rather than attempting to 'read' performances as texts, we might instead focus more directly on the physical, sensual and visceral (Magnat 2016).

As I will discuss below, my own theatrical training has been most heavily influenced by practices developed in Anglo-American and Western European contexts, mostly spearheaded by white men. These influences unavoidably shape my understanding of the performative political phenomena that I observe and participate in, and they also inform the creative practice that I undertake with others. I am firmly aware that in this respect, my work replicates the historical neglect of non-Western and Black and Global Majority performance knowledge. Limited as I am by the narrowness of my own scholarly and skills-based theatre training, I attempt to confront this issue by placing practice-based knowledge at the heart of my research. By engaging with others through the medium of Applied Theatre practice, I hope to tease out co-produced knowledge that is influenced by the experiences of people very different to myself. In order for readers to better understand this research, I conclude this chapter by summarising my own Politics-and-Performance journey as it has unfolded over the past two decades. This is followed by a summary of the key practitioners who have influenced my work and whose ideas inform the analysis and discussion in the chapters to follow.

Practical Bases

My academic career has followed an unusual path, moving from BA and MA study in Theatre to a doctoral degree in Politics. In an academic context, I have been steadfastly weaving together performance and politics since 2007 – at least, this was the date when I began to present my academic work in Politics and IR circles, inflected with knowledge drawn from my past training and study in Theatre. I came to the field of Politics as a result of my Applied Theatre work, which involved using theatre and performance practices in intercultural conflict resolution workshops and international community development projects. It was here that I gained an understanding of the way that participatory theatre projects can foster new modes of communication that help groups bridge their internal diversity and tackle sensitive topics important to their collective future. I developed a growing curiosity about the relationship between creative interpersonal activities and institutional and governmental politics. Spurred on by Theatre mentors who urged me to focus more explicitly on performance theory, I tentatively brought my knowledge and experience to the field of International Politics, where I found myself learning an entirely new language and conceptual frameworks.

Since 2013, I have worked full time in academic Theatre departments; I now have the luxury of exploring political topics in action with my students and colleagues in dedicated studio spaces on a near-weekly basis. My specialisms are broadly aligned with the sub-field of 'Applied Theatre', a term which describes non-commercial applications of theatre that possess a driving social or political agenda and that are most often undertaken in conjunction with people with no prior experience of theatre or performance.[3] Most recently, I have initiated a series of workshops that are designed to tackle digital populism by engaging with divisive political topics through the medium of performance. This practice has been designed to bring alternative viewpoints into being within the space of the workshop, using creative activities to illustrate experiences ranging from the painful to the joyous. I make use of puppetry, voice work and improvisation to encourage participants from diverse backgrounds to creatively explore their own experiences of a political issue while engaging deeply (and creatively) with the experiences of others. These workshops have to date only taken place within the United Kingdom due to the challenges presented by the COVID-19 pandemic; however, the initial work has suggested useful insights that have informed the theoretical chapters that follow in the remainder of this book.

The activities contained within these workshops are especially influenced by three key practitioners whose work has been central to my own theatrical and philosophical training – these are the figures introduced at the start of this chapter: Alfred Wolfsohn, Peter Schumann and Augusto Boal. I have had the privilege to be trained in the techniques of these practitioners, and in the case of Schumann and Boal, to learn directly from them in practical contexts. More importantly, I believe that these practitioners' work has been strongly influenced by their direct experiences of political violence; each of them developed techniques that in some way facilitate the negotiation of personal perspectives, disempowerment, and disagreement or conflict. In order to understand the centrality of conflict in their practice and the ways that it might relate to populist interactions, the last section of this chapter provides a detailed summary of Wolfsohn, Schumann and Boal's work.

Alfred Wolfsohn and the Roy Hart Theatre

Alfred Wolfsohn was born in Berlin to a German-Jewish family. In 1914 at the age of 18, he was conscripted as a stretcher bearer in the First World War. This would become the most pivotal experience of his life. Wounded in a bombing raid and mistaken for dead by his colleagues, Wolfsohn awoke from his injuries to find himself beneath a pile of corpses (Centre Artistique International Roy Hart). Wolfsohn's own words recount the horrors he experienced:

> [...] Shells burst right and left.
>
> I throw myself to the ground, my hands are clawing the earth. Often someone next to me is hit. Each time I am astonished that I have been spared!
>
> Barrage all around me. The guns from which it is coming are manned by four or five Frenchmen. I don't know where they come from, I don't

know who they are. They don't even know they can easily kill me. It's no good shouting: Jean Baptiste-Maurice-Pierre-I have done you no wrong, what do you want from me?

I keep crawling. The hours pass. The fire is getting stronger and my peril greater. I pray to God but He doesn't hear me. From somewhere I hear a voice shouting. 'Comrade! Comrade!' I close my eyes, shaking with terror, thinking: how can a human voice utter such a sound, a voice in extremis.

[...]I called for my comrades to help but no one heard and soon I was quite alone. Hour after hour, inch by inch I crawled back. After a while I heard a voice nearby moaning incessantly: Help, Help. I fought a terrible struggle with myself: should I try to crawl to him or not. I did not do it.

Wolfsohn 2012

Wolfsohn's experiences of violence lingered with him after the war, as he experienced shell shock and aural hallucinations in which he repeatedly heard the anguished cries of wounded soldiers. He was particularly haunted by the voice of the soldier he had failed to help, whose vocal tones remained with him long after his time in battle. 'Help. Help' (Wise 2007, 43). Psychiatric treatment failed to help him, and he proceeded to develop his own practice of therapeutic voice work that initially involved re-performing the voices he remembered from the trenches. Based on his experience of the extreme ways that the voice can make itself heard when the body undergoes physical or mental anguish, Wolfsohn subsequently sought to use the voice as a vehicle to enable people to access realms of their inner being that would otherwise be masked by social conditioning and the thinking mind. He had noticed that the sounds he remembered from the battlefield were not confined by the ordinary ranges of social human beings, but rather, 'their voices expressed and screamed terror and agony through every range' (Wolfsohn in Braggins 2012). This knowledge evolved into a practice that aimed to make full use of the entire range of the human voice, freeing it from social conditioning and artistic judgements and enabling people to express a full gamut of emotions. Crucially, this singing practice was not framed as an elite artistic endeavour, but rather as a manifestation of the universal nature of the human voice (Braggins 2012, 44).

In 1938, Wolfsohn fled Berlin, arriving in Britain as a refugee, where he was initially interned as an 'enemy alien' (Wise 2007, 44). He became a singing teacher and developed a reputation for groundbreaking practices that revealed hitherto unknown capacities of the human voice. As Crawford and Pikes describe: '[...] a woman could sing very low guttural notes, a man could sound high fluttering tones, both men and women could howl like beasts or cry out with broken sounds, and a single singer could scale all the voices of Mozart's Magic Flute from the depths of Sarastro to the heights of the Queen of the Night' (Crawford and Pikes 2019, 239).

Wolfsohn's most influential student was Roy Hart, who established The Roy Hart Theatre in 1969. This theatre took its bearings from Wolfsohn's teachings alongside its founder's experience in the professional theatre industry. Where Wolfsohn was focused almost exclusively on voice, Hart took the practice into the realm of avant-garde theatre, deliberately experimenting with approaches to physicality, characterisation and more (Crawford and Pikes 2019). Roy Hart Theatre now takes the form of a loose collective of practitioners from various geographical origins who take slightly different approaches to their work – but they are united by a shared practice of guiding students to explore the full range of their vocal sound-making capacities, often using physical techniques to elicit growls, screams, whispers, guttural moans and more – this cuts through the participant's typical tendencies to search for 'beautiful' or socially approved sounds (Crawford and Pikes 2019, 244).

In the work of Alfred Wolfsohn and his followers, I find an example of performance employed as a means to access and transform knowledge of the world through processes that draw on the physical body as much or more than the thinking mind. Wolfsohn's practice demonstrates that experiences of conflict can linger throughout the human body, not only as memories of personal trauma but also as reminders of moments when one's own agency, powerlessness and responsibility toward others were called into question in profound and troubling ways. Through theatrical performance, we might enable people to express this corporeally-held knowledge and bring it to bear on their interactions with others in the present.

Peter Schumann and the Bread and Puppet Theatre

The Bread and Puppet Theatre is one of the world's most well-recognised protest performance groups. Their large, vibrant puppets, often accompanied by performers on stilts, have hardly missed a major protest or demonstration in the United States over the past six decades. In addition to this, the Theatre has been developing and touring original work since the 1960s and hosting its iconic Bread and Puppet circus each year in northern Vermont. The group's name is derived from the centrality of larger-than-life papier mache puppets in their work, alongside their practice of sharing home-baked sourdough with their audiences.

The theatre was founded by Peter Schumann in the Lower East Side of Manhattan in the early 1960s. However, it might be more accurate to suggest that the roots of this iconic company stretch back to Eastern Europe in the mid-20th century: Born and raised in Lüben, Silesia, Peter Schumann experienced the perils of war at a young age when he fled the war-torn region with his family in 1944, escaping the imminent invasion by Russian tanks (Brecht 1988). The family joined hundreds of others travelling as war refugees, on foot and later by train, to a makeshift refugee village on the German-Danish border. Young Peter was allowed to take one bag of personal items with him on the journey, which he chose to fill with wooden hand-puppets (Pollak 2017). In a 1971 interview, Schumann recalled his memories of the journey: the vision of his village ablaze behind him, the frantic refugees trying to cling to the windows of the departing train, already crowded with people and stinking of vomit. Once settled in Schleswig-Holstein, Peter and his fellow youths were charged with grinding grain into flour, which their mothers would bake into bread once a week in a communal outdoor oven (Pollak 2017). At other times the refugee boys spent their days devising ways to avoid being physically bullied by locals, sometimes resorting to entertaining puppet shows as a way of mitigating local resentment toward the refugees (Andrews 2007, 185).

Schumann moved to New York City in the early 1960s, along with his wife Elka and their children[4] (Schumann 2021). The Bread and Puppet theatre was established in 1963, inspired by Peter's childhood experiences and by experimental art and theatre practices including the Bauhaus, German expressionism and Dada (Kourilsky 1974). Once in New York, Schumann connected with avant-garde artists including the Living Theatre and Allan Kaprow (Rowell 2016). Together these influences led Schumann to an interest in the relationship between bodies and objects and performance as shared event or ritual. Most importantly, Schumann's practice became distinctive for its focus on using theatre as a vehicle to enable people to encounter and engage with one another in ways that they weren't apt to do in everyday life. Drawing no doubt on his experience as a refugee, he turned to puppetry, popular performance and storytelling to develop practices that would draw together people who would not normally attend the theatre (Kourilsky 1974).

Bread, of course, has also been a central feature of Schumann's work. When the theatre moved to Northern Vermont in the 1970s, they began baking traditional eastern European sourdough and offering it for free to the public, drawing people in via their shows and establishing a sense of communal participation in the process. As Peter explains,

> The bread-eating is the motive for the puppet show … People wouldn't eat bread together unless you create an occasion for it … They only know the commerce of doing it: you buy it you chew it and you shit it out … so when you make puppet shows you feed them, and they do something together they had forgotten they could do together.
>
> *Peter Schumann in Varga 2013*

For Schumann, the fundamental purpose of theatre is to reunite people who are otherwise alienated from one another by political divisions and the demands of contemporary neoliberal society (Ryder 1995). This is achieved in part due to the unique aesthetic of the theatre, which is rooted in experiments with the forms and movements of puppets. The puppets are distinctive in their size, motion and pacing and they dwarf the audience and actors alike. This combines with the ritualistic intimacy experienced by the audience and instantiates a shift in spectatorship that arises from renewed feelings of community membership. All of this work is couched within a deep commitment to divorce the theatre from systems of production and commodification, with shows offered free of charge or at low cost in order to make them as widely accessible as possible. All in all, Peter Schumann's work offers insights into the ways that puppets and performing objects can facilitate new modes of interpersonal engagement, especially by framing potentially divisive issues within a celebration of community.

Augusto Boal and Theatre of the Oppressed

The work of Augusto Boal has been foundational to the development of the field of Applied Theatre. Scarcely any applied or socially engaged theatre practitioners exist who have not been in some way influenced by Boal's work, such is the spread and impact of his innovations. Indeed, his practices are so well disseminated that some present-day facilitators aren't always aware that he created many of the activities that they regularly use. Boal sought to develop interactive, participatory forms of theatre that outstrip traditional models of performance and spectatorship. Influenced by Paolo Freire, the project at the heart of Boal's work is to increase political engagement and confer authority and agency to parts of society who would otherwise remain marginalised, or passive. His work is broadly referred to as Theatre of the Oppressed and it encompasses a range of activities that aim to empower members of the public by enabling them to examine and debate political issues through improvisational theatre techniques. This renders theatre as a space of rehearsal for political change.

Like Wolfsohn and Schumann, Boal had first-hand experience of political conflict. His theatre career began in the 1960s in Brazil, shortly before the 1964 coup that would establish two subsequent decades of military dictatorship (Boal 1998). Having returned from studying theatre at Columbia University, Boal's early practices emerged within a high-risk context of political censorship, which was becoming increasingly uncomfortable for political artists of all stripes. Nevertheless, Boal began experimenting with guerrilla theatre and newspaper theatre,[5] using dramatic techniques to bring the political nuances of news stories to the attention of the general public. In February 1971, as he was leaving a theatre in Sao Paulo where he was directing a production, he was kidnapped by military police. Like so many other victims of the regime, Boal was imprisoned and tortured. He was prodded with electric shock devices and strapped to the *pau-de-arara*, literally the parrot's perch, a thin wooden pole from which he hung by his bound hands and feet (Boal 1998). Boal described his experience with an emphasis on his interactions with his torturers:

> [...] I was picked up in Sao Paulo and, like everyone else, I was tortured. But, as happens in the great Shakespearean tragedies, the most painful scenes are juxtaposed sometimes with scenes of ridiculous farce.
>
> [...]
>
> Among these seven mastodons, there was one who tried to justify everything with bureaucratic arguments. While he was giving me electric

shocks on the *pau-de-arara,* from which I hung naked, upside down, he said: 'You will forgive me, yeah? But I am torturing you because it's on my schedule, see? I don't have anything personal against you, honest. I'm even a fan of your plays. I haven't seen any, but I like them all, see? You know how it is, yeah? Here you do what you're told to, see? Now, you know, it's a funny old world, things change. One day it might be you who's on top and me underneath, yeah? Now if it came to that, right, you're obviously not about to forget that I tortured you, fair enough, but it was just the luck of the draw, see? I tortured you because it was on my schedule'.

Boal 1998, 150–51

Boal ultimately was exiled from Brazil and much of his work on Theatre of the Oppressed took place in Argentina, Portugal and France (Taussig et al. 1990). Perhaps because of his personal experience of political violence, he sought to develop forms of theatre that could explore sensitive political issues through processes that emphasised collective negotiation and problem-solving. His most noted techniques are Image Theatre and Forum Theatre, which involve a series of activities that engage participants in role-played tableaux and short improvised scenes to explore the realities of their political circumstances and the opportunities they contain for resistance or betterment. Part of Boal's motivation was to use theatre to mobilise people who would otherwise feel disempowered and thus decline to participate in political processes. As his account of his torture indicates, he was keenly aware of the fact that political injustices are often made possible through the complicity of everyday citizens who are unable or disinclined to step beyond their narrowly defined daily roles and take account of the broader landscape of power hierarchies and injustices. Boal became committed to theatre practices that could help people to understand the nuances and subtleties of political dilemmas and to place themselves experientially into the shoes of those who are not 'on top'.

Boal's Theatre of the Oppressed techniques demonstrate the capacity for theatrical role-play to facilitate deeper, more critical approaches to political dilemmas. His work also provides an illustrative example of the extent to which we can adapt performance practices for use by non-actors in everyday contexts. Ultimately, these techniques enable Boal to use theatre as a tool to uncover and understand the operations of power in given social or political scenarios, moving participants away from familiar avenues of political debate toward a deeper engagement with the complexities of issues.

Conclusion

This chapter began by suggesting that attention to the work of practitioners like Wolfsohn, Schumann and Boal could provide new insights about the ways that creative performance practice might impact political interactions. Following a review of recent interdisciplinary Politics-and-Performance initiatives, I also suggested that performance practice might be key to diversifying and decolonising such projects and that this point is pivotal to realising a more radical engagement across fields in line with the history of academic interdisciplinarity. In what ways, then, does practice informed by these three figureheads contribute to these aims? I believe the answer lies in the specific ways that their practices seek to use performance to produce new modes of political interaction.

As noted above, all three of these practitioners experienced at some point in their lives the direct consequences of war and/or political violence. What is perhaps even more remarkable is that the practices that they would go on to develop centred consistently on allowing individuals to express themselves in new and more productive ways, often in a manner that highlights negotiation and cooperation as opposed to political polarisation. This attitude is by no means universal within politically or socially-engaged practice, neither now or in the mid- to late-20th century when the bulk of this work was being developed; it would have been just as natural for each of these practitioners to turn to more didactic or polemical styles popular at the same time they were working – such as, for example, El Teatro Campesino or San Francisco Mime Troupe. Instead, they developed practices that feature individual self-expression within a context of group development and negotiated interaction. It seems quite likely that their experiences of violence in some way contributed to this attitude. It also makes their work highly relevant to decolonising projects because their practices are built on activities and techniques that deliberately enable the communication of pluralistic viewpoints within collaborative creative work. It is this quality that I find so compelling and relevant to the development of my own practice, and especially to the study of digital populism. Given that populism has a tendency to engender or reaffirm hierarchical social divisions, practices that facilitate broader participation in knowledge-generation are also likely to be directly relevant to populist contexts.

Based on the explorations of this chapter, in the work that follows I attempt to develop a robust interdisciplinary application of performance knowledge to populist politics. Drawing on the work of these practitioners who have transferred their experiences of violent conflict into facilitations of pluralistic cooperation, my aim is to identify key elements of digital populism that might be transformed through applications of this practical performance knowledge. This requires an exploration of the ways that performance qualities are already present within specific aspects of populist interaction, followed by a consideration of alternative approaches that are evident in performance practices like those described above. Ultimately I seek to show that the interactive qualities of populist politics might be channelled into more productive political participation through the application of performance knowledge.

2

POPULISM AND PERFORMANCE

The aim of this chapter is to map out my approach to 'populism' by outlining the chief features that I understand to align with this contested term. This establishes the empirical and theoretical backdrop for the performance practices that I explore in later chapters, which I suggest might correct some of the deficiencies of populism. The chapter begins with a brief summary of populism, drawing on previous articulations by a variety of scholars including those who advocate 'left populism'. This is followed by a more detailed account of specific characteristic elements of populism that bear a problematic relationship to pluralist democratic aims. The latter part of the chapter focuses in more detail on the ways that left populism attempts to confront these issues, arguing that digital populism thwarts the achievement of inclusive, pluralistic democracy in practice. The conclusion of the chapter introduces the benefits that a performance-oriented approach might offer to counter such pitfalls, and which will be explored in more focused detail in the latter chapters of the book.

The Problem of Populism

A plethora of scholarship has tackled the recent global upsurge in populist politics, spanning an array of theoretical and ideological perspectives. There is obviously no settled consensus regarding what populism *is,* nor even agreement about the validity of the term for analytical purposes. With that said, it remains feasible to sketch out a broad summary of populist tendencies, which is more or less agreed upon at a foundational level: A large portion of populist scholarship locates the current rise of populism against a backdrop of neoliberal globalisation, increasing wealth disparities, financial crisis, technocracy and austerity politics. The root assumption is that such circumstances have led to the public's growing sense of alienation or disenfranchisement from previously established representative

DOI: 10.4324/9780367824129-4

political processes, as traditional parties have failed to respond to the needs and concerns of ordinary people. Although there is extensive debate regarding the nature of populism, and even its legitimacy as a cohesive concept, most accounts describe it as a phenomenon that occurs when charismatic populist leaders or movements step into the vacuum created by the public's sense of alienation from traditional political parties and their leaders (e.g. Brubaker 2017; Cohen 2019; Cossarini and Vallespín 2019; de la Torre 2019; Gerbaudo 2017; Moffitt 2016; Mouffe 2014, 2018; Mudde and Kaltwasser 2012; Müller 2016). These leaders and movements typically encourage scepticism of elite or powerful perspectives, positioning themselves as marginal voices who can better or more authentically represent 'the people', and thus generate support from broad swathes of society. In this manner, populist movements have emerged in a range of geographic, cultural and ideological contexts.

'Populism' is sometimes invoked as a generalised derogatory label by political pundits – often to dismiss competing viewpoints on the basis of their perceived lack of conformity to democratic norms, their supposed confrontational nature, their reliance on partial or false information, or their zealous ideological biases. This is an oversimplified approach to the term, and it is not the case that populism has no redeeming features. Populist movements often exhibit a capacity to inspire greater political participation and the potential to give voice to issues that are primarily or uniquely relevant to marginalised sections of the public. On the other hand, advocates of populism are somewhat overoptimistic about populism's ability to truly revitalise political engagement and to respond to the diverse needs of otherwise disengaged publics. On this point it is useful to consider populism alongside the broader category of 'radical democracy', which signals a body of ideas relating to reinvigorated political participation, overlapping or intersecting with populism to varying degrees.

Radical democracy, broadly described, centres on the principle that democracy in the late 20th century and beyond has a tendency to conform to and reinforce neoliberal and neoconservative world views. (e.g. Butler 2015; Connolly 2002; Hardt and Negri 2005; Laclau and Mouffe 1985, Rancière 1995; Young 2002). For example, citing the corrupting and enervating tendencies of democracy in the present age, Rancière suggests that we now face 'post-democracy', a state in which the appearance and vitality of the demos is diminished and reduced to the mechanics of governance (Rancière 1999). A reinvigoration is required that will entail a fortification or radicalisation of the principles of liberty, equality and difference. Influenced by the illustrative efforts of the Zapatistas, Indignados and Occupy, advocates of radical democracy generally seek methods to reinvigorate democracy through extended participation and more direct deliberative processes. In this sense, populism overlaps with the goals of radical democracy insofar as it seeks to mobilise broad masses of people and spur them into more direct political action – particularly those who might otherwise remain politically marginalised or passive. However, at the heart of radical democracy is an insistence on pluralism and fluidity, in order to establish what Jane Conway and Jakeet

Singh refer to as 'a world in which many worlds fit' (2011, 689). This attachment to plurality is clearly at odds with much right-wing discourse, particularly as it has emerged in recent years in populist movements. As a result, Ernesto Laclau, Chantal Mouffe, and other advocates of 'left populism' suggest that a radically democratic form of populism is the best possible means of countering right-wing populism (Laclau 2005; Mouffe 2018).

The notion that populism can serve radical democratic ideals therefore hinges on efforts to preserve internal difference and fluidity. But as I will demonstrate in this chapter, populism as a general organising strategy possesses key weaknesses and gaps that limit the achievement of radical democratic ideals in practice, in spite of the aims that are often expressed by its proponents. This is a concern that has been raised by a number of theorists who argue that populism inherently obstructs pluralist, egalitarian democracy in practice (de la Torre 2015). My objective in this chapter is therefore to point out some of the potential pitfalls of populist political movements, evident in their organisational, aesthetic and affective features, which, although they might contribute to political potency, risk the side-lining of minority viewpoints and a tendency to gloss over crucial differences and diversity. As I will show, these pitfalls are intensified when populism is enacted through digital media. This perspective sets the stage for the later chapters which consider the extent that theatrical and performative practices might reveal information about political interaction that is crucial to inclusive, pluralist, democratic politics – and that might, when *applied*, help to ensure that the goals of radical democracy are more effectively served.

Characteristics of Populism

It is not my objective to develop a concrete definition or typology of populism within this volume; rather, I want to examine some key features of populism that can ultimately be placed under a performance-informed lens, with the aim of drawing new insights about the operations of populism as a political process. My focus here is on manifestations of populism from the United States and United Kingdom – both countries that I have lived and worked in extensively. As suggested above, my analysis encompasses both left- and right-wing populism, in the belief that the democratic deficiencies of populism cut across the political spectrum. The following section therefore outlines key features that relate to the way that populist movements are organised and maintained. I conceive of these features not as inherent or defining traits of populist movements but rather as general tendencies that coalesce in various ways to produce what might be considered 'populist politics'; in other words, some combination of a number of these features produces a constellation of political attitudes, styles, and structures that in combination challenge representational democratic norms in the name of advocating for 'the people'.

To begin with, it is becoming commonplace to observe that populism is variously defined as a discourse (e.g. Laclau 2005; Mouffe 2018; Stavrakakis 2017);

a strategy (e.g. Laclau 2005; Mouffe 2018; Weyland 2017); an ideology (e.g. Albertazzi and McDonnell 2008; Mudde and Kaltwasser 2017); and a political style (Moffitt 2016). But regardless of how we group these takes on populism, each of them is to some extent limited in its ability to accurately describe the multifarious factors that lie behind populism in its various guises. Each of the typologies that scholars have attached to populism bleeds into the others, as the features outlined overlap and inform one another. It is therefore, to my mind, most useful to draw these varying explanations of populism together with the aim of outlining key features that are common, though not ubiquitous, across a range of populist movements. From this perspective I propose the following broad outline of the fundamental traits of populism: first, the existence of a group identifying as the people, contrived to singularly represent popular interests, and who are configured as a rightful alternative to a designated group that currently enjoys greater political power; second, a leader or figurehead who attempts to connect with this group in a maximally direct, unmediated fashion, and who serves as its symbolic representation; and finally, an affective style that arouses scepticism, anger and/or fear toward outsiders, and that subversively departs from existing norms of representational political arenas.

The points noted above are apparent concerns across the various literatures on populism, and these themes also give rise to recurring questions regarding the perceived democratic capacities and deficiencies of populism. In the following section I discuss these features of populism in more detail, in order to pave the way for a deeper consideration of left populism in the context of digital mediatisation.

Constructing 'the People'

Perhaps the most fundamental characteristic of populism, broadly conceived, is its attachment to a belief that the true 'people' are presently under-represented within existing political frameworks, and that a populist movement might offer a correction to this injustice. At issue here is the way that this bloc of the people is constructed, and the implications of this for inclusive, democratic politics.

Ernesto Laclau's notion of the 'logic of equivalence' offers a useful starting point. For Laclau, the diversity of the people's unmet needs can be transformed into a unifying movement through a 'logic of equivalence' that arises from shared feelings of exclusion or disregard; by uniting otherwise disparate groups under a banner of the left-behind or the disempowered, populist politics can create a notion of the people that possesses substantial political power, as opposed to the comparatively weak positions of smaller, special interest groups (Laclau 2005). In this manner, populist movements can be crafted out of the recognition of shared demands by diverse sectors of society. While individuals or groups may experience very different circumstances that give rise to economic insecurity, physical risk or feelings of disenfranchisement, an effective populist organisational strategy can make use of these shared outcomes to forge associations based on widespread recognition of common ground. This underpins the establishment of 'the people' – a unified mass that can effectively bid for recognition from those in political power.

Left populism is generally rooted in post-structuralist philosophies that emphasise the preservation of difference within the unifying identity of 'the people', bringing it into nominal accord with broader radical democratic projects; but in practice populism always risks the obliteration of pluralism (Mudde 2009, 8). This is because the construction of 'the people' relies on the projection of a unified, outward-facing identity in the interest of achieving and sustaining political leverage. Furthermore, because the inward-facing identity of populist groups is so broad – as a result of drawing equivalence across a wide range of movements or claims – the sustenance of a populist assembly relies heavily on imagined opposition to some outside 'other' entity.

Several scholars have examined the ways that frontiers of alterity are drawn differently according to the ideological basis of populist movements, and some suggest that the nature of the imagined other is a key defining feature of left vs. right populism (Macaulay 2019; March 2017; Salmela and von Scheve 2018). Whereas Right populism tends to configure 'the people' in opposition to ethnic or racial minorities, Left populism aims to construct 'the people' as a bloc of disenfranchised subgroups impacted negatively by neoliberalism. Taking the United States and United Kingdom as examples, we can find examples of this in both right- and left-leaning movements in both countries. In the United States, Trumpian populism configured the notion of 'the people' chiefly in opposition to immigrants and foreign powers. Alternatively, left-leaning populist campaigns, such as Bernie Sanders' bids for the 2016 and 2020 Democratic presidential nominations, mainly cited economic elites as the 'other' to which 'the people' was contrasted. In the United Kingdom, a similar picture emerged, with Boris Johnson and Nigel Farage emerging as figureheads who painted the European Union as the outside enemy (including the institution itself and EU citizens living or working in the United Kingdom), while also consistently referring to immigration as a threat to the welfare of British citizens. At the same time, the left-wing elements of the UK Labour party were united under the Momentum movement in support of Jeremy Corbyn, driven by rhetoric that painted both the Conservative government and the mainstream Parliamentary Labour Party as a class of elite politicians distanced from and irredeemably out of touch with the true people.

However, regardless of the apparent differences in the nature of right and left populist othering, the pursuit of a broadly encompassing identity of 'the people' often means that the definition of the outside other is problematically vague. Because the in-group is so broad in itself, this can engender disagreement about who and what should rightfully be included or excluded. In some cases, taking too much care to accommodate diverse viewpoints can lead to political enervation. For example, Jeremy Corbyn's Momentum movement in the United Kingdom stumbled in part due to the leader's efforts to accommodate both pro- and anti-EU sentiment (rooted in varying tenors of internationalist and anti-globalist sentiments across the party). Attempting to provide a direct representation of such a diverse range of perspectives (which differed in important ways from his own past beliefs), Corbyn struggled to articulate a clear position on EU membership (Beech and Hickson 2020).

More problematically, the exclusionary logics of populism tend to produce insider/outsider statuses that reflect hierarchical divisions already present in society. For example, the propensity for right-wing populism to produce exclusions on the basis of nationality, race or ethnicity is well-documented (e.g. Featherstone and Karaliotas 2019; Mudde 2009; Salmela and von Scheve 2018). But we also saw, in the course of both Sanders' and Corbyn's populist movements, examples of racial and ethnic discrimination by small but sometimes vocal subsets (Menon and DeCook 2021; Shaw 2021). In such cases the broad umbrella offered by populism can actually facilitate greater exclusionary antagonism, because the wide range of interest groups who identify with the movement bring their existing biases to bear in ways that sometimes don't reflect the membership as a whole.

Ultimately, although the designated 'others' differ depending on the ideological orientation of movements, for my purposes, the key point is that populism gives rise to a particular treatment of internal difference and dissent. When the disaffection and precarity of disparate groups are subsumed under a singular identity, populist organising short-circuits the operation of difference *in practice*, limiting the effect that interpersonal engagement might have on individual beliefs or political leanings. Instead of creating environments in which individual difference is actively expressed and negotiated, populist leaders tend to mask difference by assuring supporters that their unique concerns are all traceable to scapegoated Others – whether this be migrants, political elites, media channels, or some combination of villainised entities. As Cohen accurately sums up,

> In short, populist strategy ultimately involves a type of identity politics that not only plays on affect and strong cathected identifications (even if one knows the relevant identities and frontiers are constructed) aimed at dividing society into opposed camps—it also tends to personalize disagreement, fostering deeply segmented and stacked political identifiers that make it very hard to discuss, compromise, or work across frontiers.
>
> *Cohen 2019, 399*

In this way, the establishment of 'the people' is fundamentally at odds with inclusive, diverse democratic politics.

Populist Leadership

The construction of 'the people' is obviously fundamental to the emergence of populist movements, but once those movements are established they maintain a particular relationship to the political systems that they operate within.

According to Margaret Canovan, populism can be viewed as a shadow of democracy, produced by tensions within democratic systems that arise from the gap between conventional electoral processes and an actualisation of popular sovereignty (Canovan 1999). The appeal of populism comes in part from its guise as a direct and unmediated expression of the will of the people. In rare cases this might take the form of a sustained alternative mode of participation that sits outside of the system, but in most instances there is an evident desire to transform movements into legitimate contenders for electoral success – in the hope of more robustly pursuing the movement's ideals through legislative means.[1] In practice this involves a specific mode of leadership that attempts to retain some of the characteristics of direct democracy while adopting the requisite organisational structures demanded by the established system of representation.

Populist leadership unfolds in different ways; in some cases, it is at the behest of a single charismatic leader who invokes broad signifiers to mobilise followers in public spaces, be they physical or virtual (Laclau 2005; Macaulay 2019). This is the model followed by the likes of Donald Trump, who styles himself as the indispensable leader who is a central, driving force of his movement. In other cases, populist communities may arise more collectively and strive for horizontal organising and decision-making – a model that Paolo Gerbaudo describes as the 'populism of the leaderless people in which the function of the charismatic leader is substituted by the self-organizing power of the connected citizenry and by a number of unifying symbols and practices, from the occupied squares to social media and popular assemblies' (Gerbaudo 2017, 18). This mode of leadership often emerges from grassroots movements that strive to maximise direct, collaborative deliberation. However, a distinguishing feature of contemporary populism is the propensity for otherwise horizontal or amorphous movements to become crystallised under a central leader.

de la Torre makes a case that populist movements are thus paradoxical in nature: they rely on a consistent articulation of their movement as one that originates in the will and interests of 'the people', yet their power is marshalled and sustained by a small group of politicians who take charge of decision-making and actions with relatively little direct involvement from supporters. Ultimately, de la Torre argues that '[…] under populism the people and the nation speak with one voice, that of a small clique of politicians and ultimately the voice of the leader' (de la Torre 2019, 68).

A key feature of populism is therefore its tendency to be sustained, if not driven, by a charismatic figurehead or collection of figureheads who can step into the vacuum left by the inadequacies of representative politics. The role of this leader is not only to persuade the public that their previously neglected concerns are answered by the movement but, more importantly, to consolidate and perpetuate the identity of the movement by opposing it to a competing power entity within the existing political system.

Masterful performances are required here – populist leaders typically portray a character that appeals to the politically disenchanted groups they seek support from, and that enables a direct association with the people they purport to represent. To negotiate such a complex role, they must style themselves (or be styled by supporters or the media) as political outsiders who defy the norms of representational leadership in their attitudes and actions. So, for example, Donald Trump and Boris Johnson have both benefited from their tendency to misspeak and make impromptu faux pas, rewarded with supporters' claims that they are just 'regular people' (Bødker and Anderson 2019; Wood et al. 2016). Such tactics can also aid populist leaders to establish identifiable links with the values and customs of the people they seek to embody – so, for example, we rarely see the former UK Independence Party leader Nigel Farage without a pint of ale within reach, even in his latest guise as television news pundit on the newly established 'GB News'.[2]

It should be noted that populist leaders do not always seek out a central position at the top of a vertically structured power hierarchy, nor do they always deliberately portray a heightened character for their supporters; for example, Jeremy Corbyn explicitly attempted to develop a leadership style that directly countered such an approach (Watts and Bale 2019). Corbyn wished to maintain a direct relationship with grassroots Labour Party members, serving as a genuine representative of their views. However, such aims are difficult to realise when movements take up a position within an elected party; when this occurs a different mode of operation is required in order to maintain power within existing electoral systems and thereby achieve the movement's policymaking goals.

Ultimately the tendency for populist movements to identify with a charismatic leader means that they reproduce the representational logics otherwise apparent in the democratic status quo. Populism is therefore not only a 'shadow' of democracy, to use Canovan's term, but in many ways a simple mirror in which the mechanisms of representative authority are co-opted and reproduced in a manner that continues the enervation of popular sovereignty. Any aspiration that populist leaders might have for horizontally organised direct democracy is ultimately subsumed by the system that they seek to retain power within. In this sense, populism's ability to address the inadequacies of representative democracy is limited.

Emotion in Populist Politics

Populism is also marked by distinct aesthetic and emotive features. As I explain in Chapter 6, I view aesthetics and emotion as intertwined and interdependent aspects of performance experience; in this section I will discuss some of the key aesthetic traits of populist content in conjunction with related emotive themes.[3]

In the first instance, populism is regarded as a phenomenon that arises in part because of the side-lining of emotions in other forms of political organisation – that is, it responds directly to the over-privileging of rationality and reason in mainstream representative democracy, which results in the neglect of constituents' experiences and everyday concerns. Where political systems over-emphasise the rational pursuit of middle ground, this can leave citizens to feel that the impact of policymaking on individuals is not duly considered. Especially when trauma and suffering increase as a result of economic decline and austerity policies, pragmatic, rational political processes can appear to disregard or dismiss the magnitude of personal experience. Along these lines, Mareike Gebhardt suggests that populism is a response to liberal democracy's 'sober regime of rationality and reason' (2021, 131). In contrast to these more impassive forms of political interaction, populism is marked by heightened emotional content, including anger, fear, humour, mockery, and playfulness (Bos et al. 2013; Sakki and Martikainen 2021; Salmela and von Scheve 2018; Wirz 2018; Wodak 2015).

This emotionality is directly linked to the efficacy of such movements; as Chantal Mouffe describes, affective and emotional dimensions are vital to establishing a sense of collective identity in populist movements (Mouffe 2014). She sees theatre specifically, and the arts more generally, as potential fora for vibrant political engagements because of their capacity to generate dynamic affective impacts (Mouffe 2020, 193). The effect of intensified emotionality is also concretely borne out in electoral results: Dominique Wirz has studied emotional content in populist communications and demonstrated a direct link with electoral success (Wirz 2018).

Perhaps the most commonly discussed emotional quality of populism is its deliberate generation of fear and anger. A number of scholars have considered the extent to which populism rests on references to crisis, so much so that perceptions of crisis are generated even where it does not substantially exist in reality (see, e.g. Brubaker 2017; Homolar and Scholz 2019; Kurylo 2020; Steele and Homolar 2019). Populist leaders make incendiary references to, for example, bogus asylum seekers, migrant terrorists, corrupt elites, or the 1%, in the interest of affirming the internal identity of their movements; significantly, these statements not only function to demarcate the movement's insiders and outsiders; they also generate fear and anxiety on the part of listeners, and they produce the affective economies that fuel populist identities (Gebhardt 2021, 132). Fear is also closely linked to feelings of anger, which are further encouraged when populist leaders blame political opponents for failing to address the threats posed by scapegoated Others, thus building on the anxieties that have already been stimulated among their followers (see, e.g. Taggart 2000, 11) In this way populist fomentations of fear and anger coalesce to create a fundamental attitude of distrust, and this ultimately short-circuits people's engagement with new or different ideas and perspectives.

More sanguine emotions are also frequent in populist movements. Pride, for example, is often felt in response to a growing sense of empowerment and a perceived ability to dominate others or see them demoted in political hierarchies (Wirz 2018). Hope emanates in a similar fashion as populist leaders, having intensified feelings of fear and anger among their followers, go on to provide a vision of a more positive future that is dependent on their electoral success (Wirz 2018). Humour and playfulness are also common in populist communications, particularly through the prevalent defiance of the 'politically correct' and the celebration of transgressive behaviours or 'poor taste', especially when the primary targets of such behaviours are political opponents (Kurylo 2020).

Overall, populism often celebrates emotional qualities that are not normally associated with the usual business of politics, or that are considered blatantly inappropriate to the political realm – especially one that has become coloured by the sober rationality of middle-ground consensus. A heightened emotional range that expresses the affective impact of politics on individuals can reflect the populist movement's embodiment of the true people. But the common feature of the qualities discussed above is their tendency to reaffirm the antagonistic attitudes of populism more generally. Emotions ranging from fear and anger to hope and playfulness can be channelled in a manner that encourages an oppositional stance against outsiders or opponents. In this respect, the emotional elements of populism can coalesce with its organisational structures to effectively constrain inclusive pluralism.

It is clear that the construction of 'the people', the comportment of populist leadership, and populist affect all combine to conjure a unique environment that impacts the negotiation of internal difference and dissent. In most cases, it is likely that these features will support the overarching divisive and antagonistic characteristics of populism. However, advocates of left populism believe that these outcomes are not inevitable and are most likely to occur in the context of right-wing populist movements. Left populism, for some scholars, might be mobilised as a means of countering right populism; furthermore, by embracing a distinct approach to political engagement it might be possible for populism to enhance democratic pluralism rather than curtail it. Before considering the ways that digital media impacts populist interactions, it is therefore necessary to focus in more detail on the tenets of left populism specifically.

Left Populism

Throughout the following chapters I discuss elements of performance practice that are relevant to populism of all ideological designations – but I am particularly attendant to the arguments made by advocates of left populism, in order to critically assess the extent to which populist politics might be made more accordant with radical democratic principles through the application of performance-based knowledge. I want to stress that it is not my intention to conflate left and right populism, nor to downplay the gravity of right-wing populism by focusing on the challenges presented by its left-leaning counterparts. But left populism shares many of the flaws of populism more generally, which I feel applied performance practice might be particularly well-equipped to address. Given this, it is useful to summarise some of the key arguments of left populism.

As noted above, left populists see populism as a route to the renaissance of politics, offering an alternative to the otherwise stultified processes of representative democracy which have succumbed to elitism, technocracy and third-way politics. Since populism has already arisen among the political right, accompanied by nationalism and xenophobia, scholars like Laclau and Mouffe argue that a left-leaning populism must be developed to counterbalance this. However, in practice left populism exhibits many of the same structural and operational tactics that characterise populism more generally, although these are coloured somewhat differently (Laclau 2005; Mouffe 2018). This gives rise to a key point of division among scholars of populism. On the one hand, champions of left populism offer a number of compelling arguments and proposals that add nuance to the challenges outlined in the section above. Critics, on the other hand, suggest that left populism is nonetheless doomed to succumb to these weaknesses and ultimately fail in its radical democratic goals.

To begin with, left populism is distinct from populism more generally in terms of its approach to difference and Otherness; while it is essential for any populist movement to configure itself ontologically in opposition to an external other, left populism attempts to establish this in a more inclusive and flexible manner. Jean Cohen provides a useful summary:

> Left populism's strategy is to draw the frontier differently. [...T]he claim is that left populism is inclusive rather than exclusive, that it challenges social and cultural hierarchies, radicalizes and democratizes democracy, and is oriented to social justice. Left populism mobilizes previously marginalized, discriminated-against or newly excluded sectors of society, opening up the political system to new actors and giving voice to representatives of those ignored by existing parties.
>
> *Cohen 2019, 395*

The crux of the justification for left populism is therefore its ability to attract and respond to a greater diversity of participants, thus creating a more inclusive model of democracy that is more authentically representative of the whole of society. The identity frontiers required by such a movement are explicitly drawn in ways that seek to ensure the inclusion of previously disregarded or disenfranchised groups.

However, despite these laudable aims, left populism is still faced with challenges with regard to its capacity to accommodate internal difference in practice. Attempts to create greater inclusivity might simply result in paying lip service to many disparate groups while inadequately representing the perspective of many of them. Left-populism advocates counter such claims, in part by celebrating the potential for populist movements to create empathy for people whose lives are very different to one's own. They consider the possibility, for example, of people from very different cultural, geographic and economic backgrounds finding common ground on the basis of similar experiences of loss or precarity (Butler 2004; Reinelt 2019). Problematically though, this view risks obscuring the relative privilege or disadvantage of those involved and also overemphasises the likelihood of achieving political consensus between very different subjects, without knowing anything more about their backgrounds or political beliefs than the fact that they have both experienced risk, loss or trauma (Conway and Singh 2011). In this way it is limited in its ability to achieve inclusivity in practice.

In addition, left populism attracts criticism for the extent to which it remains dependent on demarcations of insiders and outsiders, in just the same way that right-wing populism does. Even when the construction of identity frontiers is rooted in social justice aims, as, for example, when the economic elite or the over-represented are configured as the chief ontological outsiders, some theorists stress that left populism still exhibits a reliance on an oppositional outside other, retaining a fundamental attitude of confrontation (de la Torre 2019). Left populists attempt to address this by asserting that the frontiers of difference should never be settled but rather configured as always shifting and always in the process of reconfiguration. As such, left populism establishes a fluid and uncertain orientation to ontological others.

Rather than a crystallised populist movement based on unchanging ideologies and identities, left populists subscribe to the notion that the movement will always be subject to contestation as the many multiple frontiers of difference within it shift and realign in an ongoing, unpredictable process. This brings radical democratic goals back to the forefront of populism; As Gebhardt reminds us, instability is essential to radical democracy:

> [... T]hese borders are never final, never done, never completed, never 'truly' given, but always made. They are haunted by their inability to perfect: to finally and forever manifest. They, instead, always fail perfection. This is the strength of radical democracy not its flaw since the formulation of 'we' becomes open, ever-changing, and amorph. The populist moment within radical democracy does not turn regressive. If it does, radical democracy is transformed into something different. To qualify as radical democratic, the populist moment always needs to keep its openness feeding on both its progressive potential and radical instability.
>
> *Gebhardt 2021, 144*

This is supported by Chantal Mouffe's concept of 'conflictual consensus', which champions the continuance of ongoing internal debate and contestation, couched within an indisputable framework of liberty and equality. Conflictual consensus seeks to acknowledge and perpetuate the essential role of debate and disagreement, and ultimately difference (Mouffe 2005).

In this vein, a key point made by Mouffe centres on the development of agonism, as opposed to antagonistic politics. Agonism and engagement is the focus of the next chapter in this book, but I introduce the topic here to provide a reminder of what is at stake when populism becomes a dominant mode of political interaction. Ernesto Laclau's discussion of antagonism stresses that the process of identification against an external force inherently depends first on the recognition of that external other. He distinguishes populist politics in this way from genocide, for example, in which the beliefs and actions of the group would be based upon non-recognition of an other's legitimate existence (Laclau 2005). Mouffe develops this idea and argues that left populist political conflict 'does not take the form of an antagonism (struggle between enemies) but of an agonism' (Mouffe 2018, 91). Agonism suggests a respectful struggle between adversaries in which there is greater emphasis on the benefits of ongoing contestation rather than the pursuit of definitive victory or defeat.

This is a point that I find most promising when viewing populism through a performance-oriented lens; by considering populism as a process, we might bring interactive, interpersonal experience more squarely into the frame of analysis – and in doing so, we might begin to understand the prominent influence of these features on democratic political deliberation. However, it must be acknowledged that in practice agonism is not often achieved within populist movements. Despite the good intentions of left populism, it too often remains rooted in a fundamental recourse to combative notions of insiders and outsiders or 'the people' vs. the elite. Ultimately, while left populism espouses hopeful principles that suggest ways of pursuing inclusivity and pluralism within populist politics, it remains too susceptible to the structural and affective traits that are evident in populism of all ideological stripes. This is in no small part due to the way that digital populism exacerbates these weaknesses, and this is the focus of the next section of this chapter.

Digital Populism

When we add a tendency for populism to be enacted via digital media, the concerns outlined above become even more pressing. While left populism might seek to preserve inclusiveness and a fluid approach to difference and identity, the characteristics of digitally mediated communication often truncate such possibilities; instead of lingering on differences and engaging thoughtfully with alternative perspectives, social media users are all too often encouraged to partake of a performance of either/or, for or against. In this section I will outline some of the key traits of digitally mediated political communications, demonstrating the ways that social media can present obstacles to the pursuit of pluralistic democracy.

It is important to note at the outset that digital populism as a term refers to a range of characteristics relating to online and digitally mediated interactions; it encompasses not only the algorithms that determine what content is successful and for whom (what some theorists refer to as 'algorithmic populism'), but the full scope of changes that occur when interpersonal communication and interaction moves into a disembodied, digital sphere (Baldwin-Philippi 2019; Kim 2008; Maly 2020). For this reason we need to consider the ways that digital platforms shape the experience and actions of users, but also how users' behaviours change when enacted online.

Fundamentally, it should be recognised that digital media platforms are entangled with other cultural and political complexities that influence their integrity as sources of seemingly unbiased information. Although they appear as relatively benign platforms that provide a medium for the free exchange of viewpoints, in actuality the design and operation of social media channels are influenced by the cultural perspectives of their designers, as well as by societal behavioural norms that are upheld by the community of users who populate them (Finlayson 2020, 5). In this respect the levels of pluralist engagement that are achievable within digital populist contexts are already constrained by the influences of the political and cultural perspectives of those who design and interact with them. This results in a number of limitations that frequently exacerbate the weaknesses of populism more generally.

To begin with, we can consider the ways that digital mediatisation complicates the foundational construction of a unified bloc of 'the people'. At first glance, the potential of social media seems promising on this front. When politics moves into online environments it is generally thought to enable more people to participate, and to provide for more democratised production of content – at least insofar as a far greater range of individual people may produce content, as opposed to content being selected and curated by media professionals (Klinger and Svensson 2015). Akin to this, some researchers suggest that social media users are exposed to a greater range of information sources than non-users (Margetts 2018). These points underscore the pluralising potential of digital media. However, it is necessary to look more closely at the ways that this potential unfolds in practice.

In the first part of this chapter I stressed the ways that the establishment of 'the people' brings with it a risk of heightened political exclusion, based on populism's need to construct the broadly defined 'us' against a unifying outward 'other'. To understand the role that social media plays in this, we need to account for the ways that platforms deliver content to users.[4] Broadly speaking, digital platforms support the division of users into like-minded camps that exclude others. In the first instance, these digital social worlds can encourage users to downplay similarities in experiences or identities that underpin social group formations in real life. Instead, social media offers individuals greater opportunities to forge common links with others who espouse similar interests or values (Gerbaudo 2018, 8). This happens in part due to the natural consequences of 'following' people similar to oneself; but it is further exacerbated by social media algorithms that curate content for users based on popularity and resonance with the users' browsing history (Maly 2020). This is important because it has a direct consequence on the range of content that users will encounter.

Furthermore, social media algorithms shape the information that will be displayed to particular users on the basis of market-driven values, prioritizing '[…] hierarchy, competition and a winner-takes-all mindset' (Van Dijck 2013, 21). This runs directly counter to principles of pluralist inclusivity. It puts users into competition with one another and divides them into shallow, interest-based camps on the basis of profit-generating business models. Altogether, although a greater range of content exists in the digital sphere, social media still cultivates homophily, the tendency of similar individuals to form ties with each other

(Colleoni et al. 2014, 318). Despite the fact that the internet offers the possibility of engaging with more numerous and diverse viewpoints, in practice this potential isn't fully realised.

Populist leadership is also impacted by digital mediation. Although populist leaders and movements position themselves as the voice of the people and often use digital media in an effort to reinforce this notion, the characteristics of social media have a tendency to reinforce top-down political organising (Davis and Taras 2020). This is partly because the online presence of populist leaders tends to be mono-directional: users form 'interest relationships' with politicians whereby they follow the leader's social media feed and post content about that leader, but there is little to no direct engagement on the part of the leader themselves.

This mode of engagement is further problematised by the fact that social media platforms facilitate selective and strategic communications by leaders. Due to the temporal gap between posts and responses, populist party leaders (or their social media coordinators) are able to speculatively post experimental content and then gauge the reaction from followers, strategically modifying or building on that content accordingly (Gonawela et al. 2018). Furthermore, political parties are becoming increasingly savvy users of the data footprints generated by social media accounts in order to tailor their communications or other engagements[5] (Bennett 2015; Gonawela et al. 2018). This has been developed into fragmented, granular-level political engagement since messaging can be tailored for particular groups or regions based on detailed data about the political leanings of particular demographics. Ultimately this facilitates micro-targeted presentations of multiple variations of political scripts while minimising the importance of dialogue and engagement that would otherwise be necessary for building and sustaining political movements. In this way, populist leadership, enacted online, can become a masterful theatrical performance of unification rather than a genuinely unifying movement.

The emotionality of social media is also exacerbated within online environments, primarily because there is a symbiotic relationship between the heightened emotions of populism and the achievement of visibility on the part of users. Social media platforms operate within the structure of an 'attention economy' which necessitates competition for other users' attention and response (Davenport and Beck 2001). Significantly, highly emotional, simplified and confrontational communications are typically the ones that are most often liked and reposted (Engesser et al. 2017, 1285–86). In effect, this encourages the circulation of heightened performances of emotion by users who wish to increase their visibility and impact in digitally mediated spheres. As a result, digital media environments become marked by a heightened emotionality that dovetails with the populist appetite for emotional content.

It is also crucial to keep in mind that the competitive pursuit of visibility on social media platforms significantly diminishes horizontal engagement. In the first instance this occurs because of the incentives for users to control the visibility of other users in a manner that will support their own online popularity. As

Daniel Dayan explains, this environment motivates users to exert their influence with a view to regulating the visibility and popularity of others:

> Not only do such media allow publics to acquire visibility, and to acquire visibility on their own terms, but they also allow them to define the visibility of others, to become organizers of visibility. [...] Beyond the search for visibility, it consists in the possibility for any citizen of becoming a 'visibility entrepreneur' and thus of performing a function that journalists see as a task but that many others perceive as a privilege. Visibility entrepreneurs wish to emulate what they perceive as the crucial power of journalists: the divine power of 'conferring visibility'. Conquering such a power is attempted today on a mass scale.
>
> *Dayan 2013, 143*

Savvy users draw on the algorithmic foundations of social media platforms to garner a false appearance of their own popularity while also diminishing the visibility of others. This is often achieved by paying others for clicks and reposts or making use of bot networks to generate supportive or denigrating content as the circumstances require (Maly 2020). In political contexts, the distribution of visibility and invisibility established in such environments is likely to reflect existing social divisions and exclusions. As a result, digital media platforms are likely to further the invisibility of some groups, significantly limiting opportunities for engagements with difference.

Finally, it must also be acknowledged that digital populism thwarts true democratic engagement due to the fundamental presence of misinformation. The pervasiveness of this problem is significant; for example, by the time of the 2016 US presidential election, Facebook users were engaging more with fake news stories than factual information (Morris 2020, 3). James Morris provides a reminder of the emergence of this phenomenon, alternatively referred to as 'post-truth' or 'fake news':

> The prominent phrase in this disruption, already a cliche a few months after its emergence, was 'fake news' (also known as 'alternative facts' by some on the right-hand side of the political spectrum). Pundits and academics were soon describing the new era as 'post-truth' [...] arguing that we have entered a phase where facts are radically devalued in favour of shallow appearances and confirmation bias, fuelled by the meteoric rise in our usage of online social media over the last decade. Some have even argued that truth itself has been weaponised.
>
> *Morris 2020, 2*

As I've already described in the introduction to this book, the term 'post-truth' originated from the pen of a playwright, a fact which I believe to be more than coincidental. Especially in social media contexts, there is a clear overlap between the phenomenon of misinformation and theatricality more broadly. As social media users become increasingly conscious of the presence of misinformation, they deploy a cynical and sceptical mode of engagement with others, especially those with whom they are comparatively unfamiliar, or who they already consider political opponents. In this manner they become akin to theatrical critics who evaluate the integrity and worth of others' contributions and bring their existing world views to bear on their verdicts. Ultimately, instead of dialogic engagement, post-truth digital populism hinges on theatrical spectacle.

Altogether, the prominent role that social media plays in contemporary political communications significantly impacts the ways that people interact with one another. This is especially important when considering the relationship between left populism and digital media, given the centrality of productive modes of interaction and engagement within left populist philosophies. There can be little doubt that social media increases the rapidity of movement-building and potentially unites a greater number of people. However, this occurs in part because digitally mediatised interactions mask fine details of difference that would otherwise require engagement and deliberation; instead the environment is dominated by popularly promoted content that attracts mass support or opposition.

Conclusion: Redeeming a Left Populism in Practice

In the discussion above I have outlined my scepticism about populism, and particularly the potential for a 'left populism' to establish a truly effective alternative to the stultification of representative democracy. My objections pertain primarily to the characteristic features of populism that stymie pluralist democratic processes, and which are greatly exacerbated by digital media. Too often, populism of both left and right varieties seems to champion electoral success at the expense of true collaboration, dialogue, empathy and respectful debate.

However, and despite the challenges presented by digital populism, I maintain that there may yet be strong potential to construct popular movements that to some extent embody the principles espoused by left populists. To achieve this it might be illustrative to return to radical democratic initiatives like the Occupy Movement, where we can find a clear example of a unified collective emerging from disparate individual circumstances, based on opposition to a shared external opponent – in this case the economic '1%'. A crucial point that distinguished the Occupy Movement was that in practice the Occupy assemblies operated through a constant, open-ended process of story-sharing, listening, and dialogic communication (Taylor 2011; Writers for the 99% 2012). The celebration of ongoing interaction, and the centralisation of uncertainty and incompleteness, demonstrated the potential that these traits might achieve in the context of other political processes and movements, left populism included. In contrast to most contemporary populist movements, Occupy stressed, above almost all other considerations, the principle of collaborative *making* in an environment of uncertainty. Occupy might be seen as a victim of its own success in this regard, as multiple viewpoints were given airtime and thus the complexity of socioeconomic and political issues became clear; but it illustrated key principles that mark it out as a very different entity to recent populist movements.

Perhaps, then, the most compelling arguments for the potential of left populism come from theorists who focus on populism *in practice*. Crucial to this point is the emphasis that left populists place on the continuance of difference within a movement that is never a fixed entity but rather an ongoing process (Laclau 2005; Marino 2018; Reinelt 2019). Performance theorist Janelle Reinelt suggests that populist equivalences can leave plenty of room for internal differences if they are understood as always-unfinished, unfolding in action; she refers to this as a 'highly mobile version of populism' which is inherently 'performative' (2019, 62). This being the case, and remaining cognisant of the challenges posed by digital media, it seems apt to question what performance knowledge might bring to the puzzles of populism.

Theatre and Performance scholars and practitioners have addressed populism and its inspirations from a number of angles. This can range from performance studies analyses of the structures and logics of populist movements, to critical aesthetic perspectives that position theatrical performances as a means of resistance to populist exclusions (Asavei and Kocian 2020; Reinelt 2019). Some have explored the ways that staged performance might offer robust challenges to the inadequacies of contemporary liberal democracy, such as Rimini Protokoll's explorations of post-democracy in *State 1-4* (Rimini Protokoll n.d.). Others are keen to consider how theatre might facilitate left populism. Florian Malzacher, for example, suggests that theatre might offer a useful complement to radical democracy and agonistic politics:

> Theatre is not only a social but also always a self-reflexive practice, despite the fact that conventional approaches have been neglecting this. Theatre is a paradoxical machine that marks a sphere where things are real and not real at the same time and proposes situations and practices that are symbolic and actual at once
>
> *Malzacher 2020, 172*

Work like this provides a foundation for furthering our examination of the role of performance in different kinds of populism and also for making a case for the inclusion of new performance practices in radical democratic and left populist movements.

To achieve this goal we need to seek out creative practices that might reinvigorate political participation through heightened experiences of pluralist interaction. This requires careful attention to theatrical and performative practices that can facilitate inter-relational experiences that lead to new and different practices of pluralism; ones which foreground the expression and experience of differences while retaining the potential for sustained cooperation or cohesion. In other words, rather than seeking equivalence across difference, I am suggesting a practical approach to doing and making politics based on working within difference, thus pursuing transformation not through the amalgamation of many claims of disaffection but rather in a commitment to the process of responsive, engaged, dialogic politics. This is an aim that resonates strongly with Chantal Mouffe's concepts of conflictual consensus and agonism, but I seek to inflect it with an emphasis on the way that such principles might manifest through interactive performance practice. In the remaining sections of this book I aim to interrogate the ways that Applied Theatre and performance might contribute to such initiatives, on the basis that these practices have often sought to bring people together to create effective interventions into representative politics, and to re-imagine the form that democratic politics might take. This is obviously a goal shared by proponents of radical democracy and left populism. Perhaps by bringing these fields into consideration we can come closer to realising their aims in practice.

3

ENCOUNTER AND ENGAGEMENT

As the previous chapters have established, digital populism is marked by notable shifts in the ways that people interact and engage with one another in political contexts. To unpack this idea further, this chapter turns to a deeper examination of qualities of interpersonal engagement. I am using the term engagement here to refer to the nature of encounters and interactions that occur between individuals or groups, especially those that take place in the context of pre-existing differences or oppositions. Fundamentally, in what ways do the established codes of political frameworks tend to engender some types of engagement and render others unlikely? What are the attitudes that flow from these delimitations that condition the qualities and scope of interactions to follow? This is of course an issue of concern to a number of politics scholars who write about radical democracy, populism, and political performance (e.g. Butler 2004, 2015; Connolly 2002; Mouffe 2018). For projects that seek to reinvigorate democratic participation, engagement is crucial. But I am also cognisant of the fact that modes of encounter and interaction are naturally a primary area of concern for Theatre scholars and practitioners, given that field's interest in issues of spectatorship and participation. Throughout this chapter I aim to demonstrate that theatrical perspectives on engagement and interaction can bring new insights to political debates about democratic assembly and participation.

It is worth noting at the outset that some theorists question efforts to extrapolate qualities of interpersonal interaction to civic or institutional arenas (Wingenbach 2011). This is not simply attributable to a lack of acknowledgement of the relationship between the personal and the political; rather the scepticism is primarily aimed at oversimplified extensions of interpersonal processes to comparatively depersonalised institutional frames and contexts. Given that this book attempts to engage directly with some institutional aspects of democracy, it is worth acknowledging this perspective. However, I maintain the usefulness of

DOI: 10.4324/9780367824129-5

my approach for two key reasons: firstly, I am sympathetic to the philosophical principles of radical democracy that attempt to maximise direct participation by the populace – a form of institutional politics in which interpersonal engagement is unquestionably paramount. Taking the example of Occupy and other leftist movements into account, we might consider new opportunities for individuals to contribute, through direct interaction with others, to larger frameworks of governance. Secondly, studies of digitally mediated communication substantiate the notion that changes to interpersonal interactions have impacts on higher societal levels, for example, families and communities (Baym 2015; Skoric et al. 2016). It is thus, to my mind, very plausible that we might change the nature of institutional democracy by impacting interpersonal interactions.

In this chapter I begin with a discussion of ancient Greek theatre and its influence on notions of antagonism and agonism, concepts which have been central to scholarship on democracy, populism, and political performance in recent decades (e.g. Bishop 2004; Fisher and Katsouraki 2017; Honig 2011; Little and Lloyd 2009; Mouffe 2020; Tully 1995; Wenman 2013). Agonism is a complex and contested notion, and one which reveals the philosophical departures that characterise some of the major theorists' contributions to the study of populism. This chapter provides a brief overview of key points that are particularly relevant to digital populist contexts and questions of performance. In particular I address debates about the merits of political consensus alongside Chantal Mouffe's calls for agonistic pluralism, and I argue that this approach cannot be sustained without turning our attention to the way that populist politics unfold in interactive practice. To further this line of thinking, I consider practices and concepts that originate in Applied Theatre. I show that we can supplement our understanding of agonism by positioning it as an experiential and interactive phenomenon – notably I turn to Augusto Boal's use of the term *metaxis*, which offers an illustrative example of politics in practice that deliberately eschews consensus while also avoiding antagonism.

Introducing Agonism

Theorists of agonism often make reference to Ancient Greek democracy, rendering this one area of thought in which theatre and politics explicitly overlap and intertwine.[1] As Erika Fischer-Lichte describes, democracy and theatre not only emerged more or less concurrently, but they also possessed an oft-times symbiotic relationship in which theatre posed incisive questions and challenges to political practices, and simultaneously, political institutions and practices informed the form and content of theatre (Fischer-Lichte 2002).

Democracy, seen through the lens of theatre, bears traces of the ancient performance agon: the contest of poets, aided by the actors under their direction, that would determine which poet would obtain influence and power through military or political positions in the years to follow (Fischer-Lichte 2002, 8). Most significantly, the agon was not only staged as a contest in its own right;

the contents of the main theatrical performances also thematically and formally mirrored the social and political forums that they occurred within; this was achieved through the tragic structure of performances that positioned one character in oppositional dialogue with another[2]; and this innovative theatrical device – antagonistic characters – was not only remarkable for its impact on theatre; it had a direct counterpart in the pluralistic, conflictual comportment of the polis. Thus democracy, like tragic theatre, is marked by the irreducibility of difference – that is, the essential ongoing presence of diversity and discord (Fisher 2017; Tambakaki 2017, 578).

A tragic conception of politics therefore foregrounds antagonistic contest as the foundation of all political interaction. Pluralism necessitates disagreement, and this means that the *agon* – variously translated as conflict or struggle – is a fundamental feature of democratic politics. For Tony Fisher, politics therefore becomes defined 'through the experience of its antagonisms' (Fisher 2017). By emphasising the intrinsic pluralism of democratic societies, and the inevitable conflict that flows from this, the matter that comes to the fore is how best to address democracy's antagonistic essence. There is an inherent risk that antagonism, while vital to the healthy sustenance of democracy, if left unchecked will result in violent conflict as one side or another seeks to eliminate its political foes. Antagonism is both essential to democracy, and also the force which might undo it.

In the face of this paradox, one option is the pursuit of consensus, through justifiable processes that result in widely acceptable middle ground. Perhaps most influentially, Jürgen Habermas stressed the importance of pursuing such aims through rational, inclusive, and deliberative means in order to bring about legitimate consensus (Habermas 1979, 1987). But critics argue that this approach risks a certain deadening of democratic political interaction by downplaying disagreement and stultifying what might otherwise manifest as dynamic, if antagonistic, diversity. Furthermore, theorists who stress post-structuralist perspectives critique consensus-building for the way that it obscures operations of power that delimit who is included or excluded from political processes in the first place (e.g. Mouffe 1992). An over-adherence to political consensus is believed to result in a crystallised central political bloc that disregards the claims of those destined to remain on its fringes.

It is in this sense that Chantal Mouffe has recently critiqued the depoliticising effects of consensus-building. She cites the enfeebling effects of 'third way' political parties and agendas that set out to occupy a political middle-ground, building a broadened base of support while multiplying the sense of disaffection among those sections of society whose interests remain unanswered. Mouffe objects to consensus as a political end-goal on the basis that: 'every consensus exists as a temporary result of a provisional hegemony, as a stabilization of power, and that it always entails some form of exclusion. The ideas that power could be dissolved through a rational debate and that legitimacy could be based on pure rationality are illusions [...]' (2000, 104). As such, the process of consensus results in an appearance of settled agreement which masks the circulation of internal difference and exclusions. In this sense, consensus might simply hide incidents of marginalisation and oppression. For Mouffe, since inclusive consensus is impossible, what is required in its place is a recognition of the ineradicability of conflict.

However, the possibility for antagonistic conflict to give rise to eruptions of violence or oppression, or a privileging of individual interests over communal life, requires some constraining force to modify its worst tendencies while still retaining it as a fundamental feature of democracy. In this way, both consensus and antagonism contain the potential for violence to some degree (Wingenbach 2011, 24). It is on this basis that a number of theorists advocate agonistic alternatives. For proponents of agonism, democracy should be viewed as an everlasting contest between competing visions, beliefs, and identities – a contest which is never resolvable and which never results in long-term settlement of differences. The overarching goal is to encourage respectful disagreement and debate, maintaining the presence of pluralistic conflict but containing it within frameworks or guiding principles that transform antagonism from a combative contest into a process of respectful democratic engagement (e.g. Connolly 2002; Honig 2011; Mouffe 2005, 2018).

Theorists of agonism take up a range of positions, but for the purpose of examining its relevance to digital populism and interpersonal engagement, I want to highlight one key point of departure: following Karagiannis and Wagner, we might distinguish between Arendtian agonists on the one hand, and Schmittian agonists on the other (Karagiannis and Wagner 2008). Agonists who follow Arendt (or an interpretation of Arendt broadly aligned with republicanism) adhere to a notion of the individual's civic duty to the polity in its entirety. (Karagiannis and Wagner 2008; Wingenbach 2011, 61). For Arendt, the ideal public realm is marked by engagement in conflict, but in a manner that seeks to passionately contest individual perspectives in the interest of the public as a whole – but Arendt differed from Habermas by downplaying the rational, deliberative mode of consensus-building, preferring to emphasise the playful performance of one's ideals, in action with adversarial others (Arendt 1998; Roberts-Miller 2002, 589). Significantly though, Arendt stressed that to facilitate this, it is first necessary to establish an environment in which there is 'some broad agreement about the nature of the common good' (Karagiannis and Wagner 2008, 329). The problem here is that a staking out of the 'common good' automatically necessitates exclusions, which has the potential to undermine the radical participatory goals of left populism. This leads other agonists to lean more heavily on the writings of Carl Schmitt, understanding the existence of struggle or conflict, the agon, to take primacy over everything else, thus rendering any firm agreement about the 'common good' impossible (Schmitt 1996). This perspective has the advantage of enabling greater inclusivity and genuine plurality, though it risks engendering antagonistic violence.

As a result, recent theorists of radical democracy and agonistic politics negotiate this terrain by seeking approaches that retain irresolvable conflict as the root of radical democratic political engagement but contain the necessary features to ensure that this conflict is couched within an attitude of respect for adversaries. In recent years, Chantal Mouffe's writings have become one of the best-known and frequently critiqued examples of this nature (2005, 2014, 2018). Mouffe, building on earlier work with Laclau (e.g. 1985), puts forward a notion of agonism that positions it as a means of transforming Schmittian conflict by insisting on the constant presence of antagonism, alongside efforts to ensure that the frontiers of conflict are continually being redrawn. In other words, Mouffe and Laclau insist on the fluidity of conflict, and envision it as a constantly shifting thing. Their ideal of political conflict is one that manifests in multiple unknowable ways and defies overly exclusionary frameworks based on notions of shared morals or 'the common good' (Laclau and Mouffe 1985; Mouffe 2000, 2005). For Mouffe, the necessity for a recognition of some common moral ground is sufficiently answered by an insistence on 'liberty and equality' (Mouffe 2005, 32). In this way, Mouffe selects a careful path between the republican and Schmittian approaches to agonism, in an effort to draft conflict and disagreement into a productive mobilising force for left populism. Mouffe's 'agonistic pluralism' celebrates a Schmittian-inspired acknowledgement of friend/enemy conflict, recharacterised as a fluid, respectful and constructive mode of political engagement; by insisting on the impossibility of settled consensus, alongside an adherence to base principles of liberty and equality, Mouffe hopes that left populism can provide a truly pluralistic frame for democratic engagement - one which prompts wider and reinvigorated participation (2018).

The Inadequacies of Agonism

Left populist invocations of agonism generally posit a remedy for political disenchantment brought about by consensus-building and the stultification of politics by leaders and processes that don't respond to or inspire people. This remedy relies on an approach to political engagement that 'embrace[s] the irreducibility of radical pluralism, and work[s] to cultivate a politics in which no particular set of values, identities, or rules may establish itself as beyond contestation' (Wingenbach 2011, 64). This requires a practical approach to politics that prioritises the *facilitation* of respectful dialogue in the face of powerful differences and division. However, when left populism attempts to instantiate agonism in practice (perhaps especially digitally), more often than not, it fails to achieve respectful adversarialism. Instead it results in more deeply entrenched desires to eradicate, silence, or shut down the other side – often through deliberate misreadings, obfuscations and combative rhetoric.

This failure tends to manifest differently depending on the level of the populist movement at which they occur. An interesting dichotomy appears between the failures of interpersonal populist political interactions on the one hand, and the representations of populist movements by their figureheads. There is a tendency in interpersonal interactions, especially when digitally mediated, to revert to combative antagonism. This might arise from a perceived need to counter what is seen as immorality on the part of political foes, or from a desire to establish a sense of broadly agreed principles of 'common good'. Often, within movements themselves, we see a clear staking out of moral claims that are viewed as lines in the sand which cannot be crossed – this may relate to anti-racism, anti-militarisation, human rights, equality and the like; but it might also extend intolerance of particular terminologies, conceptual frameworks, or associations with those perceived to be political foes (Ott 2017). Significantly, whatever the precise character of these moral hard lines, they are *enacted* in combative, frequently disrespectful, modes of engagement with opponents. In these cases differences proliferate and actively limit the extent to which people will genuinely engage with one another.

On the other hand, leaders of populist movements sometimes fail to sufficiently celebrate, and thus sustain, the existence of difference and division within their own movements. This limits the scope of the movement, as was the case when Jeremy Corbyn's Labour Party was unable to forge sufficient links between newer Momentum-inspired members and more long-standing working class Labour voters, particularly in the North of England and Scotland (Beech and Hickson 2020). The division that appeared between a left-activist Labour contingent fronted by Corbyn on the one hand and disaffected voters in post-industrial Northern towns on the other was one that might have been ripe for healing through the identification of shared experiences of precarity and political marginalisation – yet for the most part this didn't occur, raising questions about what else might have been needed for this populist movement to facilitate explorations of internal differences in a practical fashion.

A further complication for left populist agonism is the fact that political interactions are always coloured by existing social structures that grant power unevenly to various groups of people (Ahmed 2004; Butler 2015). It is crucial to consider the ways that race, ability, gender, nationality and class impact the capacity of people to participate on equal footing with one another, and this presents another great challenge for agonistic pluralism (Connolly 2002). It is not possible to instantiate a political assembly that is not already marked by the inequalities and hierarchies that pervade whatever comes before it. This means that calls for agonism are unlikely to entirely offset the divisive partisanship that is attendant to populism generally. This is perhaps even more true when we consider the extent to which political interactions are shaped by digital media contexts.

As discussed above, an essential principle behind Mouffe's notion of agonism lies in her belief that political bodies are always undergoing a process of internal contention regarding what constitutes the inside/outside (2005, 269). This means that the constitutive notions of us/them that underpin populist politics should be always in flux, always subject to revision. The exclusions that result from antagonistic behaviours and legacies of inequality might therefore be viewed as just one set of frontiers that will inevitably be reshaped through the ever-shifting agonistic reconfigurations of left populism. However, I would argue that it becomes more difficult to sustain this characterisation in the face of digital populism – because in its online-mediated context, digital populism encourages the wholesale denigration of political opponents, including sometimes their ostracisation and threats to their physical, real-world well-being. At root, agonistic values are often lost in the polarising and crystallising tendencies of digital populism. This necessitates a closer examination of some of the features of digital populism that are likely to impede ongoing agonistic interactions.

There are many facets of digitally mediated interaction that thwart the pursuit of agonism. There can be little doubt that the homophily of social media truncates the flow of differences among political adversaries; rather than enabling groups to acknowledge contesting points of view and engage in ongoing processes of negotiation, the algorithms of social media facilitate a view of the world in which internal differences seem insignificant. Perhaps more significantly though, agonistic engagement is severely impacted by the competitive bid for attention that digital media necessitates. The influence of powerful 'visibility entrepreneurs' means that online political debate is unlikely to take place in an environment of 'liberty and equality', precisely because the ability for individuals to be seen and heard is already unequally distributed (Dayan 2013). It seems likely that the competition for visibility within online environments also gives rise to antagonistic attitudes toward others. With an emphasis on entrepreneurial individuality as opposed to the common good (no matter how fluidly defined), social media exacerbates populist tendencies toward antagonistic vitriol.

The evidence for this is stark and not unfamiliar to anyone who has viewed political content on social media. Studies of Twitter and Facebook have revealed a number of forms that online divisiveness might take, covering, for example, the linguistic and rhetorical features of negative posts and the strategies used to link topical political debates to scapegoated others. Hillary Clinton was indelibly labelled 'Crooked Hillary' by Donald Trump; a similar feat was attempted by Nigel Farage who painted David Cameron as 'Pathetic David Cameron'; the same feature is also true on the left, where Jeremy Corbyn's Momentum supporters regularly referred to more centrist elements of the Labour Party as 'Blairite Scum' (Hoffmann 2018; Liddle 2017). Threats of violence, including sexual violence and property damage, abound in online exchanges, and sometimes tragically spill over into real life, as was the case in the murder of Labour MP Jo Cox in 2016. Added to this is the fact that wider social inequalities are replicated in digitally mediated debates, with 35% more black and Asian women MPs receiving abusive tweets as compared to their white colleagues (Dhrodia 2017). The fact that negative or critical messaging has been consistently more effective in generating online attention makes this all the more pressing, as it means that the homophily experienced by social media users is likely to be coloured by the disproportionately recirculated posts generated by the most divisive behaviours (Gonawela et al. 2018). All of this adds up to a context that is far from the environment of agonistic pluralism imagined by Chantal Mouffe and other left populists. Clearly, something more is required to establish an environment in which 'liberty and equality' are more likely to prevail.

Agonism as a Performance Practice

As a result of the challenges outlined above, if we wish to pursue a politics of agonism that is truly based on respect for adversaries rather than a reversion to winner-takes-all antagonistic engagements, there is a clear need to consider what kinds of creative interventions might transform such behaviours into more positive modes of interaction. What is required, to my mind, is to focus squarely on how that engagement unfolds *in practice*. This insistence on viewing agonism from the perspective of interactive practice chimes strongly with Karagiannis and Wagner's proposal for 'synagonism', which they propose as a state of co-struggle rather than oppositional struggle: '[…] synagonism can be understood as the respectful struggle of one against another, bound by rules larger than the struggle, in view of excellence winning for the benefit of the city' (2008, 324). A notion of struggle as a co-operative undertaking is promising, but the model of synagonism retains a horizon of victors and losers, albeit in the interest of enabling the best or most effective positions to win and thus benefiting society more generally. Alternatively, James Tully approaches agonistic engagements between citizens and governing forces from the perspective of participation and interaction (Tully 2014). In his support for what he terms 'diverse global citizenship', which he sees as contrary to predominant forms of modern citizenship, Tully describes the former as '[…] *negotiated practices*, as praxis – as actors and activities in context' (emphasis in original) (Tully 2014, 35). This conception requires an understanding of citizenship that is founded on interactions, and this, I suggest, is where theatre and performance might come to the fore.

If, as its proponents suggest, agonism stands as a potential corrective to the combative tendencies that are otherwise inherent to populism, we might turn to theatre and performance scholarship to glean new insights about the ways that agonistic pluralism might occur in practice. Given its roots in ancient Greek democracy, and its close ties to the theatrical development of antagonist characters in theatre, it seems obvious that theatre practice might tell us something *more* about the way that agonistic forms of engagement occur in a practical fashion. However, comparatively little scholarship seriously examines the potential for theatrical practices to promote agonism, beyond simply noting theatre's dialogic or multivalent content.

To robustly analyse this conjuncture, we need to go beyond the sometimes naïve or vague assertions that theatre can create positive change just by providing opportunities for interaction or contemplation of differences. As Claire Bishop has noted in her discussion of participatory art works, in the past there has been a tendency to over-emphasise the democratic or dialogic potential of art, based primarily on its cultural positioning and its invitation to audiences to engage with it (Bishop 2004, 78). In a similar vein, theatre practitioners and scholars have tended to make somewhat rash assumptions about the capacity for performance to create new modes of engagement, sometimes without due consideration of the social and cultural frameworks that condition spectatorship and participation. Yet, at the same time, as established in Chapter 1, we have ample evidence of the ability of the arts generally, and performance specifically, to alter modes of interaction and engagement. It is therefore important, when considering the agonistic qualities of digital populism, to consider alternative modes of encounter and engagement that are facilitated by creative performance; this provides us with insights into the capacity for theatre and performance practices to create moments in which the prevailing modes of populist engagement might be disrupted or altered, thus countering the deficiencies of digital populism. In the next section I turn to the field of Applied Theatre to develop additional insights into the dynamics of engagement and interaction in social and political contexts and to provide a new lens to evaluate and/or modify political practices that seek agonistic pluralism.

Applied Theatre and Agonistic Engagement

Chantal Mouffe acknowledges a role for artistic practices in the pursuit of agonism: 'According to the agonistic approach, critical art is art that foments dissensus, that makes visible what the dominant consensus tends to obscure and obliterate. It is constituted by a manifold of artistic practices aiming at giving a voice to all those who are silenced within the framework of the existing hegemony' (2007b). Recently she has also signalled her belief that theatre, of all the arts, is perhaps especially well placed to achieve such goals. She contends that theatre, because of its live, embodied presences, might be 'a privileged terrain for the mobilisation of affects and the construction of new subjectivities' (2020, 193). Although I will expand on the affective dimensions of populism in later chapters, here I am most interested in Mouffe's assertion that theatre can operate as a vehicle for the exposure and multiplication of agonistic differences.

Theatre offers a natural platform for the experience of multiple world-views and political perspectives. As Tony Fisher reminds us, the theatres of ancient Greece encouraged a particular mode of spectatorship among citizens, who were conditioned to bring a critical, questioning and complex attitude to the interpretation of the plays before them. As mentioned in the opening of this chapter, ancient tragedy depicted the viewpoints of contradictory characters – but beyond this, the experience of tragic theatre was also shaped by a specific approach to spectatorship:

> [...]perhaps more than simply listen, they were trained to listen conflictually— they were active spectators: hence Plato's complaint that the theatre audiences were a nuisance to the good government of the polis. We find this in the Laws: audiences are simply incapable of quietly sitting back, of knowing their place, or of dutifully attending to the poetry. A veritable democratic rabble, this participative and unruly audience, stirred by the argumentative dynamics of the theatre [...].
>
> *Fisher 2017, 10*

This potential for theatre to politically mobilise the citizenry through active, conflictual listening is not confined to the ancient Greek context. Despite the prevalence of passive, well-behaved audiences in today's commercial theatre world, the art form nonetheless is rife with examples of audiences responding in unruly, patently political ways. This suggests that theatrical creativity can play an active complementary role within radical democratic projects, or left populist projects; we might glean key lessons about engagement from the theatrical arts and ultimately consider new ways of applying these within existing democratic frames. This is a point that can be further elucidated by turning to theories of Applied Theatre and performance.

Broadly speaking, the field of Applied Theatre has a natural affinity with the principles of agonism as they are generally described. Applied Theatre practitioners are mostly united in their championing of work that facilitates and celebrates respectful engagement, usually in the service of addressing conflicts, disagreements or at the very least, thorny issues where no clear solution presents itself. Furthermore, the actual practical tools used by Applied Theatre practitioners are frequently designed with the aim of enabling multiple viewpoints to come together in a respectful environment of collaboration and cooperation. This principle is enacted from the point of project organisation, when efforts are often made to ensure broad participation, especially by precarious, marginal or disenfranchised groups. It continues in the process of the project itself, when activities are carefully designed to encourage particular types of engagement, often with a view to fostering respect and participation in the face of deep internal differences within the group (see for example, Nicholson 2014; Preston 2016).

Ultimately then, one of the strongest benefits that theatre can bring to the pursuit of agonistic pluralism is the possibility to experience and consider multiple viewpoints at once – to create an environment where we can enact or empathise with conflict, exploring multiple possibilities for collaborative resolution. Then we can experience conflict and difference as a collective and unending process, even as we are aware of our deep disagreements and the failures and limitations of the joint practice we undertake. This is not to say of course that every piece of theatre or performance has the potential to achieve this – in fact it's a highly elusive state but one which can be facilitated through particular approaches to performance and spectatorship.

Difficultating

To understand this further, I want to focus in on a few key points that characterise much Applied Theatre practice, and that inform my own work. I am especially interested in the way that performance activities can bring uncertainty and fluidity to the fore in interactions, and whether theatrical elements might therefore be able to bring these qualities to the surface in political encounters. In this section I consider the extent to which performance naturally supports the principles of open-ended conflict that agonistic pluralism is so reliant upon.

First, creative performance allows people to experiment with shifting or evolving scripts, characters and storylines rather than remaining wedded to their own immediate situations or experiences. Theatre can enable people to work through issues and concepts from the basis of individual experience, but also through character-based acting, meaning that their experience of an issue need not be entirely confined to their own past history. In other words, as Susan Davis puts it:

> Drama offers a special kind of 'living through' and 'experience' because it uses lifelike situations and issues that allow participants to have an actual experience, without having to live with the consequences of real world actions. [...] Emotions are engaged and participants may come to 'feel' differently about things through the experience [...].
>
> *Davis 2015, 67*

Theatre's capacity to enable people to envision new and different possibilities for the future endows it with a utopian quality that can be highly pertinent to the pursuit of agonistic fluidity. Jill Dolan suggests that performance is particularly adept at enabling people to depict and experience worlds that don't yet exist but that we might pursue into being. She says that theatrical experiences offer the potential to 'inspire moments in which audiences feel themselves allied with each other, and with a broader, more capacious sense of the public, in which social discourses articulate the possible, rather than the insurmountable obstacles to human potential' (Dolan 2005, 2). We might therefore consider Applied or interventionary performance practices as utopian projects that continue in spite of the ever-present threat of antagonistic conflict; they constitute an approach to interaction that enables people to creatively embody an as-yet non-existent world of respectful contestation, in which new possibilities for future political actions are vigorously explored. Rather than limiting their performances to what already exists in the present, imaginative theatre work enables people to engage in creative activities that correspond to this imagined ideal future (Vittoria 2019, 60). This idealist approach is characteristic of much Applied and political theatre practice, and it is undertaken by practitioners in the hope of leaving traces upon participants that can impact the real world in tangible, if subtle, ways (Dolan 2005; Thompson 2011).

Beyond the general utopian qualities of theatre, some specific practices are especially useful in supporting the fluidity and uncertainty that agonistic engagement requires. This is because some techniques focus on sustaining a sense of difficulty and ambiguity rather than encouraging a group to settle on a particular ideal vision of the future. In many ways, this is simply a case of using theatre in Applied contexts to bring the principles of tragedy into experiential, participatory activities. As Critchley stresses 'What the experience of tragedy invites is neither the blind impulsiveness of action, nor some retreat into a solitary life of contemplation, but the difficulty and uncertainty of action in a world defined by ambiguity where right always seems to be on both sides' (Critchley 2017). By using particular Applied Theatre techniques we can insist on maintaining this sense of 'difficulty and uncertainty' which might otherwise be lost in populist political contexts. In this sense, the most productive utopian theatrics, in terms of the pursuit of agonistic pluralism, are those that facilitate participants to linger in a space of uncertainty and ambiguity – often by experimenting with multiple different characters, evolving and shifting scenarios and constantly complicated improvisations of political phenomena.

While plenty of practitioners envision Applied Theatre as a means of achieving group consensus-building or conflict resolution, some influential practices are firmly rooted in an understanding of conflict that isn't primarily angled toward the pursuit of reconciliation or consensus but instead positions conflict as a positive and productive feature of society. In particular, the writings of Augusto Boal are elucidating on this score. It is first of all crucial to understand that for Boal, 'struggle' need not have a negative connotation. Struggle, in a Boalian as well as an agonistic sense, might simply refer to a scenario marked by competing but equally meritorious perspectives, as we find in classical Greek tragedy. For Boal, the experience of this kind of tragedy can be pleasurable, invigorating, and affectively rejuvenating. Through the medium of theatre, difficulty and uncertainty can be experienced, explored and negotiated in ways that allay feelings of anxiety, failure or anger which might otherwise come about. To understand this further, it is helpful to expand upon Boal's key body of work, called Theatre of the Oppressed.

Theatre of the Oppressed was the name that Boal gave to the body of practices he developed following his exile from his native Brazil. It is comprised of a range of activities and techniques that are designed to enable members of the public to engage in theatrical improvisations that help them to understand and debate political issues. Theatre of the Oppressed is perhaps the most prominent and widespread body of practices that have been adopted by Applied Theatre practitioners around the globe. Given its global spread, and its resulting use in a vast array of political and cultural contexts, it is no surprise that various adaptations and evolutions have occurred to suit local needs. However, the vast majority of these practices retain an adherence to Boal's core principles.

The term 'Theatre of the Oppressed' gives a nod to Paolo Freire, whose critical pedagogic philosophy was highly influential to Boal. 'Oppression' in this context is a broad term that encompasses any situation in which uneven power relations prevent equal contributions to social or political dialogue. The techniques include, for example, introductory games and exercises designed to enable non-actors to participate in a fully creative, relatively uninhibited manner; the use of tableaux vivant ('Image Theatre') to initiate participants to the value of embodied representations of social and political conflict; and in its fullest realisation, Forum Theatre. This latter activity requires participants to improvise a short scene that depicts a political or social problem, taking care to represent the relationships of power and privilege that attach to particular characters. At the conclusion of the scene, other participants are invited to suggest changes to characters' actions that might alter the course of the scene. The suggested scenes are then acted out anew with the help of other participants, providing the group with the basis for more critical consideration of the issue and reflection on potential ways of addressing it. In practice, these techniques are facilitated through the mobilisation of Boal's 'spect-actor', which refers simply to the state in which participants alternate between the roles of actor and spectator, experiencing the process from both perspectives without succumbing to the temptation to categorise themselves as either participants or bystanders. Rather, actors are always to some degree spectating the action themselves, and spectators are always ready and able to step in and 'act' when warranted.

It is of utmost importance to understand that Forum Theatre, as originally conceived, does not primarily seek 'solutions' to political problems, or desire to arrive at an agreed-upon best option. Rather, the point is in the struggle itself – the difficulty of negotiating among competing perspectives and the power complexities that underpin any given issue (Boal 2008). This struggle is explored through performance in order to mobilise the participant's faculties in new and productive ways.

A crucial element of Forum Theatre is the role of the 'Joker'. This is the title that Boal gives to the leader or facilitator of activities, and it reflects their ideal disposition as a potential trickster and complicator. There is a common notion among Theatre of the Oppressed practitioners that their leadership roles are best described not through the more common term 'facilitator' but rather by the portmanteau, 'difficultator' – acknowledging their primary function as a figure who constantly challenges and complicates the participants' moves toward consensus (Prendergast and Saxton 2016, 70). This is a crucial element of the practice, because so often participants are constrained by behavioural norms, sometimes acting overly deferentially and agreeably toward one another[3] – this impedes the emphasis on divergence and debate that are truly at the heart of Theatre of the Oppressed practices. Deeming the Joker a 'difficultator' also suggests that the experience of struggle can be a positive one for participants, and even joyful, fun and playful. Most significantly though, the difficultator prolongs the uncertainty of the performed scenario by positioning potential resolutions as something sought-after but never quite attained. For Boal, the key emphasis was on the process of trying, over and above achieving a satisfactory outcome; this is a non-competitive process of dancing through different possibilities and potentials, success or failure notwithstanding.

It is also important to note that these activities are fundamentally participatory and collaborative. Paolo Vittoria stresses the essential nature of collaboration in Forum Theatre processes, which require 'reciprocal action between subjects, not solitary actions' and '[…] responsible subjects and not passive spectators, as in the false democracy of the media' (Vittoria 2019, 61). Crucially for Boal, his techniques were intended to enable people not just to imagine alternatives but to actively play them out and thus experience them – all the time observing both themselves and others.

These principles are of utmost importance when thinking about the application of Theatre of the Oppressed within populist political environments. This is not least because Theatre of the Oppressed could easily be considered in the light of antagonism rather than agonistic pluralism. Boal's techniques could simply reinforce antagonistic attitudes to engagement, by encouraging the depiction of competing viewpoints, especially if the process ends by championing one of those viewpoints as an endpoint or goal over and above others. If a Theatre of the Oppressed workshop encouraged participants to replace an enacted scenario with a performance of a singular solution, perhaps favoured by the majority of the group, then this activity would be likely to create or reaffirm the exclusion of difference instead of highlighting and celebrating it. Boal's techniques are sometimes adapted in this way, overemphasising the pursuit of group consensus and using Forum Theatre as a problem-solving tool to seek agreement on optimal solutions or procedures from everyone in the room. This is often the case when Forum Theatre is adapted for corporate training contexts, for example. Good Theatre of the Oppressed instead goes beyond a singular or final replacement – it temporarily replaces the present with an imagined alternative but this is always in flux in the interest of multiplying possibilities, and as soon as one replacement takes the stage, another negation is already formulating. In other words, as Julian Boal and José Soeiro phrase it, 'We are talking about a way of looking at what exists from a dynamic and changing perspective instead of just searching for harmony and continuity. It's a way of understanding the world that rejects that the world— or the human being— is what it is' (Boal and Soeiro 2021, 67).

Read in a different context, this quotation could be an explicit definition of agonistic engagement by political scholars. The emphasis on a 'dynamic and changing perspective' is squarely in line with agonistic goals; but it has the added advantage of being rooted in an ongoing practice, rendering it in line with James Tully's conception of a praxis of citizen interactions. As Augusto Boal says, 'It is very easy for us to decide – in fatalistic fashion – that we are the way we are, full stop, end of story. But we can also imagine – in a more creative fashion– that the playing cards can be re-dealt. In this dance of potentialities, different powers take the floor at different times – potential can become act, occupy the spotlight and then glide back to the sidelines, powers grow and diminish, move in to the foreground and then shrink into the background again – everything is mutable. Our personality is what it is, but it is also what it is becoming. If we are fatalists, then there is nothing to be done; but if we are not, we can try' (1995, 39).

Ultimately then, Theatre of the Oppressed techniques seek to create an environment in which participants become comfortable with lingering in the spaces of uncertainty within any given social or political issue. They will understand the value of holding on to differences and unresolved tensions rather than dominating or winning out over their opponents' viewpoints.

Metaxis

Boal's emphasis on an ongoing process of dynamic mutability finds its fullest realisation in his concept of *metaxis*. This is a relatively lesser-known concept of Boal's, but one which I argue is directly relevant to the practical enactment of agonistic pluralism. Boal defined metaxis as 'the state of belonging completely and simultaneously to two different worlds: the image of reality and the reality of the image' (1995, 43). Couched within his practices of Image Theatre and Forum Theatre, Boal means that these activities can enable a participant to simultaneously be fully conscious of their own experience of a real political situation while also being fully committed to a theatrical process of representation that is based on, but different to that situation.

Theatre scholars have sometimes compared metaxis to a state of liminality, but this doesn't quite get to the heart of what Boal intended. Metaxis is not simply a state of in-betweenness, and certainly not one marked by linear progression toward transformation; it is rather a situation in which the participant deliberately holds on to the experience of being both oneself and another at the same time – in the same way that an actor experiences the playing of a role. When this occurs, the participant lingers in a state of duality wherein they are aware of themselves and their ideological dispositions but are also committed to experiencing, through creative, theatrical play, the possibilities and conditions experienced by others. This results in a state of consciousness that involves holding two different worlds – and the viewpoints attached to them – in mind at once (Carroll 1996, 74).

Tor-Helge Allern has examined the origins of Boal's term metaxis and suggests that it may have been inspired by the Greek term metaxy (Allern 2001, 79). This provides some useful insights regarding its political potential: 'According to Plato the human existence is a place *in-between* the extremities of ignorance and knowing, mortality and immortality. In his search for answers to basic questions about his existence man will be in *metaxy*' (Allern 2001, 79, emphasis in original). This suggests that while the theatrical framing of Boal's activities is essential to their democratic efficacy, there is also a clear link with real-world impacts. This comes about because fundamentally, Boal's metaxis doesn't simply enable people to 'try out' the roles or experiences of others – there are real emotional and psychological consequences:

> The oppressed creates images of his reality. Then, he must play with the reality of these images. [...] The oppressed must forget the real world which was the origin of the image and play with the image itself, in its artistic embodiment. He must make an extrapolation from his social reality towards the reality which is called fiction (towards theatre, towards image) and, having played with the image, he must make a second extrapolation, now in the inverse direction, towards the social reality which is his world. He practises in the second world (the aesthetic), in order to modify the first (the social).
> *Boal 1995, 44*

It is crucial that Image Theatre positions itself firmly as a creative theatrical undertaking in order to facilitate maximal immersion in the activities and to enable participants to benefit from a convincing exploration of another person's experiences; but this also has a further impact on the 'real world' as participants learn something from their theatrical experimentations that can be brought to bear on their understanding of a political issue – and this comes about because the theatrically-suffused practice of Theatre of the Oppressed allows genuine metaxis by relocating personal experiences into a realm of artistry and play rather than real-world politics.

If we add Boal's metaxis into debates about agonism, we might reframe respectful, adversarial political contestation as a process of theatrical experimentation; in other words, agonism in practice would benefit from enabling groups to imaginatively play out alternative ideas collectively and cooperatively. This calls for the facilitation of constant disagreement and difference through practices that enable participants to perceive and act in two worlds at once – the world of their own reality, alongside the fictional, theatrical, aesthetic world of their creative explorations. This seems like a plausible and practicable goal, given the extent to which populism is already being enacted in quasi-fictive online worlds. Digital media already offers a space in which people engage in intense political debate, alongside acknowledged elements of theatricalised display, so surely it is no great leap to suggest that we might make use of this medium in more imaginative ways in order to facilitate experiences of lingering in-between conflicting perspectives. If sufficiently realised, metaxic practices might enable participants to experiment with alternatives in a non-combative, cooperative fashion, one which facilitates a heightened sense of the possibilities and impacts of both the real world and its imagined possibilities. As Jonathan Neelands phrases it, this application of performance principles might result in '[…] togetherness in argument rather than conflict between strangers who cannot imagine each other' (Neelands 2016, 33). For this reason, we might opt to pursue *metaxic agonism*; that is, heeding Chantal Mouffe's emphasis on agonistic pluralism, alongside James Tully's notion of agonistic citizenship as praxis, Boal's metaxis might offer us a set of clues regarding the ways that performance practices can instantiate pluralistic engagement in action. To explore this further, I conclude this chapter with a brief discussion of the ways that Theatre of the Oppressed, Voice, and Puppetry can add to this goal.

Realising Metaxic Agonism in Practice

The section above outlines the principal ways that Theatre of the Oppressed facilitates agonistic engagement. In Applied Theatre practice this is exemplified through Image Theatre and Forum Theatre work that encourages participants to explore multiple characters' perspectives while retaining a sense of their own experiences and world views. For example, one activity I frequently use when exploring political topics is group-generated tableaux that depict the varying experiences of each participant in a given situation, for example, border-crossing or job interviews or a university campus. These scenarios, enacted through spontaneous individual images, inevitably reveal differences in power and privilege within the group. Similarly, I often adapt Image Theatre by requiring participants to enact an image of their own experience of a situation, followed closely by a representation of the experience of a character assigned to them. This character is outlined on a card with essential factual details, based on real-world examples. These activities strive to instantiate an attitude of metaxis among participants, which bears out in the discussions of political topics that follow. After creatively experimenting in embodied ways with perspectives other than their own, participants go on to discuss political topics in a more nuanced and careful way – often feeling somewhat unsettled or frustrated by a lack of conclusion or resolution, but nonetheless having developed their own viewpoints with a greater understanding of others'.

What is most significant about this is that it reveals important points regarding the ways that a metaxic attitude might be facilitated in other, 'non-theatrical' interactive processes; referring to the examples drawn from Theatre of the Oppressed, it is clear that activities that require imaginative role play incorporating physical and narrative depictions of multiple characters possess this potential, and these qualities might easily be extended to a variety of interactive fora. It is also useful to briefly consider what vocal practices and object-based activities might bring to the table.

Voice and Puppetry

There is a close link between vocalisation and interpersonal engagement; Roy Hart practitioners and others who centre voice within their work often remark on the way that one leads into another. Often times we think of voice as an individual practice – something which emanates from and is refined and honed within the individual body, which only latterly comes together with others. Yet in Roy Hart practices, even when people are engaging in solo vocalisations, there is a direct impact on engagement with others. This comes about in a number of ways.

First, Roy Hart techniques are fundamentally rooted in a practice of heightened listening and attention. This might begin by listening and attending to the sounds one's own body is making, becoming aware of the wider vocal range that occurs when, say, leaping across a room or huddling in a crouched position or extending one's arms overhead while moving on tiptoes. But this mode of heightened listening can be easily extended to interpersonal dynamics. Practitioners who focus on the therapeutic elements of Roy Hart exercises have especially observed the capacity of the techniques to foster 'deep' or 'careful' listening. This refers not only to an ability to be attentive to the voices of others but rather a mode of listening that is generated from the chorus (or cacophony) of voices that one is a part of – a participant experiences their own vocalisations but simultaneously hears – and feels – the vocal expressions of others (Magnat 2021). This creates an environment in which different, even competing world-views are literally put into conversation with one another, and in an embodied way the individual participants attend to both their own self-expressions and the possibility of alternative responses.

It is crucial to understand that this is not just a practice of dialogue presented in the form of non-linguistic communication – the phenomenon of the voice is key to generating the multiple and fluid perspectives that are experienced and negotiated during the activities. This is because, as Adriana Cavarero explains, every vocal expression betrays the political and cultural situatedness of the speaker and is charged with particular emotional, artistic, and social elements (Cavarero 2005, 30). As Alfred Wolfsohn himself discovered following his time in the First World War trenches, the voice carries markers of our past experiences, our past interactions with others, and the beauty and pain of these experiences can literally make themselves heard in unexpected breaks and slides in a person's voice. As a result, the vocalisations that happen in workshops are not simply a matter of conscious self-expression but tap into layers of past social and political experiences – this is especially important when we put these practices into group contexts, because choral explorations of political issues can generate an environment where a multitude of perspectives is expressed and experienced simultaneously – not dissimilar to Boal's metaxis.

In my recent workshops I have been struck by the impact of collaborative vocal exercises on participants. One exercise in particular demonstrates the potential for voice practices to establish a new mode of engagement in pluralistic contexts – this is the use of soundscapes, which I facilitate by drawing on Wolfsohn and Hart's techniques of expanded vocal ranges. I begin by asking participants to consider a specific social or political context or event – this might be, for example, the departures lounge of an airport, a job centre or a crowded bus. Each individual is tasked with developing a non-linguistic sound that represents some element of that scenario that has personal significance for them. Various instructions are given (asking the participant to bounce a ball, hop up and down, lie on the floor, or high-five others in the room) in order to alter the physical stance and movement of participants while they continue their vocal work, thus interrupting the conscious control they can exert over their voices. Ultimately these voices are put into concert with one another, creating a landscape of sound made up of varying perspectives and experiences. Consistently, everyone begins with a different volume and a different rhythm, yet over the course of the exercise they begin to align with one another. In doing so, participants report that they become simultaneously aware of their own contribution while experiencing, both aurally and physically, the contributions of others.

Puppetry too has a part to play in establishing sustained, productive agonism. Puppetry can be used in activities derived from the Theatre of the Oppressed and has several key advantages. First, the use of puppets in collaborative explorations of political issues has the advantage of offering a degree of distance to those involved who may otherwise feel re-traumatised by the enactment of their experiences. Puppets are also particularly useful for work with diverse groups that may include people with mobility limitations, as carefully designed puppetry activities can alleviate the extent of physical exertion or range of motion needed by participants. Furthermore, the construction of papier mache puppets can be a collaborative process, and this means that individual participants feel freer to make their own, relatively small contributions as they are freed from a sense of responsibility or sole ownership from the end product. What results is a hand-crafted puppet that bears the markers of multiple individuals' experiences and perspectives. Similarly, participants in Forum Theatre tend to be more willing to critique or confront a puppet-image as opposed to one that is embodied by fellow participants (Grant 2020, 21). In this way, puppets facilitate a maximally inclusive environment.

Puppetry is also adept at fostering metaxic engagement by participants. This is particularly true in activities wherein the puppeteer is visible to the audience. Such practices produce a kind of 'double vision' in which the spectator perceives the material object of the puppet simultaneously with the imagined character the puppet represents (Grant 2020; Tillis 1992). This is of course true in the spectatorship of human actors playing characters, but the effect is heightened in puppetry because of a third body (the human puppeteer) who is visibly controlling the actions of the puppet. The resulting 'double vision' suggests a strong possibility of creating metaxic environments for participants. As Grant describes it,

> we can hold two perceptions of the puppet event in our mind at the same time, simultaneously acknowledging both its reality and unreality. The effect of this is to imbue the puppet with something of the emotion manifested by the puppeteers whenever they display an empathetic connection with the puppet they are manipulating.
>
> *Grant 2020, 16*

The metaxis of puppetry is intensified, in my experience, when multiple operators are manipulating the same puppet. In these cases, there is an obligation on all of the puppeteers to work cooperatively (so as not to literally tear the puppet limb from limb, and also to produce some kind of coherent action or expression); but this requires them, usually silently, to negotiate between their own often divergent approaches to kinaesthetic expressions of emotions or intents – and this inevitably draws on their own embodied differences which have been conditioned by their differing past experiences or even present-day ideologies. As a result, multi-operator puppets embody multifarious perspectives arising from the collaborative negotiation of a political issue – live, and with a great deal of uncertainty – and are observed by both the operators and other participants who (temporarily) spectate.

Taken together, the voice and puppetry practices I have drawn on point to some specific qualities of interaction that might support more positive modes of political engagement. The first of these is a genuine and sustained attentiveness to others, concurrent with an attitude of deep listening. This can be fostered through activities that require close attentiveness to the communications and actions of others, especially where collaboration and work in concert is required. In addition, there seems to be significant value in activities and frameworks that enable people to express ideas and emotions through distanced objects or avatars. By enabling participants to express a range of perspectives through objects at a remove from their own bodies, they become more willing to communicate about controversial or sensitive topics and better able to put these ideas into agonistic circulation with others. At the same time, all three of the practices I am engaging with also suggest the centrality of embodiment in interaction – this might be felt through the use of the physical body to represent ideas or experiences in new ways, or through the resonance of the voice with others – or even through a heightened perception of bodies brought about by the presence of the non-human within interactions. This points to the need to consider embodiment in greater detail to better understand its role in political interaction, and this is the focus of the next two chapters.

Conclusion

This chapter has examined political engagement to explore the ways that performance practices might support the pursuit of agonistic pluralism. It has introduced Boal's concept of metaxis as a means of understanding the extent to which performance practices might support agonistic engagement by facilitating ongoing negotiation, fluidity and uncertainty. In addition to exploring the principles behind Forum Theatre and Image Theatre, I have introduced some examples from voice and puppetry work that supplement Boal's practices. Ultimately, this exploration attempts to show that practices like the ones described above differ in crucial aspects from the performative social interactions that characterise most digitally mediated political interactions. Especially in cases where political engagement is marked by populist tendencies – such as antagonism, or an over-emphasis on exclusion as opposed to cooperation – digitally mediated interactions are often characterised by a pursuit of foreclosed outcomes and a truncated approach to communication and listening. On the other hand, the theatrical practices I am working with demonstrate that it is possible to foster the very opposite qualities in groups, even when exploring highly divisive political issues.

PART II

Political Embodiment in Digital Populist Contexts

4

EMBODIMENT AND PERCEPTION

Bringing the Inside Out

This chapter delves further into the ways that performance practices might facilitate new modes of interpersonal engagement that can counter the more detrimental elements of digital populism. The focus here turns to the role of embodiment in populist political interactions, and how insights drawn from theatre and performance might point out new or different approaches. This is the first of two chapters that consider aspects of physical presence within political encounters; Chapter 5 emphasises the ways that people physically interact with external environments, exploring corporeal experience from an 'outside-in' perspective; here though, the focus is on ways of bringing personal embodied knowledge to the surface of interactions with others – an 'inside-out' perspective.

This chapter begins with an initial overview of treatments of embodiment in politics scholarship, in order to put forward an argument for greater emphasis on material, corporeal experience rather than the more frequently discussed semiotic body. This argument is based on the assertion that the material body serves as both an archive of knowledge and experience and as a site of ongoing knowledge production; it should therefore be granted due attention within political practices. The chapter then turns to an examination of the ways that bodies are invoked in populist political organising, considering both the signifying aspects of the body and corporeal sensation. This provides the basis for a further evaluation of embodiment within digital populism, which makes clear that aspects of embodiment change significantly in online mediated contexts. In the final part of the chapter I turn to theatre and performance theories to examine the challenges involved when attempting to bring corporeal sensation to the fore of political interaction. I draw on Alfred Wolfsohn's voice work to argue that applied vocal practices offer a particularly promising route in this respect, and I supplement this with examples drawn from political puppetry and Forum

DOI: 10.4324/9780367824129-7

Theatre in order to demonstrate that performance practice might counter the diminishment of corporeal experience within digital populism.

The Meaning and Matters of Bodies

It almost goes without saying that the concept of embodiment has been increasingly taken up in Politics and IR scholarship in recent decades. Fundamentally, scholars are more and more inclined to consider the physical human body as a primary site at which global politics occurs. This body of work serves as a much-needed counterpart to studies of politics that emphasise states, institutions and policymaking. Perhaps most obviously, feminist researchers in particular have considered the extent to which personal experience is not only inseparable from politics but also that politics is conducted, mediated, perceived and communicated through personal bodies (e.g. Cohn 1987; Haraway 1991; Sylvester 2013; Wilcox 2015).

The bringing-in of bodies to global politics has led to a proliferation of analytical frameworks to address it. Broadly speaking, it is possible to distinguish two general ways that the body has been approached in political theory: first, as a discursively constructed entity that is shaped by political and cultural forces and that bears outward-facing evidence of the nature of these forces; this body can therefore be read and interpreted via its status as a semiotic surface. Alternatively, some scholars place more emphasis on material, corporeal substance – considering the physical phenomena that occur within and among bodies, which also play a crucial role in political processes. It goes without saying that these aspects of the body – the representational or signifying presence of the body *and* lived, experienced corporeality, exist in tandem with one another and cannot be easily separated. Nevertheless, political scholarship tends to be marked by an emphasis on one of these strands of thinking, sometimes at the expense of the other, and this gives rise to debates over the relative merits of the various approaches to embodiment. It is therefore useful to begin a consideration of embodiment in populist politics by positioning my discussion accordingly.

In actuality, despite a wealth of promising research on the nature of the body and its role in politics, there remains comparatively little treatment of the body's material presence and the experiences that emanate from perceptions of this materiality. Instead, a greater portion of research is oriented around the body's signifying capacities, positioning it as a kind of 'text' that can be read, or as a supplemental aspect of discourse (Coole 2007). It remains comparatively rare to find Politics and IR research that foregrounds the physical experience of bodies as a primary form of knowledge. This comes about in part because of the fact that corporeal difference has historically been drafted as evidence of sex and gender hierarchies. Women, ethnic minorities, differently abled people, and people of colour have been considered to be *more* corporeal – that is, more intensely and pervasively attached to and driven by their physical substance in a manner that limits detached intellectual reason. Social hierarchies have thus constructed those at the bottom as both more corporeal, and more irrational – and therefore less legitimate as political actors (Alcoff 2006; Grosz 1994; Mcclintock 2013).

In response a great deal of scholarship, especially feminist scholarship, has aimed to demonstrate the ways that physical bodies themselves are products of social processes, shaped and disciplined by discourse and performativity (e.g. Butler 1996; Grosz 1999; Irigaray 1985). These perspectives have revealed pivotal insights about the role that society and politics play in the manifestation of bodies, and how the experiences of those socially disciplined bodies then influence subsequent bodily acts.

However, if we focus too much on 'reading' the body as a surface then much gets lost (Coole 2007; Grosz 1987, 1994). This is because, as Diana Taylor suggests, material bodies carry knowledge that is not consciously perceived or expressed by the intellectual mind (2003, 2020). This is a perspective reinforced by Diana Coole who suggests that bodies exercise and experience their own modes of power (Coole 2007, 414). This means that we need to attend to the non-discursive, physical realms of human interaction in order to establish a more balanced understanding of political phenomena – in other words, we should turn our attention to a lived body that experiences the world corporeally, including interactions with others, through its material presence and substance. This should not entail a neglect of the ways that the body is affected by social and cultural processes, but if we are to take seriously calls for agonistic pluralism, we need to be equally attendant to the ways that bodies operate at a corporeal level. Without this, we risk overlooking points of difference that are contained within the interior materiality of bodies. In the following section I outline some key theoretical principles that will pave the way for a closer consideration of material corporeality in populist politics.

The Materially Experienced Body in Political Interaction

As noted above, the body contains knowledge and understanding that exceeds the confines of the conscious mind. The corporeal body, in conjunction with but differently to the thinking mind, bears knowledge, memory and insights about the world it interacts with. As Amanda Machin describes, bodies '[…] have a knowledge of their own gained from interacting as a part of the world. We do not consciously reflect upon how we open a door, or use a knife and fork or smile, instead there is a pre-reflective consciousness at work, as part of our human being-in-the-world' (Machin 2014, 75). This knowledge can supplement what we cerebrally apprehend so that by tapping into what the body knows, particularly in interaction with others, we might gain new insights about the world that otherwise remain obscured from our intellectual faculties.

At the same time, it remains important to recognise that embodied knowledge is not created hermetically but rather through the body's encounters with the world around it. The body is constituted multidimensionally and reflexively, through its simultaneous perceptions of itself alongside the sense of things external to it. The body possesses 'active, agentic sentience' based on its interiority, in conjunction with and alongside its exteriority, leaving it vulnerable to influence by outside agents (Coole 2007, 415). This means that knowledge generated by and contained within the corporeal body is the result of self-perception *and* interaction with the world around us.

When we frame embodied knowledge in this manner – that is, as a body of insights contained within the physical substance of the fleshed person, yet dependent on external interactions for its construction – we can begin to apprehend the complexity of its contributions to political phenomena. In Chapter 6 I give detailed consideration to the ways that the external environment impacts the body's perceptions of itself and the larger world; here though, I want to focus specifically on the ways that political experiences are perceived, responded to and remembered by the body's physical organs and surfaces. It is therefore useful to expand on a few specific points relating to corporeal experience that will be relevant to the discussion of embodiment in digital populism below.

To begin with, this complex, lived body is marked by multiple layers of somatic perception, occurring within internal levels (for example, sensations emanating from internal organs) as well as external, outward-facing levels (including external surfaces that come into immediate contact with the outside world). Performance theorist Drew Leder characterises these dimensions as the internal, 'visceral' body which gives rise to interoception, and the outward-facing surface-level body which facilitates exteroception and proprioception (1990). By considering these various sites of corporeal perception, it becomes clear that the body possesses complex, multidimensional knowledge that arises from the various ways that these sensing bodies encounter the world. Furthermore, because of the complexity of embodied perception, expressions of bodily knowledge are distinct from communications that are dominated by intellectual processes. As a result, when embodied knowledge is brought to the fore in interpersonal activities – that is, the knowledge that I refer to in the chapter title as the 'inside' aspects of personal corporeality – multidimensional perspectives are put into circulation with other physical bodies such that further knowledge is co-produced in a highly dynamic and nuanced manner (Garner 2019; Vettraino et al. 2017).

Embodied perception is also highly fluid and often ambiguous. A focus on material embodiment acknowledges the extent to which perceptions of ourselves and others are a constant ongoing process rather than one that is fixed, finished, or rooted in a sense of the fixity of others. As theatre theorist Phillip Zarrilli puts it: '"the body" I call mine is not a body, or the body, but rather a process of embodying the several bodies one encounters in everyday experience [...]' (Zarrilli 2004, 655). In other words, the body is not a fixed entity but changes and responds to its environment and its own ongoing ever-shifting needs. It also changes throughout the course of a person's life, altering in sometimes unpredictable but highly impactful ways (Jenkins 2005, 2).

These points suggest that the body inherently defies foreclosure or delimitation. It is always open to change, whether through the impact of external forces (human or non-human) or through its own corporeal processes that necessarily alter its perceptive faculties. By understanding embodiment as an always-changing process of encounters, we can understand the benefits of embodied perception within political interaction, particularly as a means of retaining a sense of openness and fluidity – a principle that, as described in the last chapter, is essential to agonistic pluralism. Of course, this potential is always met by the potency of social and cultural forces that tend to condition and frame bodily knowledge in accordance with particular norms or values; but the body's inherent tendency to exceed, challenge and overflow cultural and social categorisation suggests that it might be a crucial site for co-created political knowledge. With the concerns outlined above in mind, this chapter turns now to a consideration of how bodies are foundationally implicated in populist interactions.

The Body in Populist Politics

There are many ways that the body is called upon within populism, ranging from the centrality of the physical appearance of populist leaders to the ways that populist events generate particular brands of embodied affect. A good place to start is with the pivotal role that the physical body plays in the initial creation and sustenance of populist groups. Although my primary focus is on materially embodied experience, this necessitates some consideration of the ways that this is impacted by the already-heightened semiotic role of the physical body within populist movements (Machin 2014). This is evident in the extent to which corporeal difference provides a basis for the creation of populist frontiers; that is, the demarcation of a populist movement's insiders and outsiders is often rooted in differences relating to physical appearance. This can be based on physical differences attached to constructions of race, ethnicity or other identity markers. One of the most insidious examples of this occurred in November 2015, when then-presidential candidate Donald Trump mocked the physical disability of *New York Times* reporter Serge Kovaleski. Before a cheering crowd of 12,000 supporters, Trump clutched his right arm and hand in a flailing imitation of Kovaleski's congenital joint condition (Berman 2015). While this action rightly garnered a great deal of critical attention, it was part of a pattern of physical mockery that Trump utilised to denigrate his political foes (Hall et al. 2016).

As Trump's strategy demonstrated, the physical traits of political opponents can be invoked by populist leaders to solidify the frontiers of difference that populism depends upon. But these frontiers can also be supported through actions that highlight the physical difference of the populist leaders themselves. It is clear that the physical imagery of leaders – whether intentionally cultivated or the by-product of a pre-existing set of style choices – plays an important part in enabling the public to identify with them, especially on the basis that the leader exhibits traits that signal their status as 'one of the people' or 'just like us' (Wood et al. 2016). A number of analysts have described the ways that populist leaders present specific physical images of themselves in order to appeal to broad sectors of the public and so substantiate their claims to represent the non-elite or outsiders.

In populist contexts the leader's body typically signifies political transgression and/or subversion of the standard social order. This is often enacted by breaking the codes of dress or transgressing the traditional bodily comportment expected of mainstream politicians (Casullo 2020). We can find many examples of this among British and American populist leaders of recent years. Boris Johnson is recognisable for his unkempt mop of blond hair; Jeremy Corbyn for his casual, homely clothing choices; and relatedly, in 2018 one of the most viral internet memes showed Bernie Sanders huddled in a workaday winter coat and hand-knit mittens at the inauguration of Joe Biden. By contrast, women in populist leadership roles negotiate a different set of physical codes in order to establish their rightful association with 'the people'. For example, Alexandria Ocasio-Cortez has demonstrated a savvy ability to conform to societal gender norms while actively presenting such efforts as a burden that she shares with other hard-working women in the wider world. This is achieved through carefully crafted social media posts and selfie videos, including a 2020 'beauty secrets' tutorial (Ocasio-Cortez 2020). Examples of this nature suggest that the physical traits displayed by populist leaders are deeply enmeshed with existing social norms.

Accordingly, when considering the signifying aspects of populist bodies we need to be attendant to the ways that differences in physical appearance already significantly impact notions of who rightfully belongs in political spaces and who might be legitimately excluded. In this sense populist leaders do not achieve their popular status solely because they transgress physical and behavioural norms; they also, knowingly or not, navigate the complex ways that power and marginality are already mapped onto some physicalities more than others. Given that the leader's presence in political spaces provides symbolic representation for the groups who identify with them, the presentation of their physical characteristics can tacitly signify the parameters of the populist movement they represent. The populist leader's body can gesture toward the inclusion of other bodies who might have been previously excluded, or alternatively it can reinforce a narrow definition of who rightfully belongs within the movement and who should be excluded (Casullo 2020).

The points above underscore the importance of accounting for the signifying capacities of bodies within populist movements. With that said, the somatic registers of the body are also strongly implicated. Populism often goes hand in hand with the staging of large assemblies of people at political rallies or demonstrations, providing an opportunity for collectively experienced physicality; but similarly, the very nature of populism generates heightened emotional fervour as people respond to the movement's iconoclastic, mobilising force. These traits have a direct impact on the corporeal experience of participants. Speaking of political participation more broadly, Diana Coole suggests that 'a quickening of the heart, a rapidity of breaths, a clenching of the fists, an adrenalin rush, a blush, a frown, might indicate a preparation for resistance that is inscribed in the exteriority of the flesh and communicates to others a silent call to common action' (Coole in Machin 2014, 79). Such experiences surely proliferate within populism. Certainly we can find examples of this nature across the populist spectrum, from anti-Austerity demonstrations to MAGA rallies. In these events, shared bodily presence is amplified through physical experiences undertaken in concert with others, and this reinforces a sense of identification among a potentially broad community of populist supporters.

Given the centrality of embodiment in populism generally, it would seem that this should also be a key feature of digital populism. However, the comparatively disembodied nature of online interaction raises the question of whether the body, in both its signifying and experiential capacities, is altered when populist politics moves to an online sphere. To understand this in more detail we need to look more closely at how embodiment occurs through digital media.

It is worth noting at the outset that the role of embodiment in digitally mediated interactions is contested, particularly with regard to the extent to which participants in online interactions are attentive to and influenced by corporeal presence. It is certainly true that the semiotic function of bodies is no less apparent in online political contexts, where images of bodies abound. Social movements are often promoted through imagery of bodies that bear markers of the movement's organising values or agendas – this might range from displays of vulnerable bodies in order to generate empathy, to displays of bodily power or identity that aim to consolidate and motivate group members (Asenbaum 2019). Significantly, the bodies that appear in social media contexts are marked by the same histories and politics as those that are present in the 'real' world, and virtual bodies are subject to the codes and conventions that mark interpersonal interaction in the physical world (Elund 2015). The prominence of symbolic physicality is only intensified by the proliferation of user-generated images and video content, which bring embodied significations even more to the fore (Beusch 2006). In the competitive context of the social media attention-economy, users compete to generate the most attractive, shocking, or in some way remarkable images of bodies – both their own and others – and the most outstanding images will be the ones that garner the greatest circulation. Clearly the semiotic elements of embodiment are central to political engagement in online environments.

At the same time, we also need to consider the role of corporeal sensation in online environments. This aspect is somewhat more difficult to definitively assess. A number of theorists contend that there can be no easy distinction between the kinds of embodied perception that occur in 'real-life' as opposed to virtual or digitally mediated environments (e.g. Bakardjieva 2005; Beusch 2006; Hansen 2011; Munster 2006; Van Doorn 2011). This is because, although our political experiences are altered when they are digitally mediated, the body is never absent from any interactions. Even when comparatively static and remote, the body remains a powerful receptive channel that responds to stimuli and influences cognition. It should also be recognised that the material body participates in an active way when a person engages with social media. Bodies do not simply sit passively in front of screens or gently tap away at keyboards; there are additional elements of physical touch, movement, vocalisation and respiration that occur and that play a role in online perception and interaction. The digitally mediated content that we interact with requires embodied interaction from online participants; text, images, video files and the like might all be viewed as material with which the user's body corporeally interacts (Van Doorn 2011).

Although digitally mediated environments do entail embodied perception, it might be more productive to focus on the ways that corporeal experience is altered in such contexts. There are several aspects to these changes. In the first instance, the multidimensionality of embodied perception is reduced in digitally mediated contexts. In physically present experiences, the body is implicated through many shifting modes of perception, rather than primarily visual or auditory modes. In digitally mediated communications, aspects of physical perception like touch and movement, although not eliminated, are notably diminished. This has implications for the extent to which the different levels of embodied perception are mobilised and inform one another, and it ultimately changes the nature of embodied knowledge that is created and circulated in such contexts.

We must also consider that embodied perception and communication changes due to the temporal frames of digitally mediated interactions. For example, there is a relative lack of spontaneity in digital communications. As compared to face-to-face encounters, online interactions enable participants to rehearse carefully crafted content and responses through a delayed cycle of actions and reactions. The interval between posting and reacting provides a temporal break in communication that allows users to carefully refine their self-performance. With regard to embodiment, this has the effect of reducing or eliminating spontaneity and the unconscious physical gestures that would otherwise be a key element of human communication (Pooley 2010, 78). As discussed above, these elements of communication arise from the body's visceral layers, and ordinarily possess the capacity to communicate different, sometimes unintentional aspects of embodied knowledge; digital mediatisation, through its ability to interrupt interpersonal communication and enable carefully orchestrated responses, effectively diminishes the presence of this authentic, corporeal knowledge.

A further effect of the minimisation of the corporeal is the intensification of cynical perceptions of other users' content. As outlined in Chapter 2, social media users are deeply aware of the presence of fake news and echo chamber algorithms. This cynicism is further fuelled by the relative absence of physical co-presence in the online environment. The absence of the spontaneous embodied communications noted above also imparts a greater degree of ambiguity in online interactions (Finlayson 2020, 5). When a person's body is not physically present with us, we can more easily call into question the authenticity of their identity and the claims that arise from it. This intensifies the scepticism that users are apt to level at communications that are unfamiliar or discordant to them.

Ultimately, the relative absence of corporeal perception is likely to fuel the antagonistic tendencies of populism. A number of analysts have described how the characteristics of online interaction intensify aggressive and insulting behaviour (e.g. Chadwick et al. 2018; Dhrodia 2017; Finlayson 2020; Hannan 2018). To an extent, this can come about in conjunction with populism's rejection of established institutional political behaviours; populist figureheads garner respect and trust from followers by demonstrating their difference from the political status-quo, and this can include a recourse to insults, aggression and hyperbole, especially in the less-formal environments of social media. However, it is also likely that the online valorisation of deliberately offensive or provocative behaviours is far less likely to occur in situations where one shares an embodied physical presence with others; the subtlety of material, physical interactions provides a basis for more nuanced communication and engagement with others; when this is lacking, as it is in digital media environments, complexity, fluidity and uncertainty are unlikely to flourish.

It is clear that political interaction *does* change when it is primarily pursued in digitally mediated environments. Digital populism undoubtedly mobilises embodied perception, but in ways that often exacerbate exclusions and antagonism. In order to address this issue, we might consider what performance practices can tell us about embodied interaction that could be extrapolated to other frameworks of political interaction.

Corporeal Perception in Applied Theatre Practices

Attentiveness to corporeal perception is a core aspect of much Applied Theatre work. Indeed, it is extremely commonplace in theatre practice more generally to explore ways of re-attuning participants to a sense of their materially embodied existence. The pursuit of activities that can reawaken an awareness of mind-body interconnection – and thus produce new modes of embodied perception – has been a driving aim of avant-garde theatre, and especially actor training, throughout the 20th and 21st centuries. The longevity of the search for effective practices of this nature speaks to the challenges inherent to it. Practices that seek to bring corporeal knowledge to the forefront of activities have often evolved into lengthy, sometimes demanding training programmes. More recently, the spirit of such endeavours has been carried over into Applied Theatre circles as practitioners increasingly understand the value of corporeality to social and political projects. From the latter perspective, the goal is to identify activities that can prompt a change in interactions such that corporeal perception is reawakened and plays a more significant part in interpersonal communication (Bird and Sinclair 2019; Plastow 2015).

Despite the long-standing interest in this topic, performance theorists are deeply aware of the difficulties of achieving corporeal awareness in practice. Drew Leder offers a useful summary of the difficulties involved in such projects. He notes that although the mind and body are inseparable and intertwined, nonetheless, our habituated experience means that we often become unaware of our body in day-to-day actions:

> While in one sense the body is the most abiding and inescapable presence in our lives, it is also essentially characterized by absence. That is, one's

> own body is rarely the thematic object of experience. When reading a
> book or lost in thought, my own bodily state may be the farthest thing
> from my awareness. I experientially dwell in a world of ideas, paying little
> heed to my physical sensations or posture.
>
> *Leder 1990, 1*

This 'world of ideas' may become an exclusionary focus whenever an individual
is immersed in an intellectually oriented agenda – for example, when playing
goal-oriented sports or enacting a choreographed dance performance. There
should be little doubt that the supremacy of the 'world of ideas' is also experienced when people are actively engaged in political actions – for example, when
they take part in political debates, consume information about political events or
enact ritualistic participation like voting or campaigning.

This reversion to a dominant thinking mind is a feature even of political
events like mass protests, demonstrations, or political rallies. At the outset, such
examples offer an illustration of the intertwined nature of the semiotic and corporeal aspects of the body. When people are engaged in political activities that
highlight the socially and culturally constructed semiotics of their bodies, then
this might have a secondary effect of drawing attention to their material experience of bodies – as, for example, when women gather on the US National Mall
to protest a populist president's boasts about sexual assault; or when protesters
demonstrate about race relations by holding up their hands in a highly charged
performative gesture. Similarly, when bodies gather together in a stadium, anticipating the entertainment to be derived from a transgressive politician's fiery populist rhetoric, the body comes more to the fore in perception as hearts race and
the reverberations of the cheering crowd are felt through internal tissues. These
examples illustrate the use of the physical body as a value-laden sign system, but
they might also have the potential to reawaken participants to a sense of their
own material bodily substance (Butler 2015). In this way, actions that invoke the
thinking mind might also give rise to greater attention to corporeality.

However, while this holds true for those present at the event, it is unlikely to
occur in any pervasive manner as long as digital media engagement is a prevalent element of political action. Even as participants are sensing their own corporeality to a greater degree in these situations, they are often simultaneously
preoccupied with the 'world of ideas' as they consider the need to document and
circulate their experience for others. Furthermore, far more people engage with
such events through these circulated digital representations, such that intellectual reasoning and rational engagement far outstrip corporeal sensation. In this
way, even experiences that momentarily reawaken participants to their corporeal
existence are often largely experienced through the spectacle of social media,
subsumed into the cycle of cynical performance and spectatorship required by
these platforms.

If digital mediation therefore has the effect of increasing immersion in Leder's
'world of ideas', it is ever more important to find ways of reinvigorating democratic

practices with a conscious awareness of embodied perception. In the following section I turn again to the practices of Alfred Wolfsohn, Peter Schumann and Augusto Boal, providing examples of the ways that their practices have sought to re-establish a sense of material embodiment on the part of participants. As in the previous chapter, the aim is to identify approaches to interaction that might be applied to foster more positive engagements with political difference.

Corporeality in Theatre of the Oppressed

To begin with, corporeal attentiveness is a key feature of Augusto Boal's work. Many of Boal's techniques were specifically developed as tools to foster modes of communication that could draw on corporeally archived knowledge, enabling the expression of ideas and sentiments that have not yet been filtered through rational intellectual processes. Boal is particularly interested in how bodies archive political knowledge and experience. As Kelly Howe describes, 'before Boal even talks about how power relations might shape what a spectator says or thinks, he zeroes in on where a body can or cannot move in a theatre— and how those norms articulate power' (Howe 2021, 76). Boal believed that experiences of political injustice remain present within the flesh of the human actor, and to bring this to the fore we must begin with work that enables people to sense, through their physical being, the circulations of power among those present in any given space. To develop this ability, Boal created an extensive range of games and activities geared toward non-actors, designed to help people become attuned to the material body's ability to both sense and convey relationships of power (Boal 1995).

Theatre of the Oppressed is especially useful for understanding the relationship between the sociocultural construction of bodies and the experiences of politics that they subsequently archive. In Theatre of the Oppressed activities, a key objective is the exploration of how social and political norms discipline bodies, conditioning them to behave in particular ways in specific spaces, or in relation to other bodies demarcated in different categories to their own. However, Boal's work doesn't rest on exploring these social conditions of the body at a surface level – instead, he is much more interested in how that conditioning is manifested within the interior complexities of the physical body, and how participants can be encouraged to sense this, and then experiment with changes through creative imaginings. Once participants have been encouraged to develop their ability to physically express differences in power, activities can advance to explore memories of past oppression or injustice.

As introduced in the previous chapter, the activities conducted in Boal's Image Theatre require participants to form a still image, sometimes individually and sometimes in a group tableaux, to encapsulate a feeling or sum up an experience. These 'images' are then examined and manipulated by other participants – sometimes through physical rearrangement, sometimes through adding complementary poses, or perhaps through repositioning the various images in relation to one another. This can take multiple trajectories, from a group collaborating to explore one person's experiences, to a collective debate and negotiation of the core elements of a social or political issue. Regardless, the focus is on experimenting with and refining the physical expressions. Participants are encouraged to attend to fine details of their own and others' physicality, and by engaging with this in a sustained fashion the focus begins to shift more toward physical sensations.

In my own practice I often minimise the use of words when participants are creating and revising the tableaux of Image Theatre; instead I ask them to select a colour or a shape or a printed image in order to put together a collaged representation of their *sense* of the images, rather than immediately wresting the physical pictures back into linguistic modes of expression. By working with the same themes or issues over a sustained period of time, participants are guided toward expressing the sensations and knowledge contained within the interiority of their bodies rather than accepting a simplistic narrative articulation. Such activities enable each participant to physically explore the life-worlds of others and in doing so imagine political complexities from a new, corporeally oriented perspective (Grant 2020, 6). This is a key advantage of materially embodied performance practices, as they enable participants to creatively expand their own corporeal senses with reference to the memories and perspectives of others.

Corporeal Puppetry

Puppetry practices can also enhance our understanding of how corporeal knowledge might be accessed and communicated. Although it is typically considered a humble art, often associated with child's play, circus, and popular entertainment, puppetry also has a long association with the artistic avant-garde, especially from the early 20th century onward (Bell 2001).[1] A large part of this association with experimentation comes from puppeteers' interest in the relationship between puppets and spectatorial perception, and Peter Schumann has undoubtedly made significant contributions in this vein. Schumann has strong beliefs about the politics of puppets, and particularly the ways that they possess a capacity to alter our perceptions of embodiment and agency. In the first instance, his notion of puppets goes far beyond either the soft, cuddly types associated with children's entertainment on the one hand, or the celebrated popular entertainment forms like Punch and Judy shows. Schumann says that 'puppets are insurrectionists and therefore shunned by correct citizens – unless they pretend to be something other than what they are, like: fluffy, lovely or digestible' (Schumann in Bell 2001, 46). Here we see that Schumann's notion of a puppet is something that is potentially dangerous to the political status quo; furthermore, his puppets bear a resemblance to the rye bread he serves up alongside them – they cannot be quickly digested but must be chewed upon, thought about, sometimes spat out and sometimes imbibed for physical and spiritual nourishment. Clearly, Schumann's puppets don't belong primarily to the rational, intellectual world.

Having encountered Schumann's Bread and Puppet theatre regularly since my childhood, I am convinced that the subversiveness of the papier mache beings is closely linked to the relationship that exists between puppets and human corporeality. Schumann's puppets often call to mind something otherworldly in the slow, methodical pace of their movements and their larger-than-life presence. At the same time, they are often deeply human-like, possessing a certain grace, humility and profundity in their sanguine papier mache features. Nevertheless, it has to be acknowledged that puppets are inanimate, non-human objects that on the surface at least appear to be patently disconnected and distanced from material human flesh. It is this point that Peter Schumann is most interested in challenging through his creative work. It is not accidental that the seemingly naïve rendering of his puppets seems to endow them with an unprepossessing, timeless humanity. Schumann worked over many years, drawing inspiration from puppet theatres from around the world to create a style of puppet that could provoke an awareness of human fragility among his spectators. From the earliest phases of his work he sought to use his creations to explore the 'interior' levels of spectators (Brown et al. 1968).

This centrality of non-human materiality in Schumann's work will be explored in more detail in the next chapter. For the purposes of the present discussion the significance of this work lies primarily in the effect that the puppets can have on their human operators. This becomes a key element when Schumann's ideas are transferred to Applied Theatre settings. In these contexts, puppets need not be limited to representations of fictional characters or public figures; they can also serve as avatars for their human counterparts, offering a means to creatively select or heighten particular aspects of their identity or experiences. Puppets can therefore be thought of as an extension of the human body, serving as the vehicle through which the operator communicates their own personal perspectives. In this manner, puppets facilitate trans-embodiment, in which the actor's body is transferred to and mobilised by the puppet (Mello 2016, 49). Puppets can offer a comparatively benign vehicle for the creative communication of personal memories or political perspectives such that transmission of corporeally held memories are detached from the person's own physical presence. In effect, puppetry makes it possible to explore and communicate embodied memories that are difficult or potentially unpopular.

In addition, trans-embodiment does not simply entail a human actor consciously manipulating the movement of an otherwise-inanimate puppet; crafted accordingly, the puppet also responds to the unconscious elements of the actor's movements. In my own workshops I typically make use of very lightweight papier mache puppets that are also large and loose-limbed. This construction makes the material puppet susceptible to even small movements of the human operator's body. Puppets can therefore be thought of as prosthetic extensions of the human body, responding to and making visible the physical excesses of otherwise intentional gestures – vibrating with the actor's muscular tension or floating in rhythm with the actor's breath (Cappelletto 2011). This renders them amplifiers of the corporeal knowledge that is borne by human bones, tissues and skin.

It is clear that puppets provide multiple avenues for the communication and perception of corporeal knowledge, and this might prove useful for a range of political contexts. However, Schumann's practices also suggest a broader point that is highly relevant to issues of digital mediatisation: his work shows that the transmission of corporeal knowledge doesn't necessarily depend on the individual's own physical presence. It might well be generated through trans-embodiment, which can be facilitated through a range of creative – and mediated – approaches to political interaction.

Voicing the Body

Of the three practices that have informed my own work, the vocal experimentations of Alfred Wolfsohn and Roy Hart most explicitly seek to attune participants to knowledge contained within the corporeal body. In the final part of this chapter I aim to demonstrate how their work provides an avenue for the foregrounding of corporeal perception in ways that thwart the spectacle-orienting tendencies of digital populism outlined above. First, I explore the practical ways that vocal activities can highlight embodied knowledge. I then focus more specifically on Wolfsohn and Hart's approach to the eight-octave voice, which provides insights into the ways that corporeal experience might be expressed in a manner that resists spectacle-driven representation.

The exploration of voice and vocality seems to be a relatively common route for performance practitioners who are interested in the social, political and therapeutic impacts of corporeal perception (Linklater 1976; Newham 1994; Smith 1973). Through a wide array of practical approaches, theatre professionals have sought to develop activities that might enable participants to heighten their awareness of the voice's material properties and in the process discover something about the ways that the voice exists in an inter-relational, embodied sphere. Within this body of work, Wolfsohn's ideas stand out for the way that he addressed the corporeal mechanics of the voice alongside a recognition of their constraint by social and political forces. Wolfsohn's perspective holds great potential as a body of practice that might address the politics of vocality in a range of contexts.

To begin to understand the potential of Wolfsohn and Hart's practices, we need to first unpack what is meant by 'the voice' in social and political contexts. Voice, as a general area of concern, is one aspect of embodiment that demonstrates the ways that materially embodied experience has been downplayed in favour of the body's signifying capacities. Comparatively speaking, a wealth of politics scholarship exists that theorises the voice and vocality from a metaphorical perspective, glossing 'voice' in close relationship to agency. Even when researchers make use of vocalised data, through interview transcripts and the like, the material, embodied aspects of speech tend to be downplayed. As Rachelle Chadwick vividly describes,

> The raw corporeality of voices, their inescapable embodiment as sounds emerging from moist bodily cavities and organs (lungs, throat, mouth and tongue), their composition as mixtures of moving breath, muscle contractions, saliva flows, chord vibrations, hand gestures and signs, machine-human entanglements (as in assistive voice technologies) and unstable soundwaves, is disavowed.
>
> *Chadwick 2020, 2*

The neglect of the physical aspects of voice is not just a benign result of disciplinary emphases; it has real consequences in terms of the facets of political phenomena that are overlooked when we treat the voice primarily as a conduit of other aspects of communication. Perhaps more than any other political thinker, Adriana Cavarero has developed our understanding of the voice as a simultaneously corporeal and political entity. Cavarero addresses the 'sonorous materiality' of the voice, asserting that the historical neglect of these aspects amounts to the 'devocalisation of the logos' (Cavarero 2005, 2). Significantly, she links this to gendered exclusions, pointing out that historical female figures such as muses, sirens and opera singers possessed a mysteriously physical, non-semiotic vocal capacity – typically something to be feared, punished or ridiculed (Cavarero 2005). Accordingly, activities that enable participants to explore the material experience of voices have substantial potential for a politics of inclusivity.

These points also suggest that a consideration of vocal performance practices that are inherently concerned with the physical mechanics of the voice might prove fruitful to social science research by bringing the voice's 'raw corporeality' more centrally into the frame of analysis. In practice, vocal activities can provide insight into both discursive and material realms – like Schumann and Boal's practices discussed above, voice can offer a medium for bridging personal perspectives with an awareness of the shared experience of having a sensuous body (Waitt et al. 2014, 286). Vocal activities can help groups to become aware of multiple layers of experience and express knowledge of the world that otherwise tends to be cloaked by socially and politically conditioned frames of interaction.

In the first instance, this might entail making participants aware of how the voice can reveal more about themselves through its capacity to give expression to subconscious experiences and memories – in Wolfsohn's own experience, his voice revealed important facets of his wartime memories, which were unavailable to his conscious mind. After several failed attempts at addressing his aural hallucinations through more traditional therapeutic routes, Wolfsohn found that vocalising the screams he heard in his mind could help to alleviate the war-related trauma that he continued to experience (Wolfsohn 2012). This use of material vocal experience drew directly on the phenomenon of corporeally archived memories and knowledge (Taylor 2020). Accordingly, Wolfsohn's experiments led him to conclude that the voice has an ability to communicate aspects of personal experience that exceed the self that is consciously presented to the world. Whether addressing intense traumatic experiences or simply employed as a general tool for human development, vocal experimentations might enable people to confront aspects of their past history and present identity in a way that outstrips other approaches.

This point is especially impactful in regard to interactive experiences of voice. The voice, as described in the previous chapter, possesses a capacity to communicate complex and nuanced viewpoints within group contexts. But when we focus on the voice's corporeal essence, this point becomes even more weighty: the voice, through its capacity to carry evidence of corporeally held knowledge, can communicate multifaceted political experiences within group contexts, even exceeding the efforts and understanding of the speaker themselves. The voice accesses the body's experience and knowledge of the world and brings forth an expression of the human, fleshed being that, in its messiness and unpredictability, overflows carefully constructed outward representations. As Don Ihde puts it, 'Sometimes, and against the will of the speaker, what is spoken is not desired. The wheezing voice of the emphysemiac, of the too-far-along smoker, bespeaks the interior state of the body and its pathology' (Ihde 2007, 195). In populist contexts, this means that the voice defies the constitutive exclusions of any political identity group because it has the potential to bear vivid markers of traits that participants would otherwise keep hidden – or equally, that they are not consciously aware of themselves. In doing so, the voice brings uncertainty and multidimensionality into interpersonal interactions.

Alfred Wolfsohn's practice, and perhaps even more so the subsequent work of the Roy Hart Theatre, suggests many ways that these features of the human voice might be applied for the benefit of political interaction. Neither Wolfsohn nor Hart's practices were confined to the singing voice and certainly not to vocal training in pursuit of socially and culturally defined skill or value. Instead the emphasis is on creative exploration that enables people to express themselves using an expanded vocal range – and this typically includes everything from dulcet tones to grunts and wheezes. As Wolfsohn himself said, 'when I speak of singing, I do not consider this to be an artistic exercise, but the possibility, and the means to recognise oneself, and to transform this recognition into conscious life' (Wolfsohn 2007). And, as expressed by Roy Hart, '[...] singing, as we practise it, is literally the resurrection or redemption of the body. The capacity to "hold" the voice in identification with the body makes biological reality of the concept "I am"' (Hart 1967).

In this vein, Wolfsohn's and Hart's explorations of 'the 8-octave voice' are especially relevant. Over time, one of the trademark features of both artists' practice became the pursuit of an expanded vocal range that could enable participants to vocalise across six to eight octaves. At the heart of Wolfsohn's and Hart's approach to the 8-octave voice lay a recognition of the ways that adult human voices have ordinarily been conditioned across an individual's lifetime to correspond with social and cultural norms. Gender is by far the most indelible of these norms, but other aspects of culture – class, race, etc. – also contribute to the range and registers that an individual tends to think of as their 'own' rightful 'voice'. The ordinary human voice is capable of approximately 3 1/3 octaves. Wolfsohn asserted that any human voice could be trained to vocalise across at least 6 octaves but that this went hand in hand with heightened emotional and physical sensitivity (Hart 1967). The 8-octave voice thus offered a means of exploring both an extended vocal capability and a refined sensorial engagement with the world.

In pursuit of such goals we can use playful activities that help to de-emphasise social and cultural notions of what a skilful voice might sound like. This is realised in practice through techniques that mobilise the physical body, vibrating or jarring the fleshed organs that produce the sounds we call 'voice'. In professional Roy Hart practices this involves carefully trained teachers applying pressure to specific parts of the body, sometimes with significant force, to release sounds that the student was not aware they could produce. In an applied context, though, we can adapt this by engaging participants in movement-based activities that jostle and jar their voices and defy their efforts at control. Instructing participants to jump, stomp, crawl or gesticulate while vocalising has the effect of gently nudging the voice from the channels that participants intend for it to follow. As a result, when we come to express political sentiments vocally, the voice is better positioned to outstrip the consciously crafted intentions of the person and express some degree of otherwise-hidden corporeal knowledge.

Ultimately, vocal practice of this nature has great potential to directly address some of the challenges presented by digital populism. Where social media environments encourage aggressive or offensive behaviour because of the diminished sense of shared physical vulnerability, the use of the voice – especially in spontaneous, extraordinary ways – requires people to act in a manner that often feels uncomfortable and socially risky. In the process it can reawaken a sense of shared vulnerability that might be conducive to political engagement. Similarly, the experience of vocality, both as a means of self-expression and through exposure to the resonant voices of others, might prove effective in countering the modes of cynicism that are prevalent in digital populism, precisely because the embodied voice so clearly expresses uncontrollable and unintended aspects of human experience. In addition, Wolfsohn and Hart demonstrated that practices that access and communicate corporeally archived knowledge often reach their greatest heights when they actively pursue failures and uncertainties rather than conformity to existing standards. This suggests a relationship between corporeal knowledge and failure, a topic that will be addressed more directly in Chapter 6.

Conclusion

In this chapter I have argued that embodiment is a central element of political perceptions and one which deserves greater attention – particularly in terms of the interiority of the material body and its role in sensing, archiving and communicating experiences. This level of bodily sensation is clearly present in populist politics, and it interacts with and reinforces the way that power and identities become inscribed on physical bodies in the real world. It is therefore significant that corporeal perception is largely downplayed in present-day digital media platforms. By considering Applied Theatre practices that utilise physical improvisation, puppetry, and voice, I have introduced illustrative exercises that demonstrate the potential for performance to reinsert corporeal perception into political interaction. Of particular note is the way that some practices can encourage critical interrogation of socially and culturally conditioned bodies by attuning participants to the sensations, memories and knowledge contained within the inner material body. Explored collectively, such approaches might result in altered perceptions of the individual's own body as well as its relationship to the world around it.

5

EMBODIMENT AND RELATIONALITY

Bringing the Outside In

The previous chapter established the centrality of corporeal perception to populist politics, and the ability for performance-oriented activities to re-attune people to corporeality in a manner that might aid democratic engagement. The present chapter is similarly concerned with the role that embodied experience plays in political interaction, and how this differs in digital populist contexts from the tendencies of in-person interactions. Here though, the focus is on the relational aspects of embodied experience, and especially the ways that performance highlights the fact that bodies are constituted through their interactions with the material world around them. In this sense, the focus now shifts to the importance of exterior influences, as opposed to the earlier focus on interiorly held knowledge.

In pursuit of this, the chapter considers interactions with the non-human as well as the human, and the ways that these external entities are experienced through tactile and kinaesthetic encounters. This forms the basis of an argument that applied arts might provide insights about the current limitations of digitally mediated interactions which could help to supplement inclusive democratic projects. My central argument is that haptic encounters with the external world can disrupt our assumptions about individual agency and identity; and in so doing, they open up a space in which our encounters with other humans might be equally profound in terms of altering our sense of ourselves and our relationship to others. In other words, by engaging in disruptive haptic activities with non-human or external matter, we might find new ways of relating politically to other people.

The chapter begins with a brief discussion of recent treatments of relational materiality in political scholarship, with an emphasis on considerations of non-human objects, touch, and movement. This makes the case that haptic interactions have important political functions, a perspective that is then brought

DOI: 10.4324/9780367824129-8

to bear on a consideration of the presence of these features within digital populism. The remaining section of the chapter explores the insights about tactility and kinaesthetics that can be derived from a closer focus on puppetry, voice, and Theatre of the Oppressed. It concludes by bringing this knowledge into conversation with the goals of agonistic pluralism.

Introducing Object Agency and Haptic Encounters

In earlier chapters, I discussed topics of engagement and embodiment – here I delve into these issues from a slightly different angle, through an examination of interactions with non-human objects and haptic encounters. These are important features of both Applied Theatre practices and populist politics. In part, this chapter aims to counter the primacy that is often given to the visual and auditory senses in political scholarship and instead celebrate physical sensations of touch, movement and bodily resonance. It is important to acknowledge at the outset that the senses are fundamentally intertwined and synaesthetic in nature. They have emerged as historically and culturally constructed delineations (Sedgwick 2003; Serres 2016); but I wish to place an emphasis momentarily on the ways that haptic engagements and sensations can distinctly impact political interactions. This approach furthers the discussion of corporeal attentiveness introduced in the previous chapter, but shifts the emphasis to relationality with the external world.

This chapter draws primarily on theories of new materialism, which enable a consideration of the complexities of materialisation, positioning materials of all kinds on par with human existence in terms of their vitality, agency or interactivity. While not disregarding the impact of discourse and culture, new materialist perspectives enable a critical examination of the ways that human perceptions, beliefs and behaviours are extensively shaped by encounters with external things. For the purposes of this chapter, I begin with three key theoretical areas of concern that are especially applicable to digital populism, pluralist democracy, and Applied Theatre practice. These are: the agency of non-human objects; issues of haptic engagement; and the ways that the two former points can result in heightened perceptions of inter-relational subjectivity that is co-produced between the human actor and the objects they encounter in the world around them.

The Agency of Objects

This chapter is premised on the assertion that our perceptions of political issues, and the ways that we bring these to bear during our encounters with others, are fundamentally shaped by our corporeal encounters with the world around us. This requires a closer consideration of the materiality of the external world and its capacity to bear upon us. Fundamentally, this line of thinking necessitates a rejection of the dualistic categorisations of subject/object and human/non-human. These binary categories are historically and socially constructed and neglect more up-to-date understandings of matter and physics, which reveal the extent to which all things are intertwined and imbricated (Barad 2007; Coole 2013). In general, new materialist thinking rejects a notion of agency that is tied to a particular type of being or to specific capacities for cognition, rationality or self-consciousness (Coole 2013). As a result, we can view humans in parallel with non-human entities, and consider the non-human as fully capable of both acting and being acted upon. Jane Bennett aptly describes this as '[…]the capacity of things – edibles, commodities, storms, metals – not only to impede or block the will and designs of humans but also to act as quasi-agents or forces with trajectories, propensities or tendencies of their own' (Bennet in Harris and Holman Jones 2019, 6).

The recognition of non-human object agency is accompanied by a shift in ontological thinking, leading to an understanding of all things as co-existent in a co-operative state of flux. All things have agency; no thing is fixed or definable, but always open to change or reconfiguration through interaction with other things (Asenbaum 2019; Coole 2013). For Diana Coole, 'Emphasis falls […] on the shifting associations between and within entities that are incessantly engendering new assemblages within open systems. Porous membranes, rather than fixed boundaries, allow such systems to interact with and transform one another' (Coole 2013, 456). Significantly for my purposes, this gives rise to an understanding of agency as a quality that is inherently tied to interaction. Notably, Karen Barad characterises this as 'intra-action', an unpredictable process in which innumerable entities, human and non-human alike, are co-constituted through unpredictable processes of encounter and affectivity, producing constellations of bodies, subjectivities and beings in the world around us (Barad 2007, 394).

The implications of this are politically significant: if we give serious attention to the agency of material objects, and if we acknowledge that materialities are always in flux, then this enables profound shifts in thinking about interrelation, interaction and agency. The dynamism of any 'being' or 'thing' comes at least in part from its encounters with things other to itself. Accordingly, Jane Bennet is prompted to ask, 'How would political responses to public problems change were we to take seriously the vitality of (nonhuman) bodies?' (Bennet in Harris and Holman Jones 2019, 6). There are multiple points to consider in this respect. First of all, by recognising the agency of the non-human objects and materials we encounter, we must also acknowledge that these objects are marked by social hierarchies, cultural stereotyping and injustices in similar ways that humans are[1]; this awareness might prompt us to become more sensitive to the precise manner in which those same processes are inscribed on our own human bodies, and the bodies of others.

An awareness of object agency therefore has the potential to disrupt our settled assumptions about identities, bodies and human agency. At issue here is the proposition that encounters with agentive objects might challenge fixed worldviews by unsettling taken-for-granted presumptions about ourselves, others and the world around us. At times, encounters with material objects conform to the expectations and hopes of the human actors who consider themselves in relative control; other times though these encounters are unpredictable, fractured or messy – and in these moments, interesting political insights might occur. The subsequent demand for a reorientation between the human and the non-human can lead to a disoriented sense of power or vulnerability, effectively queering our sense of ourselves and the world around us (Ahmed 2006; Harris and Holman Jones 2019).

Ultimately then, it is clear that there is great political potential in practices that can shift human thinking about our relationships with the material world around us, and ultimately our relationships with one another. To explore this further, this chapter now turns to a consideration of our haptic encounters with objects to provide more details about what occurs corporeally when we engage with external, material worlds.

Touching, Being Touched and Reaching-Toward

As noted above, a key point for new materialists is the extent to which bodies – both human and non-human – manifest in the world through their interactions with others. This reliance on encounter and interaction brings a second conceptual strand to the fore: the ways that bodies are materially figured through haptic sensation. It is useful to note here that the fields of Psychology and Communication Studies broadly distinguish between two different types of touch – the cutaneous, tactile elements of touch that involve the contact made between skin and external surface; and kinaesthetic encounters which involve moving and reaching-toward. The term 'haptic' is used to designate experiences where both tactile and kinaesthetic perception are involved (Haans and IJsselsteijn 2006, 150). In this section, I summarise key points about tactility and kinaesthetics before applying this to an examination of digital populism.

As noted above, my interest in physical materiality is centred on the ways that we interact with the surfaces of things that we ordinarily consider to be external to ourselves – and subsequently the ways that these interactions might shape the way that we reflect on ourselves and relate to others. Erin Manning's influential work on the politics of touch is helpful in this pursuit. Touch, for Manning, encompasses both the tactile and kinaesthetic aspects of haptic encounter. She defines it as 'every act of reaching toward', and suggests that the act of touching 'enables the creation of worlds' (Manning 2007, 17). Touch is therefore a fundamental aspect of our relationally produced experience of the world: 'I reach out to touch you in order to invent a relation that will, in turn, invent me' (Manning 2007, 17). Furthermore, touch is not a definitive act that fixes or crystallises the object being encountered. Rather, it is a reciprocal interaction that leaves an ephemeral imprint: 'Touch is a trace, always deferred, always leading toward another moment, another imprint, another touch' (Manning 2007, 141). This perspective endows acts of touch with the characteristics of performance – as an interactive exchange that is always disappearing, but always contains the potential to transform all participants, through repetitions and re-enactments.

Manning also places an emphasis on 'the sensing body in movement', highlighting the 'relational matrices' it encounters and makes possible (2007, 15). Bodies that touch, whether animate or inanimate, are not fixed in time and space but rather are in a constant state of movement. Political projects that seek to delimit identities, categories, agencies and potentials often rely on fixing these categories in a non-moving framework. Bodies then become stabilised in their assigned categories or subject identities, and this contributes strongly to nation-building projects or other political institutional initiatives that rely on unified, knowable, fixed nature of people and things (Manning 2007, 16). As a result, calling attention to processes of touch means celebrating the moments of fluidity and uncertainty between bodies, and this can lead to destabilising otherwise hardened political assumptions. This suggests that creative acts that involve reaching out and connecting physically with the external world have profound potential to disrupt otherwise settled assumptions about human subjectivity. Touch can constitute a radical moment of change. To understand this further, we need to consider the ways that the haptic senses are present within populism, and especially digital populism.

Haptic Encounters in Populism and Digital Populism

Conjunctions between new materialist thinking and populism studies are relatively rare. Scholars of populism tend to emphasise discursive, ideological and stylistic features of populism rather than its material manifestations. Yet, as discussed in the previous chapter, populism obviously does manifest in material ways, experienced differently according to the role one plays. In its fundamental reliance on exclusionary frontiers, populism establishes inward- and outward-facing surfaces – these are not only rhetorical allusions to walls or metaphorical bodies, but increasingly, these conceptual delineations take on real-world physicality. The best examples of this tend to be found in right-wing populism – for example, the frequent scapegoating of migrants and foreign nationals is rhetorical in its origins, but it becomes physically present in the world through the erection of concrete walls, barbed wire, and border control policing. Populism also has a tendency to generate physical violence, as we saw all too clearly on January 6th, 2021.

Furthermore, the populist celebration of 'the people' is frequently experienced through material encounters. This is evident whenever populism manifests in large-scale, in-person rallies or demonstrations. The haptic experiences that result from the physical proximity of like-minded political actors have a significant effect. Tactile and kinaesthetic sensations come to the fore when bodies brush against one another, communicating through linked arms, hugs or simultaneous gestures (Parviainen 2010). Populism is undoubtedly experienced in a more material manner than other modes of democratic interaction, as people more frequently engage physically with other supporters of the movement, but also with objects like placards, hats and banners (Green 2010). All of this suggests that populism should be considered in terms of its material presences, and especially for the way that it engenders specific modes of relationality through haptic encounters. For the purposes of this chapter, this point will be explored through a focus on digital populism.

To begin with, we can consider the role of agentive objects in digital populism. We might approach this by first considering the ways that digital devices and platforms often act on their own agendas and impact users in unexpected ways. For example, there are a multitude of examples whereby technological devices – mobile phones, tablets, laptops, etc. – defy users' attempts to control them. All of these devices rather notoriously interrupt our intended business by presenting their own demands that must be responded to – an urgent ringtone, a warning of a failing battery; incessant buzzing notifications; or simply the tendency to fall from our hands at inconvenient moments. This interrupts the processes of engagement in political interactions, because it injects additional, unexpected aspects of a user's own life and experiences into what would otherwise have been a ring-fenced engagement with digital political content.

In addition, the content housed within such devices also exhibits agency, independent from human input. Increasingly, communications and technology scholars are investigating the agency of digital platforms and their impact on human users. In this respect, the algorithms, echo chambers and marketplaces of social media need not be thought of only as the products of unseen tech designers or digital media corporations; we might also consider these as characteristics of the non-human technologies and devices that we otherwise think of as benign mediums for communication – they are increasingly understood as complex entities that defy human efforts to reasonably control them (Pickering et al. 2017). This fact becomes especially significant when we consider the role of bots within social media networks. Social bots, created to reinforce support for specific political positions or campaigns, are estimated to generate between 10% and 20% of social media content, rendering them significant players in this political landscape (Keller and Klinger 2019; Varol et al. 2017). They may be comparatively benign or malicious, and they often have ambiguous relationships to their human operators (Woolley 2016). Significantly, social media users are increasingly aware of the presence of social bots (Stocking and Sumida 2018).

The question that results from the above is, can the agentive aspects of digital devices create a sense of ontological disorientation for users? In order to begin to answer this question, we need to turn to how social media users experience such encounters in practice. As established in Chapter 4, some theorists emphasise the extent of human corporeal involvement in digitally mediated interactions. It seems obvious though that although corporeal sensations remain present in digitally mediated exchanges, there is a comparative lack of tactility and movement involved. Nevertheless, some theorists stress the role of touch and tactility within digitally mediated political communication (Richardson and Hjorth 2019). An emerging field of 'haptic media studies' emphasises the presence of touch within digital technologies, from touchscreens to vibrating notifications. Additionally, new research is exploring the potential for expanded kinaesthetic interfaces that replicate sensations of movement and active tactility (Zasúlich Pérez Ariza and Santís-Chaves 2016). It is believed that growing innovations in haptic technology might be crucial to interaction, communication and self-perception (Richardson and Hjorth 2019, 4). In addition to this, other scholars suggest that even the non-physical aspects of objects can also be understood as material surfaces which users interact with. For example, we might consider not just the deliberately added-in haptic sensory features of digital devices, but also the unseen yet impactful waves of electrical, magnetic, and light energies (Koefoed Hansen 2011). Taken together, these points make a case for the haptic nature of our engagement with digitally mediated communication.

To some extent, the increasingly haptic features of digital technology strive to instantiate 'social presence', defined as the feeling of being co-present with and able to freely communicate with other 'real' people (Biocca 2006). Developments in virtual reality and other immersive technologies increase this sense of co-presence in a shared time and space. This would seem to provide the basis for considering digital technologies as entities that users materially interact with, and that thus provide the potential to contribute to users' sense of subjectivity and relationship to the world around them.

Returning then to the question of whether the agency of internet technologies impacts users' orientations to themselves and the world around them, the answer must be a cautious affirmative. This is because, despite the potential for digital media to function as agentive objects, the degree of hapticity involved in these encounters remains significantly diminished from what we tend to experience in everyday 'real' life. Despite technological advances that seek to increase 'social presence', I maintain that the dominant features of digital media, as they usually operate at present, still function to downplay material interaction. Instead, following Drew Leder, users are subsumed into a primarily cerebral, and also primarily visual and auditory focus on the content featured on devices (Leder 1990). Clearly though, digital media has the potential to offer encounters with the external world that might reawaken a different mode of self-perception by users; this suggests that we might glean further insights by turning to Applied Theatre practices to understand how these qualities might be more effectively brought to the surface for participants.

Insights from Applied Arts and Performance

Theatre and performance scholars and practitioners have long been interested in the ways that objects and non-human entities not only contribute to meaning-making, but also have the capacity to destabilise spectators' perceptions of human subjectivity in the process (Schneider 2015). Performance theorists also share an interest in co-production and co-presence, and the ways that these can impact human perceptions of agency. In this sense, theatre and performance practices are well positioned to reveal new insights about the ways that relational perceptions can be impacted by encounters with the non-human world around us. Ultimately, the arts have an ability to not just embody new materialist principles, but to actively pursue the underlying political project of using those principles to instantiate a new mode of being for participants in relation to the world around them. In the remainder of this chapter, I review the ways that Boal, Wolfsohn and Schumann have developed practices that possess potential to destabilise human participants' understandings of agency and interrelation. I begin with a consideration of how Boal and Wolfsohn exemplify approaches that highlight relationality between human participants, and then extend these insights to the work of Schumann, which firmly incorporates non-human objects.

Boal, Bodies and Touch

Although Augusto Boal typically emphasises creative practice between human bodies, the games and activities that provide the foundation of Theatre of the Oppressed are explicitly aimed at fostering perceptual connections between the individual and the group. Of particular interest is Boal's extensive use of touch and person-to-person contact in activities that seek to alter participants' perceptions of themselves and others – particularly within diverse, multifaceted groups (Boal 2002). As a result of years of experimentations in a range of global contexts, Boal derived a number of insights about the benefits of tactile encounters with others. One illustrative example of this is an activity that he called 'Colombian Hypnosis'. Named after the location in which Boal devised it, Colombian Hypnosis is an activity that involves 'connecting' one part of one's own body with another part of an other's body, through an imaginary thread – so, for example, the palm of my right hand might become 'attached' to your nose, and through my own movements, I can then control the pace and direction at which your nose will travel through the space, with other parts of your body following in whatever way is necessary to retain a precise and consistent connection between us.

Boal has developed an entire arsenal of games and activities that heighten people's ability to engage with one another in a co-operative and constructive manner (Boal 1995, 2002); but I find Colombian Hypnosis one of the most illustrative of the ways that bodies in motion encounter one another materially. Conducted entirely in silence, the relationship created between the two participants is primarily a physical one. Because they are in constant movement, and because a good deal of concentration is required to maintain the 'hypnotic' connection, participants tend to arrive at a heightened sensitivity to the surfaces of their own body, and the surfaces of their partner. This results in a giving-over of one's own body to the joint project of the pair. Each body becomes part of a moving sculpture and the body both acts and is acted upon in equal measure.

This is a useful exercise in Applied Theatre contexts because it begins to establish corporeal cooperation and interrelation without the risks associated with actual physical contact. However, it is especially significant in the context of this chapter because it enables participants to effectively experience 'touch' across distances. Although there is a complete absence of contact between participants, a strong connection exists which emulates physical contact. This demonstrates that profound experiences of touch can occur even when no actual contact is made between entities. Although Boal's practice does not frequently involve non-human elements of the external world, his work demonstrates that relationality can be established through tactile and kinaesthetic activities that occur across distance and without the benefit of linguistic communication. This is obviously not dissimilar to the innovative kinaesthetic interfaces that are being developed in conjunction with digital platforms.

Boal's work is also significant here because Colombian Hypnosis stresses a sense of what Erin Manning refers to as 'reaching-toward'. It requires participants to continually and constantly buy into the connection, to sustain the imaginary thread connecting body to body. I often find that participants engaged in this activity develop a particularly strong sense of physical connection – tasked with maintaining the connection with another body in movement, and unable to communicate verbally, the connecting points of the body tingle with awareness of the other's movements. It is a sensation of always-anticipated contact. By mobilising the corporeal body in this way, orienting it toward the input and feedback of others in collaboration with our own, participants become attuned to a revised sense of agency that is rooted in relationality. This gives rise to a physically sensed state of interdependence – one that is couched within Boal's quest for metaxis among participants. As a result, the haptic engagements of Colombian Hypnosis demonstrate one way of creating a relational orientation toward others that is inherently fluid and transformational (Coole 2013). Touch, in this activity, is not a means of knowing and defining the other; rather, it provides an avenue for ongoing uncertainty and porosity. Manning puts it thus:

> Relation exceeds self and other, expressing the desire not to seek a commonality in the particularities that differentiate us but to engage the difference as the untouchability that will forever draw me outside my 'self'. Untouchable, I realize that I have no self, that I exist in relation, that I am in relation to my own untouchability. My body is not One.
>
> *Manning 2007, 74–5*

Voice and Exterior Materiality

Alfred Wolfsohn's vocal practices also address exterior materiality. We typically think of the voice as an entity that is contained within our own individual bodies, only collaborating with others through conscious effort. Yet Alfred Wolfsohn and Roy Hart's vocal practices reveal the extent to which the voice itself functions as a *thing* in the world that sometimes seems to exist independently from the person attached to it; As discussed in the previous chapter, voices have a dynamism of their own, distinct from the human consciousness that generates them. Furthermore, this sometimes-independent voice can be brought forth in ways that alter our perceptions of selfhood and interdependence.

To begin with, the sounds emanating from bodies are produced by a complex interplay between air, space and biological features and with sufficient provocation they can outstrip the control of the singer. Without doubt, voices operate as a medium for reaching-toward others in a relational way, especially when cultivated to outstrip social or cultural conditioning and speak otherwise hidden personal truths. But additionally, we might consider voices as entities in their own right, as they move around spaces in unpredictable ways. Bodies experience vocal sounds through both creation and reception (Chadwick 2020; Thatcher and Galbreath 2019). In the space in-between creation and reception, voice exists as a sometimes-unpredictable thing that is not dissimilar to the vibrations and light waves offered up by digital devices. Voices produce sound waves that resonate with other entities, both human and non-human, passing through surfaces and physically altering interiors, through sonic wave vibrations (Cavarero 2005; Chari 2020). The vibrations of noise production move from one body to another, and bodies impact the sound waves which in turn resonate against other bodily surfaces. Sometimes windows or metal frames vibrate subtly; curtains move; glass surfaces can be covered with condensation. In this way, although the voices we sense emanate from the interior surfaces of another body, we can also experience the voice itself as an independent object in the world.

If we consider the voice in this way, as an entity endowed with a degree of independent agency, we might also attribute to it the potential to prompt new awareness of relationality. Chadwick asserts that this might be possible because of the relationship between the voice and our natural environment:

> [...]with every breath we pull into our lungs we underline our relational dependence on more-than-human bodies and environments [...]. As bodies, we are not closed systems or self-contained individuals but radically interpermeated by (industrial and organic) plant and algae breaths, gaseous air molecules and planetary winds moving air across the globe[...]. Our bodies are always already more-than-human and our breaths inter-mingle endlessly with the breaths of plants, factories, machines, animals, algae and bacteria.
>
> *Chadwick 2020, 2–3*

In other words, as voices transform breaths into sound waves, they are already dynamised through the incorporation of external material – the substances that linger in the atmosphere, bearing traces of other elements of our physical environment.

This perspective underscores the nature of the voice as an interdependent entity that might offer a window onto our imbrications with the external world. But to make the most of this potential, it is necessary to use the voice in a way that attunes both speakers and listeners to this orientation. A key feature of practices derived from Wolfsohn and Hart is the point when one hears a voice emanating, apparently from one's own body, but sounding – and feeling – very little like the voice one thinks of as one's own. As the exercises and games proceed, the voice begins to move beyond its culturally induced constraints, as well as the constraints developed from individual experiences and beliefs. It gains in strength and resonance and becomes something unfamiliar to the body and mind that produces it – and in the process, participants feel a profound sense of disrupted identity.[2] Although moments like this are most likely to occur after an extended engagement with Wolfsohn-Hart practices, they demonstrate the potential for the voice to operate as an almost-independent entity, one that has power to outstrip the controls of its 'owner' and to force that person into a new orientation with the world around them.

The Agency and Relationality of Puppets

The practices described above suggest that Applied performance might provide essential clues regarding the ways that people become attentive to material relationality. However, of the three bodies of work that have informed my own practice, puppetry undoubtedly offers the greatest potential in this regard. This is largely because from the very start of his work Peter Schumann has been thinking of puppets as objects endowed with agency (Brown et al. 1968). From the mid-1960s onward, Schumann was perceptive of the link between object-agency and human relationality, and he has maintained this interest up until the present day (Schumann 2018). Accordingly, in this section, I explore the materiality of puppets and their corresponding potential to disorient perceptions of individual subjectivity and agency.

For Peter Schumann, puppets are subversive beings that have an innate potential to move spectators toward an appreciation of human/non-human interconnectedness. In the late 1990s, he wrote,

> We who think of ourselves as subjects don't even know donkeys well enough, not to speak of fence posts and rocks, to which we assign the job of object, because we haven't discovered their individuality yet. As a donkeyman – which means: related to donkeys and therefore also to fence posts and rocks – I shy away from that particular definition: object. Object exists only because we are deceived into being subject, and as subjects we are subjects of a republic in which the prisons grow faster than any part of the growth factor [...] Objects have been performing under the whip of subjects too long and are now disobedient and can't be counted on any longer. They avoid real contact and meaningful relationships and divorce

themselves from the intentions of subjects. They used to be good and close to our hearts. They almost liked us and seemed to be grateful for our attention, but were deprived of their dignity by the throw-away philosophy, which resulted in the object's revenge: garbage.

Schumann in Bell 2001, 48–49

Schumann's words, developed without reference to quantum theory or new materialist thinking, feel ahead of their time. They pose the question of whether there is something unique about performance work with puppets that naturally lends itself to an awareness of such themes. Regardless, Schumann is clearly if quietly aware of a profound fact about puppets: they are beings with agency of their own.

It is almost commonplace for puppeteers to espouse, only slightly tongue-in-cheek, that their puppets really do have a life of their own and their own agency (Bogátyrev 1999). I have come to this sense in my own puppetry practice, particularly in group workshops. While my attention is directed to the human participants I share the space with, very often the puppets make their presence felt in unexpected and influential ways: their paper creases create rigid joints that operate according to each one's unique biology, impacting their movements in defiance of operators' efforts; the angle of their gaze, ostensibly controlled by the puppeteer's manipulation of a head or neck, is actually determined by the complex ways that the folds and creases of their face interact – meaning that they sometimes fixate on areas of the room or other objects hitherto unnoticed by the humans. Outdoors, the puppets conspire with the elements, taking flight at the hands of the wind and pulling against the straining arms of puppeteers; sometimes they weep and blur when it rains; often their weight increases throughout a long day, and they become more and more burdensome and more and more controlling of their puppeteers. Jane Bennet describes this uncanny sense of the dynamism of objects as 'enchanted materialism' – an understanding of inorganic entities as beings that are to some extent independent from human will and capable of acting in unexpected ways (Coole and Frost 2010). Notably, this perception has the potential to disrupt our sense of our own individual selfhood and reorient us toward our relationships with the world around us. To understand how puppetry establishes this in practice, we need to consider some key features of Schumann's work in more detail.

First, it is important to keep in mind that from the start of Schumann's artistic development he was familiar with Oskar Schlemmer's experiments with masks, automatons and marionettes and the ways that these could be used to prompt audiences to think differently about embodiment (Bell et al. 2013). As a primary leader of Bauhaus theatre workshops in the 1920s, Schlemmer experimented with the use of sculptures, masks and objects that surrounded the actor's body with the effect of revising both actors' and audiences' consciousness of embodiment. In his *Stick Dance* from 1928, Schlemmer strapped lightweight poles to the body of actor/dancers, thereby changing their perception of their bodies in space.

But additionally, this practice also changed spectators' perceptions of the dancers, altering their sense of themselves in the spaces they co-occupied (Le Feuvre 2019). Schumann's work bears evidence of a similar approach, as his larger-than-life puppets possess the ability to change spectators' sense of their own bodily dimensions within the shared performance space; this effect is heightened by the fact that spectators are often expected to become participants through communal processions and call-and-response interactions with the puppets. When working with puppets in Applied Theatre settings, I find that this effect holds true, but it is also supplemented by the sensory experiences that occur when participants themselves become the puppeteers. In such cases, there is an altered perception of where the physical human self ends and the puppet body begins.

In addition, Schumann's practice has obvious haptic elements due to the crafted nature of the puppets. This operates at two levels: first, spectators' perception of the handmade puppets and second, participation in the making process. To start with, Schumann's papier mache puppets are memorable for their handcrafted beauty and elegance. Although sophisticated in their facial expressions and physical gestures, they bear the hallmarks of naïve crafting traditions. Craft-based practices are defined in part by their processes of making, and crafted objects reflect the cultural and historical situation of their makers. Crafted objects therefore function as records of the past, whether historically distant or recent, and this might evoke new sensations or insights when those objects are encountered by others in the present. As Nicole Burisch explains,

> [...] crafted objects might be viewed as especially appropriate, embodied, or representative forms of documentation. In this view, crafted objects function as records of all the actions that took place over a given time, with the 'event' or act of making physically inscribed upon them.
>
> *Burisch 2016, 67*

They also give rise to associations with the imagined crafter and their context, thus evoking a degree of haptic relationality (Burisch 2016). When people view Peter Schumann's puppets, with their characteristic marks of hand-craftedness, they encounter a record of other persons' pasts. By calling attention to their materiality, the puppets invite spectators to view them not only as the fictional characters they represent, but also as the products of other people's prior labour and creativity. In addition, due to the uneven, lumpy surface of the papier mache materials, Schumann's puppets invite tactile engagement. Acts of touch are already implied in the marks that the makers' fingers have left on their surfaces, and this overtly tactile surface invites further reaching-toward by those who encounter them.

When these features of Schumann's puppets are extrapolated to applied workshop contexts, the impact of tactile crafting is further heightened. This is because the puppets made in workshops do not simply exist to be spectated from a distance – they are brought to life through hands-on processes that require participants to encounter their component parts through tactile engagement. In my own practice, I take this one step further. The puppets I make use of in workshops are often collaboratively designed and crafted and they bear physical markers of multiple participants' past political experiences. They might be partially constructed from official letters, photographs, messages from loved ones, overdue bills, newspaper cuttings or other mementos that call to mind traumatic or indeed joyful experiences related to political events or policies. These component pieces are objects that, although originating as benign pieces of paper or cloth or ink, were changed by their interactions with political entities. They now function differently, and they therefore impact the people who creatively work with them in different ways. We rework these objects into the skin and fibres of a puppet body – sometimes tearing or twisting them, allowing the material (the textured surface of official letters, the glossy surface of photographs, the fragile fibres of newsprint) to prescribe the ways that we can work with the objects and the shape of the face that will result. In doing so, these objects reclaim a vitality of their own, one that is neither wholly resistant nor any longer firmly within the grasp of powerful political or economic institutions.

This is often a highly poignant experience for those involved, and it speaks strongly to the ways that objects are bound up with human experience, and vice versa. The ability to serve as physical archives of people's experiences is an important feature of puppetry, because it provides avenues for people to physically interact with multivalent embodiments of experience which is not only semiotic in nature, but that, through the traits outlined in the section above, offers a means of reworking people's perception of their own body and the bodies of others (Astles 2009, 99).

Regardless of whether a papier mache puppet is made by the participant or simply spectated, a key element of perception that comes into play is kinaesthetic empathy. This is a concept that has received growing attention from both performance scholars and cognitive scientists in recent years. Kinaesthetic empathy suggests the possibility that, by watching another being's physical movement, the onlooker might sense themselves to be physically involved in a similar way. Historically this concept has been an influential theory within dance studies in particular, but in recent years it constitutes a body of research reinvigorated by the discovery of mirror neurons. These special nerve cells are remarkable due to the way that they are similarly discharged whether a person undertakes an action themselves or simply views it from a distance. In effect, the body primes itself to be able to act in concert with the actions it perceives from others. Mirror neurons are also thought to play a key role in the ability to understand others' actions (Heyes and Catmur 2022; Mazurek and Schieber 2019).

Significantly, studies have shown that non-human actors can also stimulate mirror neurons in spectators (Press et al. 2005). This means that puppets almost certainly possess a capacity to stimulate kinaesthetic empathic responses to their movements that have the potential to transform onlookers' sense of themselves (Grant 2020). As the puppets of Bread and Puppet theatre move enigmatically before spectators, they activate specific neural processes that impact perception of both the spectated objects *and* the viewer's own body. The significance of this is profound. Puppets, presenting themselves as tactile objects with agency, and sometimes bearing the material traces of other people's past political experiences, might move in ways that are shaped by the influence of their makers' contributions. The experience of this movement is perceived by spectators through cognitive mechanisms that, in some respects at least, position them as if they occupied the place of those puppets and all that has created them. As a result, spectators gain a material experience that outstrips their own location in the world.

Conclusion

This chapter has suggested that inter-relational haptic encounters are a key aspect of interaction that is diminished within digital populism. Although some degree of kinaesthetic and tactile sensations are still present when we encounter one another through digital media, these features do not reflect the complexity and centrality of hapticity in human communication more generally. This is an important point to consider when seeking methods that facilitate agonistic pluralism. When haptic engagement is diminished or absent from interactions, it is far more likely that antagonistic exclusions will prevail.

In *The Minor Gesture* Erin Manning proposes a new politics of touch that seems particularly appropriate to the pursuit of fluid, inclusive agonism:

> A politics of touch calls forth a democratic movement toward justice that releases judgment indefinitely. In practice, this means experiencing justice as the opportunity of postponing a final decision even while engaging fully in an act of reaching-toward. To engage fully is to admit responseability. A politics of touch recognizes that there will always be time(s) for another judgment, for another justice that itself will call forth the irreducibility of time.
>
> *Manning 2016, 141*

This perspective echoes the concerns of Chantal Mouffe, and also of Augusto Boal's pursuit of metaxis. It reinforces the importance of reinserting hapticity within political interactions, a goal which I have suggested is ripe for development through practical, performance-inspired approaches. The work of Wolfsohn, Boal and Schumann demonstrates a sustained interest in re-attuning participants toward the physically embodied position of others – facilitating them to 'reach toward' the external world around them in a manner that opens them to being touched themselves. Interactions with non-human objects are particularly promising in this regard, because they profoundly reorient human perceptions of selfhood and agency. This suggests that the divisiveness of populism could in part be addressed through the facilitation of creative, haptic encounters within political contexts.

PART III

The Affective and Aesthetic Dimensions of Populism and Performance

6
FEAR AND FAILURE

So far, this book has established the need for practices that can help to sustain genuine pluralistic engagement in order to mitigate the antagonistic tendencies of digital populism. I have introduced Augusto Boal's concept of metaxis to suggest that performance theories and practices might provide ways of enabling political participants to retain a sense of their own perspectives and motivations while simultaneously immersing themselves in alternative worlds marked by different values, needs and imagined futures. The concept of metaxis supports the aims of vigorous, agonistic democracy by configuring pluralist participation as a multi-layered experience comprised of one's own perspectives together with the imaginatively lived-through perspectives of others. By privileging performance-informed modes of interaction that generate metaxic practices, frontiers of identity become intrinsically ever-shifting and mobile, as each participant endeavours to experience alternative perspectives as if those perspectives were their own.

To explore this claim further, the previous two chapters turned to a consideration of embodiment to explore the ways that heightened awareness of corporeal presence and encounters might help to counter the antagonisms that digital media encourage, and thus enable greater generation of metaxic attitudes. In the two remaining chapters, I turn to aesthetic and affective elements of populism and related Applied Theatre practices. The first of these chapters focuses on sensations of fear and failure, both of which are often considered as obstacles to productive engagement. In the final chapter, I turn to concepts that are more typically associated with positive outcomes: pleasure and beauty. Before examining these topics specifically, this chapter begins by considering recent scholarly treatments of aesthetics and affect, outlining the theoretical territory that Chapters 6 and 7 engage with. Following this, this chapter explores the role of fear and failure in populist political movements, focusing especially on the ways that these aesthetic and affective elements colour digital populist interactions.

DOI: 10.4324/9780367824129-10

This leads to a discussion of theatrical activities that have been utilised in my own recent Applied Theatre practice, which suggest the potential for performance practices to transform fear and failure into more productive experiences. The chapter concludes by positing ways that these insights might be applied in broader political contexts.

Approaches to Aesthetics, Emotion and Affect

It is perhaps useful to begin by setting out my approach to affect and aesthetics, and the relationship between these in political contexts. Although these concepts are often approached separately in academic studies, there can be little doubt of their overlapping nature. Although a thorough discussion of philosophical and analytical approaches to aesthetics and affect is far beyond the scope of this volume, I want to emphasise a few key points about their interrelationship that will inform my discussion below.

To begin with, I understand 'aesthetics' as a consideration of the sensorial aspects of any given object, event or phenomenon. By this definition, aesthetics is not constrained by values of beauty or taste, nor must it be tied to the pursuit of refinement or resolution of sensations. The notion of aesthetics that I refer to is one that encompasses the broad expanse of our sensorial perceptions of the world, as well as their expression through creative mediums (Armstrong 2000; Eagleton 1990, 13; White 2015). This perspective enables a broad view of the aesthetic nature of a multitude of events and interactions. It is also important to bear in mind that aesthetic experiences are complex and stretch beyond immediate cognitive perception; they invoke aspects of memory, imagination and embodied perception (Haseman and Winston 2010). Aesthetics must therefore be understood alongside affective experiences, because aesthetic encounters go hand in hand with affective sensations that provide opportunities for the disruption of existing political sensibilities (Rancière 2010). To take the topic of this chapter as an example, fear-related affect is often produced or intensified through linked aesthetic themes such as failure. Savvy political leaders are able to colour their speeches, events, and interactions with an aesthetic of failure in order to capitalise on the circulation of fear in society more generally.

It is this approach to aesthetics that is most relevant to the performance practices I am investigating, and it also chimes with the view of aesthetics that is explicitly described by Augusto Boal. In Boal's last book, *The Aesthetics of the Oppressed*, he called for aesthetics to become an inseparable element of Theatre of the Oppressed, referring to a conjuncture of sensorially perceived emotional and intellectual stimuli. The Aesthetics of the Oppressed, he said, 'is essential, in so far as it produces a new form of understanding, helping the subject to *feel* and, through the senses and not just the intelligence, to *understand* social reality (Boal 2006, 36). Boal's linkage between aesthetics and affect ('feeling') therefore underscores the intertwined nature of these two concepts and suggests their essential relevance to the development of metaxic interaction.

When considering the role of affect in politics, it is notable that IR scholarship on emotions and affect has burgeoned in recent years (see e.g. Bleiker 2009; Bleiker and Hutchison 2008; Sangar and Clément 2018; Hoggett and Thompson 2012). Affect and emotion have at last been granted a place of legitimacy within the study of international politics, something which scholars who locate themselves within artistic fields might perceive as long overdue. Such research is accompanied by a growing diversity of approaches and definitions that colour scholarly treatments of affect differently, according to the philosophical or methodological roots of each. For my purposes, I am most interested in notions of affect that consider it as a phenomenon that exceeds and precedes cognitive reflection and expression (Hutchison and Bleiker 2014).

Affect can manifest through largely unconscious physical reactions, from tears running down a face to a foot tapping unthinkingly in response to musical rhythms (Hutchison 2019, 280; Kalpokas 2019, 4). Furthermore, affect bears a direct link to corporeal knowledge – according to Ben Highmore, affect can be the thing that:

> [...] gives you away: the telltale heart; my clammy hands; the note of anger in your voice; the sparkle of glee in their eyes. You may protest your innocence, but we both know, don't we, that who you really are, or what you really are, is going to be found in the pumping of your blood, the quantity and quality of your perspiration, the breathless anticipation in your throat, the way you can't stop yourself from grinning, the glassy sheen of your eyes.
>
> *Highmore et al. 2010, 118*

This is an important point to consider, given that people do not experience affect in predictable or uniform ways – rather, each individual may respond differently to the same or similar stimuli (Kalpokas 2019). Affect, when expressed through the body's outward-facing surfaces, communicates complex sensations that reflect each individual's unique perspectives or experiences. This means that affective diversity is a key feature of pluralism, and one that must be given serious consideration within the context of political assembly.

'Emotion', on the other hand, denotes the way that affect is granted meaning through socially and culturally influenced frameworks of perception and communication (Boiger and Mesquita 2012; Deleuze 1978; Gregg and Seigworth 2010). Of course, affect and emotion are entwined and interrelated in complex and messy ways, but by distinguishing these levels – affect alongside emotion – we might become attentive to the space in-between the two as a locus where something explicitly political occurs; that is, the process of transferring affect to emotion and vice versa is a process saturated by the influence of political norms, beliefs and power. To understand the importance of this to populist interactions, we need to focus especially on the ways that affect is transformed into emotion through distinctly political processes.

Fundamentally, affect, experienced corporeally, becomes understood and communicated through a process of representation to oneself and others. The sensations that we perceive within our bodies – tightened abdomens, tingling skin, lungs that don't quite fill to their normal capacity – become interpreted as specific emotions through recourse to socially and culturally established concepts. Emotions are collectively shaped and experienced, and our individual perceptions of emotions – not to mention our representation of those emotions back to others – are always coloured by the social environment in which they circulate. This means that emotions do not originate within individual realms but rather are a collective phenomenon (Ahmed 2004, 25). Situated within particular social spheres, people identify and analyse their emotions with reference to established normative explanations and values. But these norms and values are also subject to being reworked or exploited for political purposes. Hall and Ross claim that emotions '[...] are not innocent descriptors but products of often intensely political processes of framing, projection, and propagation' (Hall and Ross 2019, 1357). At the extreme, emotions might be cultivated and channelled by political movements, either in pursuit of particular short-term ends or, in some cases, as a means of ensuring the longer-term continuation of current constellations of power and identity. By taking this view, we are compelled to acknowledge that existing power structures within society must come into play when affect is socially transformed into emotion.

The implications of this for political engagement are significant: especially when rooted in populist contexts, the progress from affect to emotion is a key point at which antagonism can be fostered. This is because the expressions of emotion that develop from common affective sensations are apt to be coloured by discourses that reflect existing divisions and hierarchies within society. This is even more pertinent in the case of populism, because populism is generally associated with an increase in emotionality in its discourses, relying on emotional appeals to supporters to construct its constitutive inside/outside identities (Bos et al. 2013; Hameleers et al. 2017; Mouffe 2020; Wirz 2018; Wodak 2015). Many theorists consider this emotionality to be a logical antidote to the overemphasis on rational compromise that is typically evident in contemporary liberal democracies; populism offers a contrast in which the emotional depths of disaffection and frustration of the populace come to the fore (e.g. Rico et al. 2017; Salmela and von Scheve 2017). In addition, because populism relies organisationally on existing divisions within society, it is highly likely to amplify those divisions when affective sensations become organised into socially expressed frameworks of emotion.

In light of this, it is essential to consider methods that can enhance a group's capacities to explore emotions in a productive manner for the purpose of improving democratic engagement. What practical methods might be useful for transforming affect in productive ways that can enhance agonistic pluralism rather than servicing exclusionary populist frontiers? Both International Relations and Performance scholars show an interest in innovative methods that might enable people to become more attuned to our affect and emotions and perceive and act upon these in more beneficial ways. Erik Ringmar asserts that:

> [...] we must rebel against the dictatorship of cognition. In order to feel better, we need to feel differently. We must learn to explore new and unexpected implications, break old patterns of thought and acquire new habits. This is not a quick fix to be sure but the consequences are self transforming. The self is transformed since its body feels different.
>
> *2018, 42*

In this vein, the underlying suggestion put forward in these chapters is that theatricality might be particularly useful in moving people to 'feel differently', and that through practices that invoke the conjunction between aesthetics and affect we might create avenues for new ways of thinking, feeling and engaging with one another. In order to explore this in detail, I turn now to a consideration of the aesthetics and affect of fear and failure and their role in populist politics.

Fear and Failure in Populist Politics

In this chapter, I am considering qualities that are usually associated with negative connotations – failure and fear. It is not my intention to examine each of these concepts as detailed and distinct from one another; rather I am approaching them as linked and overlapping qualities that are encountered and experienced affectively, and also developed aesthetically, producing collective emotions that shape the future qualities of political interactions.

As we've seen already in Chapter 2, notions of risk and fear are present in populist politics at a foundational level; if, as many theorists suggest, populism is a response to the growing sense of precarity among the public in the wake of financial crisis, austerity politics, climate disaster, wars, and mass migration, then it might be just as useful to consider populism as a response to feelings of fear in an increasingly risky world. An environment in which feelings of fear and failure are ever-present is nothing new. For example, Brian Massumi pointed out nearly three decades ago that citizens are frequently kept in a constant state of low-level fear through discursive references to risk in everyday life (Massumi 1993). This state of constant fear has obviously only intensified since the War on Terror and the normalisation of vigilance against terrorism that every citizen is encouraged or even mandated to maintain. In recent years, the increasing risk experienced by individuals in economically, geopolitically and ecologically unstable times has led to increased competition between individuals – competing not only for jobs, money, and resources, but also for a sense of security and social recognition (Salmela and von Scheve 2018). Perhaps as a result of this context, political leadership can be legitimised by capitalising on fear. By channelling fear outward toward designated others (migrants, foreign nationals, subordinate or elite identities, and political opponents), and by presenting oneself or one's movement as a sound and effective response to risk, political authority can be predicated on shaping and controlling fear rather than actual effective responses to root issues (Enroth 2017).

Given the powerful mobilising effect that fear can produce, it is no surprise that it plays a central role in populist discourse. Right-wing populism is especially likely to couch references to immigration, national identity and economic prospects in terms that evoke feelings of fear, risk, powerlessness and loss (Salmela and von Scheve 2017; Wodak 2015). It is in this vein that Donald Trump and Nigel Farage have both referred to immigrants as rapists, criminals and terrorists (Gabbatt 2015; McSmith 2014). It is important to take note of the disparities between right and left populist politics in this regard; specifically, right-wing populism shows a greater tendency to direct feelings of anxiety or insecurity toward subordinated identity groups. In comparison, left-wing populism is more likely to construct institutions as the key generator of precarity, and thus the source of feelings of fear. This being the case, projects that seek to alter or mitigate the ways that affect is developed into political emotion must consider differing orientations depending on these differing ideological predispositions. It might be far easier to move left-wing populists toward an empathy-oriented exploration of fear than their right-wing counterparts. But nonetheless, as earlier chapters have established, both groups retain identity frontiers that are likely to impede their capacity to explore fear productively with those who are firmly marked out as political foes.

Fear, when considered as an affective quality, is subject to the exertion of political forces that channel it toward socially articulated emotional concepts. Physical and psychological sensations are produced in response to feelings of insecurity; these sensations exist as a result of widespread and complex social and political drivers, but they become perceived as the product of *specific* factors as a result of public political discourses. Problematically, this process is coloured by the general predilections of populist organisation and interaction, which, as I have discussed in earlier chapters, rests all too often on antagonistic attitudes toward others.

In the development of fear from affective sensations to collectively articulated emotion, populist sensations of fear are frequently transformed into expressions of failure. (Salmela and von Scheve 2017). Fear, in the context of populist discourse, might be reframed as a focus on looming failure to secure desired outcomes, either due to one's own unsatisfactory efforts or those of others. Failure speaks to an individual's sense of frustration or inadequacy in the context of neoliberal values that enshrine linear, market-oriented measures of success; or to a sense of underperformance on the part of nations or governments responsible for the welfare of their citizens. These assessments of failure are a conspicuous feature in populist speeches; In many instances, failure is invoked as a defining characteristic of individual leaders or institutions. Significantly, characterisations of failure are not necessarily detrimental to one's popularity or authority; as I will discuss below, failure can be employed to denigrate opponents, but it can also be deliberately self-performed for strategic ends. The important point is that failure, whether expressed by leaders or supporters of movements, is a prominent theme in populism, and it exists in a cyclical relationship with affective sensations of fear. To understand this further, I turn now to a more detailed discussion of fear and failure in digitally mediated contexts.

Emotions and Aesthetics in Digital Populism

The antagonistic emotional tendencies of digital populism are only exacerbated once political interaction moves into digitally mediated realms. Fundamentally, the algorithms of digital media platforms operate on the basis of their ability to stimulate affective responses on the part of users; the algorithmic distribution of content succeeds because algorithms capitalise on the affective payoff that users experience when they receive and respond to content that aligns with their existing world-views – whether that payoff stems from a position of agreement or contention doesn't matter; users experience a profound sensation of satisfaction as a result of participating in the circulation of information that conforms to their prior frames of reference (Kalpokas 2019). As algorithms identify and utilise users' histories, they capitalise on the power of affective satisfaction to drive those users' future engagements; in other words, the content that users are exposed to is based on an archive of their past, affectively informed engagements. As a result, savvy users of algorithmic data can build upon those affective drives to create a powerful platform for their own interjections (Kalpokas 2019).

Affective manipulation by algorithms also plays a significant part in the establishment of digitally mediated communities. As noted above, algorithms identify and respond to the preferences of individual users, producing individual affective responses. But they also, in effect, create communities of users who are united by their tendency toward similar affective responses to particular kinds of content (Kalpokas 2019; Maly 2020). In other words, although individual people have different affective responses to political stimuli, the algorithmic frameworks of social media effectively group people according to their likelihood to respond affectively to specific sorts of communications – and ultimately, to translate this into likes, comments or retweets. This is the basis of the infamous social media 'echo chamber', which must be understood as an affectively driven phenomenon.

Affect is therefore at the heart of creating political communities online; in all likelihood, these online communities are not the diverse groupings that would most effectively facilitate true pluralistic political engagements. But perhaps even more detrimental is the way that affect becomes expressed as emotions through interactions with others in online environments. The sensations that digital media content gives rise to are understood and expressed through socially and culturally influenced emotional concepts (Boiger and Mesquita 2012). It is in this process that antagonism, rooted in existing social distributions of power and privilege, is most asserted.

Before continuing, it is important to stress the extent to which *representations* of emotions play a central part in digitally mediated interactions. The 'attention economy' of social media and the influence of 'visibility entrepreneurs' (discussed in Chapter 2) are fed by the capacity for users to represent their own emotions in ways that generate active responses from others. This point resonates strongly with Steve Tesich's character Alex Chaney, discussed in this book's introduction. When Chaney suggests that people suffering the tragic consequences of global events should be more engaging, more dramatic, he does so in response to the vast quantity of news stories and information that he is exposed to on a daily basis. In order for a personal anecdote about political events to make a mark on him, Chaney says that he needs to be emotionally moved by the people represented in the story (Tesich 1997). In a similar fashion, digital media users need to stand out from the plethora of competing content by representing emotions in a way that can command attention. Furthermore, the pressing need to represent emotions to other users for the sake of visibility leads to an intensification of emotional content more generally, as users act multivalently as creators and spectators. In other words, the spectacle-driven nature of digital media also creates a hyper-emotional environment, as users compete to present the most emotionally moving depiction of their own experiences or perspectives.

Accordingly, the way that emotions are crafted as representations in digital populist contexts matters just as much as the circulation of actually experienced affect or emotion (Duncombe 2019). Ultimately, representations of emotions coalesce into overarching aesthetic themes, influenced by the algorithmic distribution of content that is most likely to gain traction within particular user groupings. I do not intend to suggest that there is such a thing as a singular digital populist aesthetic or emotional attitude, but it is useful to sketch out some of the common ways that emotion and aesthetics are likely to converge in such contexts; this is intended to elucidate the cultural backdrop that specific interactions occur within, and that should be accounted for in projects that seek to intervene to create alternative modes of political engagement. In this vein, it is my contention that the aesthetic of digital populism is saturated by representations of failure. This can be understood through a closer look at the qualities of fear and failure in online populist representations.

In digital populist contexts, affective sensations of fear frequently become bound up with content that highlights ruptures, frustrations and failures, which can alternately be directed in an antagonistic fashion toward others, or invoked as a marker of group identity. This results in a prevalence of representations of failure, which support both in-group identity coalescences and outward-facing antagonistic frontiers. This point is evident in content generated by both populist leaders and their followers. Taken all together, the prevalence of failure-related content in digital populism is a central feature that impacts the nature of newly generated content and conditions the quality of interactions and engagements that result.

To start with, digital media in general has a demonstrated tendency to privilege negative or divisive content.[1] We know, for example, that 'going negative' on social media platforms has previously correlated with electoral success for politicians (Ceron and d'Adda 2016; Duncombe 2019; Ott 2017). The benefits of negativity, especially directed toward political opponents, were clearly evidenced in the 2016 US Presidential election when Donald Trump's poll numbers increased significantly following negative tweets aimed at other candidates (Gross and Johnson 2016). Furthermore, when digital media converges with populism's general tendency to defy behavioural norms, social media, in its guise as a comparatively anarchic and ostensibly emancipating environment, provides a platform for individuals to conduct themselves with little regard for the strictures of political etiquette. This provides a degree of freedom to engage in derogatory or combative exchanges which, despite their positive impact on political campaigns, are often considered inappropriate in other contexts. The prevalence of negative emotions feeds on the fear-driven politics that mark populism generally, and prompts further representations of negative emotions to conform to the accordingly conditioned appetites of user communities.

The negativity of digitally mediated communications might be viewed as a simple extension of populist antagonism. But significantly, the negative communications that stem from feelings of fear are often transformed into representations of failure, especially in online contexts. As negativity dominates online environments, users seem to compete to highlight the failures of political opponents (Hannan 2018). Social media posts that depict the failures or missteps of others are among the most popular, so participation in the circulation of this content is vital to users who seek wider visibility. Any small mistake by a prominent political figure, from a physical stumble to a misspoken word, provides social media users with material that can be easily amplified.

In part, such content reflects the prominence of societal feelings of fear and insecurity that populism responds to; the missteps of others become interpreted within frames of reference that are founded on an awareness of the consequences of personal failures in precarious, neoliberal contexts. But aesthetically, it adds up to a celebration of personal mistakes or misfires. Furthermore, while content of this nature is often humorous, there is frequently a clear antagonistic bent underlying such posts. There can also be serious implications for one's personal and professional reputation if small errors are amplified through viral recirculation. As a result, failure-related content doesn't just respond to the existing prominence of fear-based political positions; it also intensifies it.

Within this context, representations of failure differ in their nature and function depending on the level of populist organisation to which they refer. In the first instance, populist movements can be invigorated by individuals' representations of their own personal failures (Wood et al. 2016). Depictions of personal financial hardship or unemployment have been a key feature of left populist organising. Alongside this, right-wing movements depict similar personal stories, especially relating to growing economic precarity and perceived loss of cultural identity (Apostolidis 2022; Nowakowski 2021). The distinguishing feature of these stories tends to be the entities that are blamed for such hardships; but fundamentally, these representations function as a way of increasing group solidarity, and in many cases increasing the scope of the movement's appeal (Apostolidis 2022; Reinelt 2019). These stories contribute to the proliferation of representations of failure. Regardless of whether this is the failure of capitalist economics to safeguard the welfare of citizens, or the failure of the state to protect against threats from terrorism, disease or job losses, depictions of failures increase sympathy internally and thus solidify the horizontal identities of populist movements (Gomberg-Muñoz 2016; Stephen 2013).

Representations of failure also play a pivotal role in the legitimation and popularity of populist leaders. As already discussed, populist movements most often require leaders who represent 'the people' and this hinges on a would-be leader's capacity to exhibit characteristics that enable followers to infer that the leader is 'just like us'. Fear plays an important part here because if leaders are to convincingly present themselves as synecdochic representations of 'the people', they must to some degree exhibit the same fears, worries or anxieties expressed by the movement's adherents. This can manifest as leaders making references to their own personal or family histories of precarity, as Alexandria Ocasio-Cortez has done in multiple tweets that refer her past employment as a waitress (Zummo 2020). It might also take the form of leaders expressing their own worries with regard to scapegoated others, as Nigel Farage did when he suggested that he would be concerned if a 'group of Romanians' moved in next door to him (BBC News 2014). In these examples, fears are expressed alongside implications of failures by those in power.

Equally, failure can be deliberately performed by leaders in order to increase their claims of authenticity. Authenticity, construed as a level of genuineness based on the rejection of campaign-oriented or political class personas, is necessary to generate a following from populist voters; representations of a leader's failures are key to this. Failures offer a powerful marker of a leader's authenticity because they build on the public's own fears of personal failure, demonstrating that even powerful and successful politicians make errors and missteps. Digital content of this nature usually starts with small mistakes or missteps on the part of individual leaders, but becomes amplified through circulation on social media platforms. Take, for example, Donald Trump's infamous tweet on 31 May 2017, in which he stated, 'despite the negative press covfefe' (Trump 2017). This tweet, bearing evidence of typing mistakes, became viral almost instantly but it generated a wide range of responses – from those who mocked its failures to those who believed it to be an indicator of Trump's authenticity, predicated upon his relatable human fallibility (Bødker and Anderson 2019). Indeed, throughout Trump's presidency, his frequent misstatements and oversimplifications were typically greeted by supporters as a sign of his authenticity (Shane 2018).

Whether representations of failure refer primarily to leaders or followers of movements, they draw on the prevalence of fear in society and channel it in the service of populist identities. The digital content that results can function as a means of consolidating internal identities, or of further distancing political opponents through mockery and derision. What works to forge a sense of commonality within can also provide the material for scorn or ridicule from without. Stories of personal hardship might attract labels like 'snowflake', for example, and mis-spellings that signal common-man identities within might attract accusations of intellectual inferiority from opponents. But overall, the points above suggest that digital populism, with its aforementioned tendencies to stimulate and perpetuate antagonism, is at least partly sustained through an affective-aesthetic convergence of fear and failure. This calls for an exploration of practices that might alter inter-actions in a way that has potential to transform sensations of fear and failure into a basis for more constructive political engagement.

Transforming Fear and Failure through Creative Practice

The notion that fear and failure might be positively transformed for political pur-poses is far from a new suggestion; scholars across Politics and Performance have not only underscored the social and political necessity of such processes, but also pointed out ways that we might begin to address this in practice. The last section of this chapter puts a few of these theoretical perspectives into conversation with the practical methods drawn from Wolfsohn, Boal and Schumann.

Fundamentally, the practices I explore here do not seek to eliminate or down-play sensations of fear and failure, nor to transform them into oppositional qual-ities like safety and success. My interest is rather in acknowledging the powerful potential of fear and failure when utilised for constructive purposes – enabling participants, as Ringmar puts it, to 'feel differently' (Ringmar 2018, 42). Along these lines, Henrik Enroth suggests that the most productive politics of fear would not centre on rejecting or downplaying it, but rather focus on embrac-ing fear in an alternative fashion. Instead of prioritising leadership or policies that effectively manage risks and therefore mitigate fear, Enroth calls for 'a new politics of fearfulness' (Enroth 2017, 68). This approach to fear would entail acknowledging fear and anxiety and mobilising it in new, more productive ways. Complementarily, Jack Halberstam contends that failure offers an anti-dote to 'positive thinking', which otherwise conditions people to intellectualise their feelings of failure as unique individual experiences, and ones which could be avoided or altered through personal choices or actions (Halberstam 2011). Approached differently, experiences of failure might provide an opening for see-ing and understanding the world in new and productive ways.

Cognisant of the relationship between fear and failure, I suggest that the antag-onistic tendencies of digital populism might be usefully addressed by embracing a politics of both fearfulness *and* failure. Taking the above points together, it seems clear that practices seeking agonistic engagement must enable participants to acknowledge and express individual fears, but to position these within col-lective, collaborative frameworks. This might usefully entail practices that crea-tively explore failure, particularly in a manner that emphasises group experiences over individuality, and that stresses the benefits of agonistic cooperation as an end goal in its own right, divorced from the pursuit of security or success.

Theatre is especially adept at altering the social production of emotion, given this discipline's deep historic engagements with emotion in public contexts. A multitude of canonical activities exist that seek to enable participants to 'feel differently' or to explore, shape, and understand individual feelings through various modes of interaction with others. Moreover, theatre in general seems to have a natural affinity with the spectre of failure. As Cormac Power notes,

> It is often said that the possibility of failure, or of something going awry, is what gives a live performance its intensity and excitement. [...] Even in the case where a performance is deemed excellent by all who see it and where no mistakes or mishaps occur, the possibility of failure surrounds and conditions the event and the way it is experienced.
>
> *Power 2010, 126*

Combined with theatre makers' explorations of affect and emotion, the fundamental role that failure plays in theatrical performance and spectatorship suggests that this medium might have much to tell us about the ways that fear and failure manifest in social and political contexts.

It is unsurprising that performance makers are innately attuned to such issues, given the nature of their work, but the task of transforming fear and failure for productive ends is far from easy or simple. All too frequently, even in creative contexts, socially constructed frameworks of emotion impede participants' abilities to apprehend and express authentic affective responses. Participants, especially those who have not undertaken previous actor training, are likely to be constrained by their perceptions of what kinds of emotional responses are expected in relation to particular stimuli, and the appropriate ways of articulating these emotions to others (Salverson 2008, 253). Culturally and ideologically prescribed understandings of privilege, victimhood and morality can get in the way of genuine affective and emotional engagement, even in the most skilfully designed creative practices. Consequently, work of this nature requires activities that can prompt participants to encounter affect and emotions in complex and unexpected ways. To explore this in more detail, the remainder of this chapter examines performance practices that enable participants to perceive fear and failure as creative social experiences rather than as individual circumstances or challenges. Such practices have the potential to counter the very basis of populism by disrupting competitive, individualist orientations. As I will show, these practices demonstrate that fear and failure can be explored in ways that lead to a heightened sense of future possibility that hinges on cooperative collaboration, thereby enhancing pluralistic engagement in political contexts.

Practicing Fear as a Social Experience

Although populism capitalises on fears that stem from conditions shared by a large proportion of the population, sensations of fear are often experienced as an individual phenomenon. When cognitively perceived and expressed with reference to social and political norms, fear becomes an emotion that is attributable to a person's unique individual circumstances. This has a direct consequence on social and political engagement, because fear of this nature frequently gives rise to shame. Fear can therefore result in disconnection from social groups, on the basis that one has failed to achieve the expected standards or conform to the ideals of that group (Sloan 2018). In this way, fear can be a significant obstacle to political engagement of any kind.

Even in cases where these feelings of fear are associated with the failings of governments, financial institutions, or elite sectors of society, fear is still often thought of in terms of individual security and prospects. In many ways, fear can be a profound obstacle to pluralistic engagement because it naturally focuses people's attention on their own short-term welfare. Faced with imagined futures clouded by unstable employment or threats of violence and insecurity, individuals have a diminished capacity to engage with others' circumstances. Of course, some populist movements, especially left-leaning ones, seek to respond to such issues by explicitly calling for empathy and appreciation of shared precarity (Butler 2015). But in practice, when a person faces the imminent risk of physical insecurity and loss, focus is often placed on the short-term welfare of oneself and one's immediate relations. Fear isn't only generated by perceptions of neoliberal precarity; it is also fuelled by crucial, real-world experiences of precarity that necessitate sharp attention to short-term material needs, and this naturally diminishes an individual's engagement with wider social issues.

In response to the disengaging effects of fear and failure, we need to identify practices that can enable a sense of fear as a shared experience. To achieve this in practice, my recent workshops have employed a number of related activities that are inspired, especially by Alfred Wolfsohn and Augusto Boal. The practices of both these practitioners incorporate activities that naturally push participants to take risks and behave in ways that they would not ordinarily be inclined to do for fear of embarrassment or failure. As such, when practised in a collaborative fashion, they are particularly appropriate for enabling groups to address sensations of fear in more constructive ways.

In recent workshops, I have explored the use of activities that encourage an initial openness to risk-taking by participants. This is a relatively common feature of Applied Theatre practice, but when positioned as part of workshops that are explicitly aimed at generating metaxic political engagement and debate, such activities take on a renewed significance. Voice, Puppetry and Forum Theatre all provide opportunities for participants to experience risk and fear, but the practices I have developed are especially intended to shift explorations of fear away from individual perceptions toward collective experiences. This goal can be approached through introductory games and activities that encourage individuals to experience risk or fear while relying on other group members for support. A classic example of this is Boal's 'trust circle' which involves one participant standing in the middle of a circle of peers, eyes closed. The main participant allows themselves to fall forward, backwards or sideways, relying on group members to gently catch and redirect their momentum (Boal 2002). Now ubiquitous in team-building contexts, this exercise remains exceptionally useful in terms of drawing out each participant's attitudes toward risk and gently extending their willingness to engage in activities that generate fear in a productive fashion. The significance of activities like this should not be underestimated; while they have become relatively commonplace in a variety of social settings, it is easy to overlook just how effectively they enable people to understand their own sense of fear and risk and how this changes within the circulations of power and identity in group contexts.

Similarly, voice work often begins with an introductory exchange of instinctive utterances, using whispers or hums to encourage participants to explore expressive sounds. In my experience, vocal exercises are the one area of activity that prompts people to feel most vulnerable and afraid to take risks, especially in the presence of others. I have begun developing activities that utilise this feature of voice work to enable participants to become more attentive to the qualities of risk and fear in interpersonal interactions. For example, one activity requires participants to use their voices collaboratively to construct an aural scene depicting the theme of powerlessness. This begins with each individual, in their own space and time, developing a sound that they associate with a moment in their own lives when they felt powerless. They are encouraged to remember the details of that experience, from where they were to who they were with, and all of the features of their surroundings. In this way, they recall the sensations they experienced at that time, and channel these into their individual vocal expression. In these initial activities, affect comes to the surface. Sensations of fear produce physical affective signs, from sweaty palms to stuttering voices. However, at this stage, it is still likely that participants will primarily explore fear as an individual experience. The significance of the activity occurs when the individual participants are asked to come together. Still sounding their own individual expression of 'powerlessness', they join in concert with the very different expressions of others. Sometimes they respond to others, often unpremeditatedly, by changing their own vocality. Gradually, the individual participants become aware of the collective creation more than their own single part in it. The fact that this aural scene is developed improvisationally foregrounds a sense of risk – participants are explicitly exploring a remembered situation in which fear might have been a natural response, but the act of improvising with their voices in front of other people accentuates the environment of risk. By expressing remembered sensations of individual experiences of risk and fear within the frame of a collaborative yet contested creation, a communal affective environment begins to be forged.

As a forerunner to Image Theatre or Forum Theatre, I often insert an activity adapted from collaborative storytelling activities. This is a challenging exercise that requires participants to focus on their own experiences of fear or anxiety while simultaneously identifying points of commonality with others. Sitting in a circle, the group is asked to construct a string of associated remarks that describe recent individual experiences of anxiety or fear. The first participant holds one end of a coloured ball of yarn and makes a short statement describing a recent experience or a worry about the near future. Keeping hold of the end of the string, the ball is tossed to another member of the group, who makes their own statement – one which is different but related to the first. The second participant holds on to their part of the string, creating a thread between the first two people; the yarn is then tossed to someone else and the activity continues in this manner until all members of the group have made at least one contribution. In the initial stages of a project, the statements made by participants will focus on comparatively minor fears or anxieties; but as projects progress, they can become more weighty, or oriented around a specific political theme at the discretion of the facilitator. We end up with a web of yarn that connects the group in multiple ways, vibrantly illustrating the common ground among the group, and the notion that fear and anxiety can be the basis of a collaborative creation. This activity is particularly useful as a forerunner of more advanced Image Theatre or Forum Theatre, because it establishes an approach to fear and risk as foundational qualities of collaborative political engagement.

Both of these exercises are useful because they foreground sensations of risk and fear; but more importantly, the embodied theatricality of the activities enables participants to begin to explore the relationships between personal fear and collective precarity, and the ways that security and vulnerability operate on and between bodies, leading to a better understanding of the ways that fear is socially and culturally constructed, mobilised, and experienced (O'Grady 2017, 6).

Practicing Uncertainty and Failure

Once workshops have sufficiently enabled participants to explore fear in a collective fashion, we move on to activities that bring the prospect of failure to the fore. Through activities that highlight indeterminacy and unpredictability, we begin to embody failure in creative ways. In recent decades, staged theatre, performance art and Applied Theatre practices have examined the value of failure in social and political contexts[2] (e.g. Bailes 2011; Nicholson 2013; Power 2010). Sara Jane Bailes suggests that performances that centre the prospect of failure alter our perceptions of what is possible because as spectators we witness moments in which actors attempt the impossible. 'It is precisely the perseverance of an event in the face of difficulty that turns impossibility from a category of negation into a strategy of hope [...]' (Bailes 2011, 125). In a similar vein, over the past two decades, Applied Theatre practitioners have steadily rejected defined end goals in their work, favouring the value of creative processes over assessments of efficacy (Thompson 2011). This enables practitioners to shift their attention away from project 'success', and explore the value that arises from unexpected disruptions or turns. As Sheila Preston explains, facilitators should attempt to 'stay with the mess' and consider difficulties that arise in the room not as signs of problems but rather as opportunities for new directions (Preston 2016, 74).

Uncertainty, and even outright failure, can therefore be desirable and beneficial in performance contexts. In recent workshops, I have observed this in practice, especially when groups tackle political topics through improvised Forum

Theatre and voice work. In Forum Theatre, participants' quest for definitive solutions to political dilemmas is perpetually thwarted, both by the joker who points out weaknesses or detriments, and by fellow participants who are encouraged to counter others' suggestions by asserting their own points of view. As groups work toward explorations of policy alternatives, for example, they are never allowed to settle satisfactorily on an endpoint but instead, each suggestion is explored in an environment of perpetual uncertainty. Each proposed approach is enacted, then challenged, questioned, and reworked into a slightly different representation, creating a cycle of suggestion, enactment, and further questioning – a cycle where undecidability prevails. The discussions that arise within Forum Theatre are rich with complications and frustrations, revealing the inevitable shortcomings of consensus-driven policymaking.

In the case of Wolfsohn-inspired vocal practices, we build on activities like the aural scenes described above, nudging participants toward expressions that relate to increasingly specific political issues. As the work develops, they are pushed to fail by extending and disrupting the voice's habituated patterns. By physically jostling the voice away from its socially condoned tones and ranges, we also defamiliarise it to the person it belongs to, resulting in a distinct sense of uncertainty on the part of participants. Failure in this case allows the participant's body to resonate with profoundly new and different sensations. When put into practice in sessions that focus on fear-related political issues, this enables participants to explore political affect differently. As such, sensations of fear don't necessarily subside, but are experienced through new and different frames of reference.

Much of the power of this work comes from the fact that participants are not only acting; they are also spectating. In the context of failure-based performances, this is a key point of consideration, because as Cormac Power has noted, performances that involve the prospect of failure foreground uncertainty and change the ways that spectators interpret them.

> Rather than offering the spectator a strategic vantage point from which to employ dominating interpretations [...] the spectator is asked to make 'tactical' decisions in relation to the piece, to improvise interpretative responses as the performance unfolds, and in a sense, to stay within the performance rather than taking up strategic interpretative positions from outside the performance.
>
> *Power 2010, 133*

Significantly then, performances of failure might reorient participants toward others – instead of positioning themselves as interpreters of others' representations of affective or emotional experience, performances might be structured in ways that encourage participants (who alternate among roles of actors, spectators, and spect-actors) to engage in ongoing interpretive engagements from the *inside*, rather than from an externally demarcated distance. This seems especially apt with regard to participatory Applied Theatre projects, where the participants themselves are engaging in performances that are deliberately designed to curtail successful culminations. Ultimately, performance practices that embrace uncertainty and failure can 'poke holes' in what would otherwise be a settled, coherent notion of future success (Halberstam 2011, 3). When unexpected things happen, or expected things don't happen, we might suddenly reconsider all of the possibilities of the space we are in and what might occur in the future. This has strong implications for political participation. Through practices that embrace an aesthetics of failure, we might enhance participants' capacity to 'feel differently'. By reconfiguring failure as a vital element of political engagement, we might create environments for deliberation that address fears and anxieties without engendering individualism and competition – as a result, failure might be better positioned to serve agonistic ends.

Conclusion

This chapter has addressed the role of fear and failure in digital populism, arguing that Applied Theatre practices might suggest new tactics for mobilising these affective and aesthetic qualities in new and more productive ways. Fear and failure exist in a cyclical aesthetic and affective relationship, and both are commonplace in populist interactions. Particularly when populism is enacted through the frameworks of social media, performances of fear and failure largely serve to reaffirm identity boundaries and provide fuel for antagonistic communications. Personal sensations of risk and fear can result from genuine precarity caused by political issues, but they can also be exacerbated and extended by leaders in efforts to generate or sustain support. Fear and failure therefore become prominent themes within populist performances, and digital media platforms provide a means of creating and circulating a proliferation of content that can both unite and divide people according to how the causes of fear and failure are apportioned, and how closely one's own fears and failures align with the characteristic discourses of specific movements.

However, despite the clear potential for fear and failure to serve antagonistic ends, the history of performance practices demonstrates that rich possibilities exist to use these affective and aesthetic qualities in politically productive ways. Some performance practices offer the potential to transmute sensations of risk and fear by contextualising them as elements of creative experience within explorations of difference. In effect, this can position perceptions of fear, anxiety, uncertainty and failure as the basis for forging connections within an environment of diverse viewpoints. As Jack Halberstam suggests, 'Under certain circumstances failing, losing, forgetting, unmaking, undoing, unbecoming, not knowing may in fact offer more creative, more cooperative, more surprising ways of being in the world' (Halberstam 2011, 2). If performance can provide a means of revealing these surprising ways of being, then it surely should be considered an important tool for transforming fear and failure into productive bases for pluralist engagement.

7

PLEASURE AND BEAUTY

As discussed in the last chapter, affect plays a pivotal role in political interaction, and it also has the potential to be deliberately evoked and redeployed through creative theatrical tactics that seek to channel emotions for more positive ends. In this chapter, I continue this discussion by turning to the aesthetic and affective qualities of pleasure and beauty. Like fear and failure in the previous chapter, these two concepts are assembled here as a conjuncture of related qualities that inform and impact one another. Scholars from both Politics and Performance have addressed pleasure and beauty, revealing their potential to lead to social and political transformation but also their capacity to feed into antagonistic or divisive attitudes.

This chapter begins by framing my initial approach to these broad concepts. This is followed by a detailed exploration of the role of pleasure in populist interactions, with a focus on the ways that digital media complicates and exacerbates the capacity for playfulness and fun to serve antagonistic ends, especially due to the prominence of competitive attitudes in online environments. Following this, I explore beauty as an aesthetic frame that bears a close relationship to pleasure and that builds on or alters the modes of engagement produced by pleasurable political encounters. This point is explored through a closer look at Applied Theatre practices that employ experiences of pleasure and beauty in ways that lead to agonistic engagement. The chapter concludes with a further discussion of Peter Schumann's puppetry practice, which exemplifies the capacity for theatrical mobilisations of beauty and pleasure to operate as a means of creating pluralist communal experiences.

Approaching Pleasure and Beauty

Like the previous chapter, this chapter addresses a convergence of two qualities that operate in both affective and aesthetic ways; the focus here is on pleasure and beauty, two concepts which are not only capacious but are also philosophically

DOI: 10.4324/9780367824129-11

and culturally contested. Pleasure might be considered to include, for example, happiness, joy, fun, playfulness, or effervescence, among other related qualities (Fincham 2016; Moore 2019). Each of these qualities has been analysed from a range of philosophical and disciplinary perspectives, from the psychoanalytical to the artistic. Likewise, beauty is a subject of much debate, often contentious for its attachment to hierarchical societal norms and notions of 'taste' (Haseman and Winston 2010; Kant 2005; White 2015); but beauty is also considered a powerful feature of political and artistic practices that seek to challenge the political and social status quo (Adebayo 2015; Scarry 2010).

To some extent, pleasure and beauty might be viewed as a simple opposition of the themes of the last chapter – pleasure could perhaps be construed as an absence of fear and beauty as an oppositional aesthetic of failure. But as will be demonstrated below, pleasure and beauty encompass affective and aesthetic features that position them differently to the elements of fear and failure discussed previously; and they also correlate with a different set of phenomena in relation to digital populism. Accordingly, this chapter aims to approach these terms as aesthetic–affective traits in their own right, engaging with distinct challenges of digital populism that relate to these qualities.

For the purposes of this discussion, my aim is to embrace the breadth and uncertainty of these terms in order to give consideration to their joint impact on political interactions; that is, remaining open to the breadth of possible affect, emotions and experiences that fall under the umbrella of the pleasurable and the beautiful enables a concerted focus on the ways that positive concepts of this nature can further antagonistic conflict; this establishes the need for a critical examination of the ways that pleasurable and beautiful sensations and experiences are framed and enacted, in order to identify opportunities to employ these qualities for more constructive social and political ends.

In this chapter, I define 'pleasure' as a heightened sensation of happiness or elation that goes beyond mere satisfaction (Fine and Corte 2017). I specifically address fun, playfulness, and fantasy within populist political contexts. 'Beauty' refers, for my purposes, to a pleasurable aesthetic experience that activates one or more of the senses in a way that sets that experience out from the ordinary or everyday. Assessments of beauty vary according to individual tastes, but I am most interested in events and experiences that have the potential to produce collective, accordant appreciations of something that is considered 'beautiful' (Thompson 2011; White 2015). As such, both pleasure and beauty are approached as umbrella terms that can be deployed in both positive and negative ways.

Populist Pleasure and Beauty

To begin an examination of the role of pleasure and beauty in populism, it might first be useful to question the extent to which these qualities are relevant in this context. Pleasure and beauty are almost certainly not the first qualities that come to mind when thinking about recent populist politics; the notion of populism, even if considered in a positive light, is more typically associated with conflict and divisiveness, or at the very least with a concerted oppositional stance. To some extent, pleasurable affective sensations tend to remain a by-product or sub-strata of the more negative emotions that are often vociferously expressed in pop-ulist contexts; nonetheless, aspects of pleasure and beauty are pervasively present in such interactions, even if at a more subtle level than emotions like fear and failure. It is essential to understand that pleasure and beauty are not incidental or minor elements of populism – in fact, they play a central role.

The presence of these qualities is actually unsurprising given what politics and performance scholars have already revealed about the persistence of pleasure and beauty within contexts of intense conflict, violence and trauma. Indeed, there is a clear link between environments of conflict and the affective power that joy and beauty can produce in such situations. Applied Theatre scholar James Thompson, drawing on his practical work in war zones, notes that pleasure and beauty become especially sought-after in times and places where ordinary life is disrupted by conflict, violence and fear[1] (Thompson 2011, 138). A related point is taken up by Elina Penttinen, who proposes a turn to joy-oriented research methods in order to highlight the prevalence of hope, happiness and healing in global politics. Penttinen shows that even in the most traumatic of circum-stances, human beings retain an overwhelming capacity for these positive feelings (Penttinen 2013). If, as Thompson and Penttinen suggest, pleasure and beauty can persevere in situations of intense conflict, then it is no surprise that they are also present within populist interactions.

Given the powerful ways that sensations of pleasure and beauty circulate in even the most conflictual contexts, it is perhaps tempting to celebrate them unre-servedly for their capacity to serve as forces of reconciliation, resilience and heal-ing. However, while it is important to acknowledge this capacity, it should also be noted that like fear and failure, pleasure and beauty can undermine agonistic pluralism. In this section, I begin by discussing the ways that pleasure is embed-ded in populist political interaction through an exploration of fun, playfulness, fantasy and competitive success.

To start with, I want to suggest that an aspect of populism that is frequently overlooked by analysts is the fact that, experienced from within, populism is quite simply *fun*. This is evident when observing the crowds gathered at Trump rallies or the demonstrators amassed in public squares at anti-austerity protests, and it is obviously a mainstay of digital populist repartee.[2] Whatever the ilk of the populist movement, those involved are motivated at least in part by the fact that the experience of participating is not only pleasurable but an active source of effervescent happiness – in other words, 'fun' (Fine and Corte 2017, 66). Two themes are especially prominent within populist fun: fantasy, involving immer-sion into vividly imagined worlds, both historical and future-oriented; and playfulness, a general attitude of non-serious transgression, rule-breaking and pleasurable indulgence in alternatives to the everyday. Both of these qualities are often strongly influenced by a third – competition-oriented gameplay, a feature that changes the effect of the first two qualities.

To begin with, populism is often underpinned by imagined happiness in the form of fantastic notions of an idealised future that might be realised if a movement succeeds. This can take the form of collective nostalgic fantasies, as is often the case in right-wing populism, but it might also pertain to a collectively envisioned utopian future that is simply thwarted by current systems of power and exclusion (Browning 2019; Kenny 2017; Silva and Vieira 2018). In many cases, it seems that populist leaders are keenly aware of the affective power generated by fantasy-driven narratives. For example, in a much-quoted passage from *The Art of the Deal*, Trump said the following three decades before he would successfully run for President: 'I play to people's fantasies. People may not always think big themselves, but they can still get very excited by those who do. That's why a little hyperbole never hurts' (Trump 1987, 58). This approach was clearly in operation within the notion of 'Make America Great Again'; Trump built up a fantasy of an America that could more or less instantly return to more affluent and secure footing if only he were elected. A similar approach was evident in the United Kingdom: Nigel Farage's UK Independence Party and the Eurosceptic elements of the Conservative Party trumpeted a vision of a revitalised Great Britain that would be significantly more prosperous and secure once freed from EU membership.

Much of the mobilising potential of fantasy is derived from the pleasurable sensations it elicits. Fantasies can transform unsatisfied needs or wishes into detailed imaginings of a past or future that might be brought into being if only the right turn of events occurs. In other words, fantasy adds a pleasurable element to discontentment because it enables people to imagine more positive alternatives. It also contains the potential to exacerbate political divisiveness. This is because fantasies are often imagined as alternative realities that would already exist were it not for some designated obstacle (Browning 2019, 231). Most often, especially in populist politics, this obstacle takes the form of political opponents or scapegoated others. Populist fantasies therefore hinge on tacit accusations levelled at, for example, political parties, financial institutions, international treaty organisations or racial and ethnic minorities.

Alongside fantasy, pleasure is also mobilised in populism through the prominence of playfulness. When political scholars consider the defining traits of populist style, transgression of behavioural norms is often at the forefront (Aiolfi 2022; Bucy et al. 2020; Moffitt 2016). Viewed from an affective and aesthetic angle, we might consider such transgressions as embodiments of a playful approach to politics. Transgressions happen in part because of the disaffection that people feel in respect to the status quo of electoral democracy. There is a widespread perception that political processes are dominated by a political-class persona, exemplified by the suits and ties of the so-called political elites. This persona is interpreted by many as a mask that obscures corruption, indifference or general lack of interest in the challenges experienced by the general public. It is therefore unsurprising that there is a growing appetite for disruptive, playful figures who seemingly mock the sobriety of politics and by extension, the false airs of professional politicians.

This paves the way for leaders like Boris Johnson with his messy hair, or Bernie Sanders with his comparatively humble clothing, to offer a visually less-sober alternative to the status quo (Farhi 2015; Winter 2020). In addition, transgression of behavioural norms can be equally apparent in the tone of a leader's actions, and a playful tone can provide as an especially vibrant contrast to the strait-laced seriousness of 'professional' politicians. Ben Anderson has observed just how effective this approach was for Donald Trump:

> People laughed at the exaggeration and perhaps at his outrageousness, but they also laughed at his insults, at his verbal and gestural impressions, at his name calling. Sometimes, it was the fun of not being serious in a world of responsibilities, the fun of being with other people in a shared situation, the fun of not being weighed down, for a time, by all the impediments to action that block, thwart, and frustrate. It was the fun of feeling liberated as finally someone other than you was publicly saying everything you were told you couldn't or shouldn't. The fun of not conforming to norms of action and thought that you never fully believed in or felt like you consented to.
>
> *Anderson 2017*

Clearly, while transgressive behaviours contribute to a leader's status as 'one of the people', they also operate as a mode of interaction that directly challenges the stultification of the business-like political status quo. For many decades activists have understood the powerful impact that playfulness can achieve against a backdrop of dispassionate political sobriety; but significantly, playfulness is not present in such movements simply because of its potential efficacy; it is also highly pleasurable for those involved, and it projects an atmosphere of fun that attracts others who are not already involved. The same process is evident in populism, where the iconoclastic playfulness of emerging leaders not only galvanises existing members but draws others in to participate in the collective spirit of fun.

Playful actions in populism can also effectively consolidate the otherwise broad identity of movements. This is because a playful tone can confer a degree of ambiguity to a leader's statements, rendering it easier to gesture toward the interests or concerns of subset groups without alienating others. An air of playfulness on the part of a leader leaves room for audiences to choose which remarks should be taken seriously and which are just part of the overarching game. Trump's Make America Great Again Movement is undoubtedly the foremost example of this phenomenon. Within his speeches and other public appearances, Trump has consistently engaged in playful behaviour, not only mocking political opponents but doing so in the manner of an entertainer rather than a politician running for office; his speeches were peppered with impersonations, insults and outrageous claims against others, but they were delivered in the style of a comic actor who pauses expectantly at the punchline to allow the audience to laugh and applaud. These actions coalesced into a mode of political performance that was often interpreted by his supporters as simply a pleasurable, light-hearted alternative to the political mainstream. They also created a mode of spectatorship that was coloured by expectations of entertainment.

Most significantly, this overall tone of playfulness enabled Trump to make ambiguous statements that helped to ensure ongoing support and cohesion for the MAGA movement; because of the overarching attitude of play, any statements by Trump that might have prompted supporters to question their loyalty (such as mocking disabled people or suggesting that protesters should be removed with violent force) were easy to overlook because of the ambiguity of Trump's intent – it was often not quite clear if he was serious or simply playing up to the crowd to generate laughter and applause; on the other hand, for supporters inclined toward more radical views, such statements could be interpreted as an indication of Trump's genuine beliefs.

The examples found within the MAGA movement are comparatively extreme, but the point also applies to populist organising more generally. It is common for playfulness to serve as a means of mitigating internal difference or conflict within social groupings (Fine and Corte 2017, 65). Given the overall heightened emotionality within populism, coupled with the need to forge alliances among otherwise competing interests, it is logical that an attitude of fun and playfulness can support efforts to downplay internal difference. In a playful atmosphere, otherwise controversial or divisive statements by a populist leader can be dismissed in the interest of sustaining the light-hearted communal culture. In this way, pleasure and 'fun' cement an internal sense of 'the people', but they can also obscure plurality rather than exercising it in the interest of productive engagement.

Alongside the unifying force of playfulness, this quality can also support exclusions from populist movements (Fine and Corte 2017). In the examples cited above, Trump created an atmosphere of fun and playfulness, but at the same time, his jokes and jibes often made reference to marginalised groups; although most of his taunts and jests were aimed at individual political foes, they operated by associating that individual with a group of people who were already implicitly established as external to Trump's movement. For example, when Trump continually called Democratic primary candidate Elizabeth Warren 'Pocahontas', often to the cheers and laughter of his followers, he was not only denigrating a potential political opponent but was also reinforcing the boundaries of the MAGA movement that hinged on ethnicity or national identity.

This is also not simply a case of laughing at others' expense – in cases like this, the playfulness of populist politics has further ramifications because the identity of the movement, constructed oppositionally to designated outsiders, encourages the repetitious circulation of the most provocative past actions. Some playful jokes, taunts or transgressions live in the memory of the group and function as reminders of past good times – in this manner, they solidify the playful culture of the movement and maintain its distinction from others (Fine and de Soucey 2005). This enables populist figureheads to make reference to the same repertoire of jokes, stories or anecdotes over and over, hitting the same punchlines. By doing so, they increase the fun of the movement overall.

It is clear then that pleasurable sensations rooted in attitudes of playfulness and fantasy are a key feature of populist interactions, and furthermore, these qualities often serve antagonistic ends. To understand why this is so often the case as opposed to the rejuvenating and healing potential of joy and beauty discussed by the likes of Thompson and Penttinen, we need to consider one other aspect of populism that contributes to its overall pleasurable qualities overall – this is the prominence of game-oriented approach to interaction.

The Pleasures of Competitive Success

To fully understand the role of pleasure in populism it is vital to consider the prevalence of competitive, game-oriented attitudes. It is not uncommon to find studies of electoral politics that liken it to the fervent competition of team sports (e.g. Forgette 2004; McDonald and Samples 2006; Miller and Conover 2015). Like other political parties or social movements, populist movements are fundamentally brought into existence in order to 'win', if winning is defined as electoral success; but there seems to be something more at work in terms of the centrality of competitive attitudes among populists. I believe that this is directly linked to the fact that victory or success over opponents is in itself *fun*. If electoral politics can be experienced in a similar way as team competitions, and if fun is already a key driver of populist interaction, then it follows that the pleasures of competition will have a significant impact on the mobilisation and sustenance of populist publics. While most political analyses of the competitive nature of populism tend to emphasise its generation of anger and hatred, here, I want to give space to the way that such competition can be deeply enjoyable for participants.

Foundationally, treating populist campaigning as a competition between one's own group and an oppositional team results in stronger in-group identification (Miller and Conover 2015). The framework of competition enables members of the group to clearly evaluate their degrees of success and superiority, and this, in turn, further legitimates the existence of the movement. As Miller and Conover explain:

> The desire for one's partisan team to 'win', whether in elections or in a broader sense, is powerful. It mobilises volunteers and drives election turnout, since in electoral terms the number of 'fans' who subscribe to your team equals victory. Because winning is so central to the survival of the team, this encourages players to try to win at almost any cost, even incivility and aggression toward opponents.
>
> *Miller and Conover 2015*

The centrality of competitive success is obvious within populist leaders' speech. Donald Trump, for example, frequently makes explicit reference to 'winning':

> We're gonna turn it around and we're gonna start winning again. We're gonna win so much. We're gonna win at every level. We're gonna win economically. We're gonna win with the economy. We're gonna win with military. We're gonna win with healthcare and for our veterans. We're gonna win with every single facet. We're gonna win so much, you may even get tired of winning. You'll say, please, please it's too much winning. We can't take it any more Mr. President, it's too much. And I'll say no it isn't we have to keep winning, we have to win more. We're gonna win more. We're gonna win so much.[3]
>
> *CNN 2016*

This is just one example of the prominence given to 'winning' within Trump's presidential campaign speeches; it became a central theme, often inserted toward the end of rallies to the increasing cheers and exhortations from the crowd.

While short-term winning tends to feature less in left populist discourse, it is nonetheless a persistent feature – often taking the form of celebrating an underdog status with an implication of defying others' expectations and fighting for longer-term success. This is evidenced in Bernie Sanders' speeches, for example, which are marked by their combination of an outsider/underdog identity alongside intimations of national crisis (Staufer 2021). Take for example, this excerpt from a speech in 2020:

> Our campaign is unprecedented because there has never been a campaign in recent history that has taken on the entire corporate establishment. And I'm talking about Wall Street and I'm talking about the insurance companies and the drug companies and the fossil fuel industry. There has been never a campaign in recent history which has taken on the entire political establishment and that is an establishment which is working frantically to try to defeat us [...].
>
> *Sanders 2020*

Similarly, Jeremy Corbyn's speeches position victory as something to be pursued in honour of the sacrifices made by historical groups, which he links with the Momentum–Labour movement:

> We should be proud of those who went before us and proud to learn from them to develop those ideas in the rest of this century to bring about the justice and equality that they dreamt of and that they fought for and this generation and the next generation can, will and must achieve.
>
> *Corbyn 2015 in Bennister et al. 2017, 112*

In both of these examples, there is a clear emphasis on competitive success through references to fighting and achieving and resisting defeat. Although more subtle than the Trumpian examples, it seems clear that populism of any ideological bent has the potential to be positioned within a game-oriented framework that stresses the pleasurable pursuit of victory, usually at the expense of some other entity, be that another country, another party, a political 'establishment', or a minority group. Although there are important ethical differences among these examples, it remains true that competition feeds into the affective pleasure that participants experience. More broadly, pleasure and happiness are sometimes treated as a finite resource that warrants antagonistic confrontation. In some cases, external opponents are suspected of possessing more than their fair share of pleasure and happiness: immigrants or EU citizens are thought to be happy and well only because 'we' are losing out in relation to them; or the wealthiest classes are enjoying life explicitly at the expense of 'the 99%' (Browning 2019, 231). Pleasure itself therefore becomes affective territory that can be gained or ceded – emotional ground to be fought over in a battle for possession.

Ultimately, the prominence of competitive attitudes, however enjoyable they are for participants, has the effect of further exacerbating the downsides of fun and playfulness discussed above. Because winning becomes the utmost goal, playfulness can lean more toward exclusionary mockery or insults; nostalgic or utopian fantasies might be pitted against one another as mutually exclusive visions of reality that can allow for no alternatives. All in all, competition exacerbates by its very nature the prominence of antagonistic attitudes within populist movements, and this extends to a tendency to channel pleasurable affects like playfulness and fantasy into tools for division and exclusion.

Pleasure in Digital Populism

The presence of playfulness and competitive fun flourish in online environments. In this section, I give further consideration to the ways that pleasurable affective sensations influence social media users' interactions in populist contexts and how they exacerbate the issues discussed above. To begin with, as mentioned in the previous chapter, participation in digital media often gives rise to a significant sense of satisfaction on the part of users as they join in the cycle of information circulation that conforms to their existing world views. There is a sense of pleasure attached to viewing and reposting content that exemplifies one's own existing views. This is intensified as online communities consolidate and flourish. When online exchanges result in affirmations of social identities and a sense of group solidarity, the subtle pleasure that goes along with sharing content reaches greater heights (Ahmed 2004; Salmela and von Scheve 2018, 583). Once like-minded communities form and interact regularly with one another, greater degrees of pleasure are enjoyed as participants not only have their own worldviews affirmed but also feel part of an identifiable network of other people (Sakki and Pettersson 2016). This leads theorists like Ignas Kalpokas to position the existence of post-truth and fake news content as part and parcel of 'a progressive shift toward politics as an algorithmic pleasure-maximizing service' (Kalpokas 2019, 1). Especially given the marketplace of visibility that characterises social media, politics ultimately becomes a competitive process in which political actors compete to produce the most enjoyable content and thereby win over a greater number of followers. As consumers of social media respond to content they find pleasurable, this creates a demand for further such content.

While participation and a sense of community provide a foundational source of pleasure for participants, the role that pleasurable sensations play comes even more to the fore due to the tone of digital populist communications. Much online political content is clearly humorous and light-hearted in tone. Perhaps the most obvious example of this is the prolific circulation of memes which offer a distinctly playful tool for communicating political positions, even when mocking political foes (Baldwin-Philippi 2019). The success of playful political content was clearly demonstrated in the 2017 UK general election when fun social media posts became an influential aspect of Jeremy Corbyn's campaign. Light-hearted memes, including one that inserted Corbyn's face and speech into a Stormzy video, were the most widely circulated during the election (McLoughlin and Southern 2021).

However, the tone of pleasurable content needn't necessarily be positive or light-hearted in its own right. Partaking of online interactions that shock or dominate others can be an extremely pleasurable experience for some users (Turner 2007). This is not simply an extension of the playful insults and mockery that occur during in-person events. In online environments, it is even easier for jokes and insults to serve divisive ends because behavioural codes are already slackened in such contexts; in order to be transgressive through playfulness, users must produce content that is even more shocking or unexpected. Online environments also enable the production and consumption of outright aggressive or violent content because of the anonymity offered to users; simultaneously, this anonymity enables consumers of such content to take pleasure in the extreme transgression of such posts without the risk of being personally associated with it as they might at in-person events.

Ultimately, digital media thwarts the rejuvenating and healing aspects of fun because of the competitive frames that surround both social media marketplaces and populist electoral politics. The prominence of competition within both of these contexts suggests that manifestations of playfulness, fun, and pleasure will most often become oriented around attempts to outplay opponents. In this way, pleasure quickly leads to acrimony.

Beauty as a Creative Intervention

This chapter has so far established the tendency for pleasurable affect and attitudes to exacerbate antagonism within digital populist contexts. The potential for theatrically informed practices to respond to this issue is further complicated by notions of beauty. Beauty can offer a potent aesthetic frame which, due to its relationship with pleasure, might condition the attitude of participants towards either cooperation or antagonism, depending on the specific ways that this quality is deployed. The concept of beauty has, of course, been long contested in scholarly and artistic circles; but in recent decades theatre scholars and Applied Theatre practitioners have shown a renewed interest in its political potential. Beauty in these contexts is often interpreted broadly, associated with experiences that activate the senses in pleasurable ways (Thompson 2011; White 2015). Theatre can stimulate the spectator through visual appeal but also through delightful smells, sonorous music, sensations of warmth, or the taste of shared food; any of these qualities might lead to associations with beauty, and theatre might be especially likely to be described as 'beautiful' when it manages to touch a range of senses (Adebayo 2015, 138). This broad approach to beauty allows for a multiplicity of ways that people might derive a pleasurable aesthetic experience from an event. It also provides the basis for an argument that beautiful encounters might effectively shape group cultures of pleasure and playfulness in ways that foster collaboration and cooperation in the face of diversity rather than competitive conflict.

Before developing this point further, it is important to note that we need to remain cautious about the potential for beauty to result in healing or rejuvenation in the face of antagonistic competition. We need to keep in mind that beauty can also fuel antagonism. This is because beauty is often considered with reference to socially constructed ideals and standards that reflect other hierarchical delineations in society; this is most obvious with regard to the physical characteristics that mark some bodies out as more 'beautiful' than others; but the point also applies in a wider sense, whenever beauty is invoked to designate some entities as more valuable than others. Beauty can appear in digital populist contexts as a means of consolidating populist identities, particularly by enabling social media users to associate themselves with visual representations of common values. Judgements of what is beautiful and what is ugly help to establish and perpetuate a political grouping's sense of shared taste (White 2015). This might take comparatively benign forms, such as content that includes identity-based objects like flags or other national symbols. On the other hand, notions of beauty are perhaps at their most antagonistic when shared values are expressed through judgements about the physical beauty of others.

In social media usage generally, there is widespread pressure for users to out-perform others in the achievement of 'beauty' according to given social standards (Duffy and Hund 2019; McRobbie 2020). When translated to populist interactions, this competitive approach to beauty often manifests as mockery of political opponents' physical features, alongside celebrations of the physical appeal of allies. For example, throughout Barack Obama's presidency, burgeoning right-wing populist contingents widely indulged in racist characterisations of First Lady Michelle Obama's physical appearance; when Melania Trump took up the role of First Lady in 2017, these same users posted pictures and memes celebrating her beauty in explicit comparison to her predecessor (Tate 2018). This example demonstrates how aesthetic judgements of beauty can be consciously employed to reinforce other hierarchical social divisions like race. Left populists also participate in such tactics. Trump himself has been the subject of innumerable jokes about his physical appearance, but the same brand of mockery has also been levelled toward centrist politicians such as British MPs Rory Stewart and Anna Soubry (Esposito and Zollo 2021).

Judgements of beauty can be deployed as a tactic to consolidate in-group identities, precisely by labelling opponents ugly or unattractive. The implication is that where beauty is lacking, so too is political legitimacy. This suggests that there is substantial potential for sensations of beauty to support antagonistic approaches to political engagement. In order to mobilise beauty for productive ends, we need to be more attentive to how beautiful experiences might unfold in practice.

Beauty in Applied Theatre Practices

In contrast to the divisive invocations of beauty mentioned above, many Applied Theatre practitioners have demonstrated a growing conviction that beautiful encounters can effectively instigate social or political transformation. The justification for using beauty for positive ends stems from a number of influential theoretical contributions. To begin with, Applied Theatre scholars maintain that beautiful experiences can serve political ends because of their capacity to disrupt our everyday orientation to the world around us (Haseman and Winston 2010; Thompson 2011). Elaine Scarry's writings on the transformational potential of beauty have been widely influential in this vein (e.g. Adebayo 2015; Thompson 2011). Scarry makes a case for the potential of beauty to wrest people from their ordinary perceptions of the world into some other mode of engagement. Eloquently, she writes that beautiful things,

> act like small tears in the world that pull us through to some vaster space; or they form 'ladders reaching toward the beauty of the world', or they lift us (as though by the air currents of someone else's sweeping), letting the ground rotate beneath us several inches, so that when we land, we find we are standing in a different relation to the world than we were a moment before. It is not that we cease to stand at the centre of the world, for we never stood there. It is that we cease to stand even at the centre of our own world. We willingly cede our ground to the thing that stands before us.
>
> *Scarry 2010, 112 (quotation from Simone Weil)*

Building on Scarry's work, James Thompson believes that beauty can create moments of pleasurable sensation that can stop people in their tracks, arresting their attention and changing their perspective on the world (Thompson 2011, 144). In this way, beauty has the power to open people up to the perspectives of others, relinquishing their own individual positions and embracing the potential to understand the world from a different point of view. This suggests that beauty might play a direct role in instantiating metaxic attitudes; when encountering profoundly beautiful things we allow ourselves to become displaced from our usual position and from our short-term self-interest or pre-existing motivations. As a result, we might enjoy an enhanced capacity to imaginatively occupy the positions and perspectives of others.

Similarly, beauty might also prove useful as a tool to change the way that people interact with one another. For example, Gareth White describes an 'aesthetic of participation' within much Applied Theatre work, suggesting that applied projects employ participation not only as a practical instrumental approach but also as an overarching aesthetic quality that emphasises the collaborative process (White 2015, 45). In a similar vein, Cynthia Cohen notes that beautiful creative interactions are characterised by a heightened attendance to the sensibilities of the receiver. She says that:

> [...] it is through beauty that a work of art issues its invitation. It is by virtue of this reciprocity that aesthetic transactions are inherently other-regarding. They involve an awareness of the other, a sensitivity akin to respect. This quality of aesthetic experience alone makes cultural work and the arts especially valuable in situations of enmity when groups act with utter disregard for the well-being of each other.
>
> *Cohen in Dwyer 2016, 130*

Where Cohen sees beauty as an instigator of sensitivity toward others, Thompson goes further to suggest that beautiful experiences might provoke further engagement and communication. He notes that profound personal sensations of beauty produce an innate need to communicate that beauty to others. He talks about beauty as something which prompts a desire to 'share affect'. While recognising that beauty is subjective, he notes that watching something we consider beautiful prompts us to become aware of its potential to move others:

> How many of us have played a piece of music to try to convince friends that it is the best song ever, or pressed people to go to a play that has overwhelmed us? Who has not, with co-participants in a theatre project, energetically reminded each other of those moments we know were the best. We accept beauty is in our eye, but we are desperate to locate it in an object (workshop, performance, song) and share that feeling with others.
>
> *Thompson 2011, 144*

Beauty, therefore, Thompson argues, might create an urge to engage with others, translating individual experience into communal experience (Thompson 2011).

These perspectives are united by their emphasis on beauty as a collective experience. They suggest that shared encounters with sensorially pleasurable objects or events can inspire us to re-evaluate our own position in the world and perhaps reach out toward others' values and perspectives. In accordance with these theorists, I believe it is crucial to pursue instances of beauty that are defined by their emphatically collective nature. To counter the pitfalls of digitally mediated populism, we need to pursue beautiful experiences that are not just attention-generating but that also have the potential to simultaneously alter our perception of ourselves and others. Performance-inspired practices might reaffirm the relationship between beauty and collective pleasure and effectively counter the divisive and competitive tendencies of these qualities that are otherwise prevalent in digitally mediated contexts. To achieve this, it seems necessary to pursue a special kind of beauty – one that outstrips the circulated representations on social media that simply reinforce existing cultural hierarchies and group identities. We need to be arrested by beauty, momentarily paused so that we might reflect differently on our relationship to others and to the world around us; but most importantly, this needs to generate a collective experience of the pleasures derived from beauty – through an aesthetics of *beautiful participation.*

The Beauty and Pleasure of Puppetry

In my own practice, I have found puppetry to be the most useful tool to establish a sense of communal, playful beauty. This is not to say that voice and improvisation don't bring their own value in this respect; in practices inspired by Alfred Wolfsohn and Roy Hart, it is not uncommon for participants' voices to suddenly resonate with profound clarity and beauty that is resolutely joyful. Likewise, Augusto Boal's entire corpus of work stems from the principle that pleasurable, playful exploration can have deeply political impacts. But within my own workshops, I find that nothing comes close to puppets in terms of instantiating an environment of collective playfulness and aesthetic beauty. Puppets, perhaps not unlike some populist leaders, seem to give participants tacit permission to abandon their everyday behavioural etiquette. They invite people to become child-like again, invoking their imagination in astonishing and wonder-filled ways.

Given that puppets can provide this powerful conjunction of playfulness and beauty, Peter Schumann's work provides one further reminder of the way that theatrical practice can produce knowledge about political interaction. It is worth keeping in mind that Schumann first began experimenting with puppet shows during his time as a refugee in northern Germany during the Second World War. During this time, he experienced the daily prospect of violence from locals who looked unkindly on the refugees (Andrews 2007). For Schumann, puppets have always offered a way of bringing together people who might otherwise indulge in increasingly hardened stances of Us vs. Them. This concluding section examines the ways that Schumann's Bread and Puppet Theatre facilitates an aesthetics of participation that emphasises collective playfulness and beauty throughout. I am referring especially to the performance practices that Schumann developed for shows at his Glover, Vermont farm. These performances – constituting the

Bread and Puppet Circus – have been held every summer since 1974 and they exemplify the ways that populist themes and attitudes can appear in environments that stress collaboration and communal celebration, even while preserving internal difference.

Fundamentally, the Bread and Puppet Circus provides a model of performance as a means of provoking communality and collaboration. In many ways, the communal development of an audience is a goal of many contemporary political theatre events, especially those that overtly take care to foster such attitudes. However, Bread and Puppet goes a step further by ensuring that their audiences are diverse in the first place. This is achieved in part through an approach to theatre making that is inherently transgressive – both politically and theatrically. Schumann takes great pains to position his theatre as one that welcomes people of all backgrounds, ensuring that it is maximally accessible. Often open to the public for the cost of a 'suggested donation', it is funded in large part through the sale of 'cheap art' sold from the company's brightly painted decommissioned school bus – these are typically vivid woodblock prints produced by volunteers in the Schumanns' barn. Although the philosophical basis for 'cheap art' was developed in the 1970s and 80s, the manifesto speaks strongly to present-day political contexts: 'Cheap art is NOT important. Cheap art defies, ridicules, undermines and makes obsolete the sanctity of affluent-society economy' (Bread and Puppet 1985). In this way, Schumann positions his art, including his theatre, as inherently NOT important, transgressing societal norms about art and culture and encouraging a defiant, transgressive attitude among his audiences. This also increases the diversity of audiences because (not unlike populist events like rallies and demonstrations) the beyond-the-norm framing of the event encourages the participation of people who would not normally attend a theatrical performance.

In addition to accessibility, active participation is also at the heart of Schumann's aims, but it is a different kind of participation to that fostered in Augusto Boal's work, for example. In the Bread and Puppet Circus, participation begins from the shared appreciation of the unique aesthetic space. Drawing on traditional forms of popular entertainment like circus and pantomime, the crowds attending the shows develop a sense of community based on sharing the same pleasurable experience. The performance space is a large grassy area with a natural amphitheatric shape. Audiences are often led to this area by flag-bearing puppeteers playing makeshift instruments; members of the crowd are asked to hold up sections of banners, and together they form a joyful procession toward the performance space. Once people have arrived and walked to the Circus performance area, they are given loaves of home-baked sourdough bread to share with the strangers who sit beside them. They sit on picnic blankets and share food and drink while the circus acts unfold before them. Schumann thus describes his 'puppet shows' as a foil for the more important aim of making people sit down and eat together. He explains that people have forgotten how to do something as simple as being together and sharing bread and that the act of doing so somehow reunites them; it allows them to engage with one another, sharing ideas, beliefs, and experiences in a way that they would not have done otherwise (Varga 2013).

It is clear from this that performance could provide a key for maximising the diversity of political groupings by creating aesthetic and emotional frames that challenge the exclusionary or stultifying environments that are common to contemporary British and American democracy. Creative approaches that gather groups of people together in unexpected ways might increase and diversify political participation. They might also provide a basis for enhanced engagement with others by creating a pleasurable atmosphere for the consideration of contested topics.

These features can be further developed by ensuring that the playfulness of the event is paired with a communal experience of beauty. The playfulness of Schumann's puppetry is profoundly beautiful.[4] The giant papier mache puppets move slowly and gracefully and their features suggest a universal, human simplicity. The characters range from peasant farmers to politicians to military generals and corporate CEOs. Very often, they engage with one another, aided by voice-overs provided by the puppeteers. Sometimes these interactions illustrate conflict, loss and other serious themes – but the beautiful and graceful aesthetic dominates the perceptions of spectators. One critic described the shows in this way:

> The giant puppets with their long flowing robes moved by sometimes dozens of members of the theater walking on stilts look like 'naked souls'; with their sheer size and simplicity, they are able to concentrate the onlooker's emotion.
>
> *Spitta 2009, 117*

Although these puppets sometimes mock one another or hit one another over the head, they employ insults and jibes within a framework of beautiful playfulness. Most often, audiences are delighted and astonished by the appearance of the puppets and this shapes their interpretation of each scene's content. In this way, Schumann utilises some of the same affective and aesthetic qualities that are evident within populism. The Bread and Puppet Circus is saturated with playfulness and fun, but when these qualities are applied to sometimes-controversial political topics, they support the development of agonism more than the competitive modes of play and pleasure that are common in digital media contexts. This is because the collective experience of beauty enhances the sense of communal participation in the event. Audience members retain a sense of their own perspectives and beliefs, but these are tempered by the extraordinary aesthetic environment that holds sway. The fun and beauty evident in Schumann's practice prompts people to step back and reorient themselves in relation to others, thus altering the atmosphere of political engagement. This has profound implications for the ways that pleasure and beauty might contribute to a reinvigoration of democracy; if genuine diversity can be maintained through maximal accessibility, and if an atmosphere of shared joyfulness and wondrous beauty can prevail, then surely a new vibrancy might be brought to political interaction.

Conclusion: Bringing It All Together

At the end of my projects, participants have collaboratively made their own papier mache puppets and masks; they have become comfortable 'playing' with their voices to express negative and positive concepts; they have explored difficult political topics using Image Theatre and Forum Theatre activities; we have had wide-ranging conversations that cover difficult themes, sometimes producing uncertainty and confusion; we feel now more like a family or a close-knit group of friends than participants in a project. In the last part of the final day, it all comes together. I typically watch in awe from the sidelines as my participants, usually by this point fully in charge of events themselves, bring their beautiful puppet creatures to life, sometimes in a way that makes it difficult to discern where human flesh ends and puppet fabric begins. Voices resonate from behind puppet faces, undulating in strange and unpredictable yet sonorous ways. The movements of the puppets reflect the postures derived from improvisations of political oppressions, but now they no longer seem oppressed – just innately human. The people move between and among the puppets they have crafted. I bring in one remaining puppet, made of thin tissue paper stretched on a willow withy frame. In the shape of a bird, it floats buoyantly among the group. They recognise the paper it is made from as the sheets that they had anonymously written their greatest hopes and fears on in the first week of the project. The bird, bearing their own personal statements but existing as an unfamiliar and unknown thing, is incorporated into their movement-play. I press a button and tiny LED lights within the new puppet illuminate it from the inside – revealing a glowing, graceful creature marked by the hopes, worries and possibilities of everyone in the room. The voices thrum.

When it works, it is beautiful.

CONCLUSION

The past few years have undoubtedly brought profound changes to global society that will impact politics for decades to come, yet the sense of dissatisfaction with political leadership continues to grow. It is perhaps true that the global coronavirus pandemic has shifted some public attention away from the deep ideological divisions exemplified in populist movements. To some extent, the worldwide threat of a highly contagious and deathly virus led to a greater appetite for technocratic, middle-ground politics in the interest of immediate public welfare concerns. However, this shift in sentiment seems to have been equally matched by factions that are bent on interpreting government policies as evidence of extreme corruption or hidden agendas. While support for populist parties and movements is always likely to ebb and flow, it is difficult to imagine that the driving factors behind populism will rapidly abate in any significant fashion.

At the time of writing, the ongoing presence of populist antagonism is starkly evident. To take just two recent examples, UK Labour Party leader Keir Starmer was harangued in a London street by anti-vaccination protesters who repeated conspiracy theories about centrist politicians' links to paedophilia. Similarly, a convoy of truckers and their supporters from across the United States and Canada surrounded a city, harassing citizens and politicians alike with demands which, although representative of a relative minority, were enormously amplified through social media in a manner that generated maximal division between insiders and outsiders. In both of these instances, participants seem to have been drawn from a range of political backgrounds and were spurred on by disparate individual concerns, but they were united under a single banner that was directed outward in aggressive confrontation. Given this state of affairs, it is starkly evident that the underlying qualities of populism – divisiveness, oversimplification, fear, anger and othering – are still very much in play in present-day

DOI: 10.4324/9780367824129-12

politics. Within this environment, the end goals of radical democracy and left populism seem as elusive as ever.

The chapters in this book have attempted to provide an introductory consideration of some of the ways that populism, and especially digital populism, impacts political interaction on interpersonal, embodied and affective levels. The book has argued that performance practices are useful both as a means of providing theoretical insights into political interaction and also in applied contexts where theatrical and performative qualities might be employed to counter the worst tendencies of digital populism. I have suggested that the acrimony and divisiveness that digital populism engenders might be productively redirected by incorporating Applied performance knowledge into future frameworks of political interaction. Through the explorations of engagement, embodiment, and aesthetics and affect, the preceding chapters have uncovered a number of salient points that might enhance genuine democratic engagement. Of course, there is far more to be said about the ways that performance is implicated in populism and how Applied performance might respond, but my hope is that these chapters have broached a number of insights that might be given further consideration by scholars and practitioners interested in vibrantly pluralist, inclusive democracy.

Fundamentally, I have suggested that a view of populism as an interactive practice enables us to consider it as a creative process; in this sense, the logics, structures and styles of populism become features that unfold in a live, interactive, processual manner. Alongside or within these features we can introduce any number of practices that might effectively alter the outcomes of populist interaction. Furthermore, this view of populism enables an approach to agonistic engagement that truly foregrounds diversity, fluidity and change.

To fully realise the potential of this perspective, we need to boldly reconsider what kinds of practices and behaviours are relevant and appropriate within political deliberation. For example, drawing on theatrical knowledge offered by the likes of Augusto Boal, we might linger on the in-betweenness of agonism, the metaxic space that exists between our own conscious identity and opinions and those of others – this is a space that is ripe for occupying with creative, imaginative play and improvisation. Creative, fictive frames can alter people's capacity for empathetic engagement with others, particularly by instituting a space for temporary enactment of alternative worlds. They can reinstate an orientation to political engagement that privileges the exploration of difference in practice; whereas populism and its attendant modes of interaction frequently obscure difference in the interest of group cohesion and outward-facing competitive efficacy, theatrical performance inherently offers a space for difference to be experienced in a sustained and productive fashion.

We might also colour this creative space of active agonism by insisting on the active presence of corporeal knowledge and perception. By introducing activities that foreground material corporeal sensation we can access aspects of human experience and values that are otherwise not readily available to the thinking mind. This has the potential to further diversify the perspectives that are brought to bear in pluralist contexts because it provides a means of accessing knowledge of the world that is retained in the body's interior realms. We can also, through practices that encourage us to reach-toward others, change our orientations to the world around us. We can explore aesthetic and affective sensations like failure, fear, beauty and pleasure in safe and productive ways, countering their appropriation by divisive political movements. All of these might free us to occupy a truly metaxic space of creative uncertainty where we can experiment with radically different approaches to political contention.

Is it too utopian to suggest that Applied Theatre and performance practice has something substantial and important to offer to the development of democratic frameworks? Or to wish for a world where such practices could be robustly incorporated into grassroots political movements or citizen assemblies? Perhaps this is so, but however utopian, this premise might be one that could result in significant benefits in terms of the public's engagement with democratic politics. The notion of injecting the serious business of politics with creative theatrical practice might be even more appropriate in light of the ways that digital media is expanding and developing. In the preceding chapters, I have focused primarily on political engagement within the frameworks of social media platforms because this is the most prominent and accessible set of tools available to the general public at present. However, I am cognisant of intriguing developments in virtual reality technology that are likely to significantly alter the nature of digitally mediated interactions. These technologies raise interesting prospects about the blending of everyday life with quasi-fictional immersive worlds, giving rise to new ways of thinking about theatricality in interpersonal interaction. But beyond this, such technologies could also greatly enhance possibilities for haptic and kinaesthetic encounters with others. Perhaps our political interactions online need not be limited to brief tweets or snapshot videos or regulated by profit-making companies whose priorities lead to algorithmic divisions. If we were to inject practical performance knowledge into such contexts in meaningful ways, we might develop virtual worlds that more fully realise the potential for digital media to serve as an emancipating, democratising platform.

This book has also encompassed a broader aim of providing an interdisciplinary study that is balanced between the fields of Politics and Performance. Although there is always scope for greater development in this respect, I have attempted to draw out two principles in particular. First, I have deliberately chosen to profile the theoretical and practical contributions of individuals whose own work was developed in response to their experiences of political violence. While more recent practitioners are currently demonstrating new and interesting ways of utilising theatre's capacity for representation and spectatorship, I find a unique approach to political interaction in the practices of Wolfsohn, Schumann and Boal. I believe this relates to their personal understanding of violence and war, which has resulted in a keen awareness of the complex ways that performance and politics are intertwined. To my mind it suggests that interdisciplinary research of this nature might benefit from paying close attention to creators whose work is rooted in the conditions of global politics that we seek to investigate and analyse.

Relatedly, this book has sought to highlight the benefits of practice-informed research. In an effort to avoid an approach that over-instrumentalises performance, I have attempted to stress the unique perspectives that theatrical practice can bring to politics scholarship. This has entailed positioning the research primarily from a performance-informed epistemological standpoint; rather than using theatre and performance in metaphorical ways or as a medium through which political phenomena is represented, the chapters in this book attempt to centre the ways that performance practitioners uniquely apprehend the world around them. What results is a concerted emphasis on live, embodied interaction. It is my hope that this work hints at the vast, relatively untapped potential of theatre practice to serve as a Political epistemology and methodology.

This project was conceived as one part of a broader practice-based research project. The next steps will involve additional creative workshops drawing on the practices outlined in these pages as a means of facilitating agonistic engagement in pluralist contexts. By involving many different communities and bringing this work to groups with very different political leanings, the aim is to uncover the aspects of theatricality that can truly serve to reinvigorate democracy in the 21st century.

NOTES

Introduction

1 I am using the term 'performative' here to refer to qualities of performance, as opposed to definitions of performativity derived from the work of J.L. Austin (1975).

Chapter 1

1 Interdisciplinary pioneers of this nature must be recognised not only for producing important insights in their own right but also for paving the way for creative work by future scholars. For a small sample of such work, see for example Danchev and Lisle (2009), Shapiro (2013), Chan (2003), Sylvester (2005), Bleiker (2009) and Weber (2006).

2 A rich array of scholarship from Theatre and Performance theorists provides evidence of the social and political functions of theatre within a range of historical and cultural contexts. See, for example Osita Okagbue (2013) on African theatre and performance; Siddheswaar Chattopadhyay (2020) on ancient Indian theatre; Benito Ortolani (1995) on Japanese theatre history; Mark Eckersley (2012) on Australian Indigenous drama; Christy Stanlake (2009) on Native American drama, to name just a few.

3 It is worth noting that the term 'Applied Theatre' is somewhat contested within the field itself, as some scholars feel that it overemphasises mono-directional interventions by outside facilitators at the expense of collaborative community explorations or problem-solving. Others contend that the word 'applied' suggests the use of theatre as a tool to achieve pre-set outcomes. For a detailed discussion of this term and its alternatives, see Adebayo (2015).

4 It was with great sadness that I learned of Elka Schumann's passing on 1 August 2021, shortly after this section was written (see Schumann 2021). Peter Schumann is without question the visionary artist who has driven Bread and Puppet throughout its history; but Elka Schumann has always been influential to the development of this work, organising the activities of the theatre, coordinating volunteers, fielding press inquiries and so forth (Brecht 1988). Given her influence on Bread and Puppet's work, it is perhaps worth noting that her own childhood was also marked by the anxieties born of political conflict. She was born in the 1930s in the Russian city of

Magnitogorsk to a Russian mother and American father (John Scott, son of Scott Nearing). When the purges began in Moscow, her father fled to France and was later expelled from the Soviet Union. Eventually, the family succeeded in securing visas to enable them to remain together in the United States. The trip was made via Japan, and in an oral history interview in 2016, Elka Schumann relates the tensions experienced while waiting in that country for transport to America in 1941 (Rowell, 2016).

5 Guerilla theatre is a technique of unexpected performances in public spaces to bring political theatre – and the issues it is highlighting – to the attention of the public in ways that traditional theatre cannot do. Newspaper theatre, which originated in the 1930s, involves the performance of short theatricalised scenes drawn from otherwise overlooked news stories.

Chapter 2

1 I am referring here to populist movements in Western liberal democracies, and particularly to the movements in the United Kingdom and United States that I refer to as examples throughout this book. This is not to suggest that populism, or more broadly, radical democracy, is limited to such contexts.

2 GB News is a right-leaning television news channel launched in the United Kingdom in June 2021. Nigel Farage is a regular host, often seen speaking to guests over a pint of ale as in his regular *Talking Pints* programme.

3 In Chapters 6 and 7 I provide a more detailed discussion of affect and emotion, including a consideration of the way that internal affect becomes translated into outward-facing emotion, conditioned by social and cultural processes. The present discussion aims to establish the prevalence of heightened emotionality within populism generally, and the impact of this on antagonistic orientations to political interaction.

4 There are of course a large number of digital media channels that offer distinct methods for the generation and display of content for users. Facebook, Twitter and Instagram have received the most scholarly attention, alongside some researchers' forays into the 'dark web'. It is the general tendencies of digital media platforms that I engage with here.

5 Many commentators point to Barack Obama's 2008 presidential campaign as an early example of the use of social media to broaden the campaign's reach and persuasiveness (Bode and Dalrymple 2016; Gonawela et al. 2018; Tumasjan et al. 2010). Since this time a number of studies have discussed the success of electoral social media campaigns, and these approaches are increasingly professionalised by industry experts who advise on social media strategies (Gonawela et. al. 2018, 300).

Chapter 3

1 I concur with critiques of political theory (e.g. Shilliam 2021) that suggest it is overly reliant on Western understandings of democracy; However, given the prominence of references to ancient Greek contexts by scholars who examine agonistic populism, it is helpful to focus here on ancient Greek theatre to further unpack the relationship between performance and politics.

2 The poet Thespis was the first to suggest that a single actor should step out in front of the play's chorus, and therefore position his character as separate from but in dialogue with the chorus. Later a second and a third actor were added by Aeschylus and Sophocles, respectively (Fischer-Lichte 2002, 10).

3 This is further constrained by behavioural norms attached to particular genders, races, ethnicities and ages and it can result in the power dynamics of the outside, 'real world' impinging overmuch on the exploration of political scenarios in the workshop setting. For more, see Boal (1995) and Preston (2016).

Chapter 4

1 While it would be a mistake to sketch overly broad generalisations about puppetry, given its rich diversity and global history, I seek to draw out aspects of puppetry practices that can tell us something about how the body is perceived, and which might be applied to further our understanding of populism.

Chapter 5

1 I concur with Diana Coole in her suggestion that the agency of objects is not exactly synonymous with human agency and is better understood as partial or non-reflexive agency. Nonetheless, a conceptualisation of the world in which objects are recognised for their agentive qualities produces important insights about the construction of identities and subjectivities that are vital to understanding populism.

2 I base this assertion in part on my own experiences with Roy Hart Theatre training, in which I became profoundly, though not unpleasantly disoriented as the voice I thought I owned became something unfamiliar and beyond my control.

Chapter 6

1 Although some differences in emotional tone have been noted between the most prominent social media platforms, such as Twitter, Instagram and Facebook, it remains true that social media overall encourages negative or divisive interactions (Dayan 2013; Duncombe 2019).

2 Frequently, failure appears on stage as a defining aesthetic, as actors and characters embark on actions that are impossible to finalise. Most especially, postdramatic theatre, which rejects traditional mimetic characters, narratives and plots, has experimented with self-conscious and ironic performances of failure as a strategy to reveal the multiplicity and provisionality of real-world identities (Tomlin 2016, 81).

Chapter 7

1 James Thompson notably cautions against an overemphasis on predetermined social and political outcomes in Applied Theatre projects. In place of measurements of efficacy, Thompson emphasises creativity and beauty as inherently productive activities (Sloan 2018; Thompson 2011).

2 I am basing this assessment in part on my own observations, especially as a participant in anti-austerity protests in the United Kingdom and in my participant–observation of right-wing political groups in the United States in 2007 and 2012 – groups that would later form the backbone of the Tea Party and latterly the Make America Great Again movement.

3 This quotation was taken from Trump's 11 April 2016 rally in Albany, New York. However, there are multiple examples of the same repetitious references to 'winning', 'winning at everything' and 'winning on all levels' from rallies throughout his presidential campaign.

4 It is difficult to convey the theatre's unique aesthetic in words; readers unfamiliar with Bread and Puppet's work might wish to access the excellent digital archive of Bread and Puppet's work available at www.breadandpuppet.org.

BIBLIOGRAPHY

Adebayo, Mojisola. 2015. 'Revolutionary Beauty out of Homophobic Hate: A Reflection on the Performance "I Stand Corrected"'. In *Applied Theatre: Aesthetics*, edited by Gareth White, 123–55. London, UK: Bloomsbury.

Åhäll, Linda. 2019. 'Feeling Everyday IR: Embodied, Affective, Militarising Movement as Choreography of War'. *Cooperation and Conflict* 54 (2): 149–66. https://doi.org/10.1177/0010836718807501.

Ahmed, Sara. 2004. 'Collective Feelings: Or, the Impressions Left by Others'. *Theory, Culture & Society* 21 (2): 25–42. https://doi.org/10.1177/0263276404042133.

———. 2006. *Queer Phenomenology: Orientations, Objects, Others*. Durham, NC: Duke University Press.

Aiolfi, Théo. 2022. 'Populism as a Transgressive Style'. *Global Studies Quarterly* 2 (1): ksac006. https://doi.org/10.1093/isagsq/ksac006.

Alaimo, Stacy. 2010. *Bodily Natures: Science, Environment, and the Material Self*. Bloomington, IN: Indiana University Press.

Albertazzi, Daniele, and Duncan McDonnell, eds. 2008. *Twenty-First Century Populism: The Spectre of Western European Democracy*. Basingstoke, UK; New York, NY: Palgrave Macmillan. http://www.dawsonera.com/depp/reader/protected/external/AbstractView/S9780230592100.

Alcoff, Linda Martín. 2006. *Visible Identities*. Oxford University Press. https://doi.org/10.1093/0195137345.001.0001.

Alexander, Jeffrey C. 2011. *Performance and Power*. Cambridge, UK: Polity Press.

Alexander, Jeffrey C., Bernhard Giesen, and Jason L. Mast, eds. 2006. *Social Performance: Symbolic Action, Cultural Pragmatics, and Ritual*. Cambridge Cultural Social Studies. Cambridge, UK: Cambridge University Press.

Allern, Tor-Helge. 2001. 'Myth and Metaxy, and the Myth of Metaxis'. In *Playing Betwixt and between: The IDEA Dialogues 2001*, edited by Bjørn Rasmussen and Anna-Lena Østern, 77–85. Bergen, Norway: Idea Publications.

Anderson, Ben. 2017. '"We Will Win Again. We Will Win a Lot": The Affective Styles of Donald Trump'. *Society and Space*, 28 February 2017. https://www.societyandspace.org/articles/we-will-win-again-we-will-win-a-lot-the-affective-styles-of-donald-trump.

Andrews, Morgan. 2007. 'When Magic Confronts Authority: The Rise of Protest Puppetry in North America'. In *Realizing the Impossible: Art against Authority*, edited by Josh MacPhee and Erik Reuland, 180–209. Oakland, CA: AK Press.

Apostolidis, Paul. 2022. 'Desperate Responsibility: Precarity and Right-Wing Populism'. *Political Theory* 50 (1): 114–41. https://doi.org/10.1177/0090591720985770.

Arendt, Hannah. 1998. *The Human Condition*. 2nd ed. Chicago, IL: University of Chicago Press.

Armstrong, Isobel. 2000. *The Radical Aesthetic*. Oxford, UK ; Malden, MA: Blackwell Publishers.

Asavei, Maria-Alina, and Jiri Kocian. 2020. 'Include Me out: Theatre as Sites of Resistance to Right-Wing Populism in Estonia, the Czech Republic and Hungary'. *Studies in Theatre and Performance* (October): 1–17. https://doi.org/10.1080/14682761.2020.1834258.

Asenbaum, Hans. 2019. 'Rethinking Digital Democracy: From the Disembodied Discursive Self to New Materialist Corporealities'. *Communication Theory* (November): qtz033. https://doi.org/10.1093/ct/qtz033.

Astles, Cariad. 2009. 'Barcelona: Earth, Puppets and Embodiment'. In *Performance, Embodiment and Cultural Memory*, edited by Colin Counsell and Roberta Mock, 97–113. Newcastle upon Tyne, UK: Cambridge Scholars.

Auslander, Philip. 2008. *Liveness: Performance in a Mediatized Culture*. 2nd ed. London, UK: Routledge.

Austin, J.L. 1975. *How to Do Things with Words*. 2d ed. The William James Lectures 1955. Oxford, UK: Clarendon Press.

Aytac, Ugur. 2020. 'On the Limits of the Political: The Problem of Overly Permissive Pluralism in Mouffe's Agonism'. *Constellations* (August): 417–431. https://doi.org/10.1111/1467-8675.12525.

Bailes, Sara Jane. 2011. *Performance Theatre and the Poetics of Failure: Forced Entertainment, Goat Island, Elevator Repair Service*. New York, NY: Routledge.

Bakardjieva, Maria. 2005. *Internet Society: The Internet in Everyday Life*. London, UK: Sage Publications Ltd. https://doi.org/10.4135/9781446215616.

Baker, George. 2004. 'Introduction to "Antagonism and Relational Aesthetics" by Claire Bishop'. *October* 110 (October): 49–50. https://doi.org/10.1162/octo.2004.110.1.49.

Baldwin-Philippi, Jessica. 2019. 'The Technological Performance of Populism'. *New Media & Society* 21 (2): 376–97. https://doi.org/10.1177/1461444818797591.

Ball, Stephen J., ed. 2012. *Foucault and Education: Disciplines and Knowledge*. Routledge Library Editions: Michel Foucault. London, UK: Routledge.

Barad, Karen. 2003. 'Posthumanist Performativity: Toward an Understanding of How Matter Comes to Matter'. *Signs: Journal of Women in Culture and Society* 28 (3): 801–31. https://doi.org/10.1086/345321.

Barad, Karen Michelle. 2007. *Meeting the Universe Halfway: Quantum Physics and the Entanglement of Matter and Meaning*. Durham, NC: Duke University Press.

Barish, Jonas A. 1985. *The Antitheatrical Prejudice*. Berkeley, CA: University of California Press.

Barry, Andrew, and Georgina Born. 2013. Interdisciplinarity: Reconfigurations of the Social and Natural Sciences. Abingdon, UK: Routledge.

Baudrillard, Jean. 1994. *Simulacra and Simulation*. The Body in Theory. Ann Arbor, MI: University of Michigan Press.

Baym, Nancy K. 2015. Personal Connections in the Digital Age. Cambridge, UK: Polity Press.

BBC News. 2014. 'Nigel Farage Defends Romanian Comments amid Racism Claims', 20 May 2014. https://www.bbc.co.uk/news/uk-politics-27474099.

Beech, Matt, and Kevin Hickson. 2020. 'Divided by Values: Jeremy Corbyn, the Labour Party and England's "North-South Divide"'. *Revue Française de Civilisation Britannique* XXV (2). https://doi.org/10.4000/rfcb.5456.

Behrens, Electa W. 2019. 'Devisers in the Dark: Reconfiguring a Material Voice Practice'. *Theatre, Dance and Performance Training* 10 (3): 395–409. https://doi.org/10.1080/19443927.2019.1637372.

Bell, John, ed. 2001. *Puppets, Masks, and Performing Objects*. TDR Books. Cambridge, MA: MIT Press.

Bell, John, Steve Abrams, and Max Schumann. 2013. 'Peter Schumann'. In *World Encyclopedia of Puppetry Arts*. Union Internationale de la Marionette. https://wepa.unima.org/en/peter-schumann/.

Bennett, Colin J. 2015. 'Trends in Voter Surveillance in Western Societies: Privacy Intrusions and Democratic Implications'. *Surveillance & Society* 13 (3/4): 370–84. https://doi.org/10.24908/ss.v13i3/4.5373.

Bennister, Mark, Ben Worthy, and Dan Keith. 2017. 'Jeremy Corbyn and the Limits of Authentic Rhetoric'. In *Voices of the UK Left*, edited by Judi Atkins and John Gaffney, 101–21. New York: Palgrave Macmillan.

Berman, John. 2015. 'Trump Mocks Reporter with Disability'. YouTube video. CNN. https://www.youtube.com/watch?v=PX9reO3QnUA.

Beusch, Danny. 2006. 'Transmitting the Body in Online Interaction'. *M/C Journal* 9 (1). https://doi.org/10.5204/mcj.2584.

Billé, Franck. 2018. 'Skinworlds: Borders, Haptics, Topologies'. *Environment and Planning D: Society and Space* 36 (1): 60–77. https://doi.org/10.1177/0263775817735106.

Billig, Michael. 2005. *Laughter and Ridicule: Towards a Social Critique of Laughter*. Theory, Culture & Society. London, UK: Sage.

Biocca, Frank. 1997. 'The Cyborg's Dilemma: Progressive Embodiment in Virtual Environments [1]'. *Journal of Computer-Mediated Communication* 3 (2). https://doi.org/10.1111/j.1083-6101.1997.tb00070.x.

Bird, Jane, and Christine Sinclair. 2019. 'Principles of Embodied Pedagogy: The Role of the Drama Educator in Transforming Student Understanding through a Collaborative and Embodied Aesthetic Practice'. *Applied Theatre Research* 7 (1): 21–36. https://doi.org/10.1386/atr_00003_1.

Bishop, Claire. 2004. 'Antagonism and Relational Aesthetics'. *October* 110: 51–79. https://doi.org/10.1162/0162287042379810.

———. 2012. *Artificial Hells: Participatory Art and the Politics of Spectatorship*. London, UK: Verso Books.

Bleiker, Roland. 2009. *Aesthetics and World Politics*. Basingstoke, UK: Palgrave Macmillan.

Bleiker, Roland, and Emma Hutchison. 2008. 'Fear No More: Emotions and World Politics'. *Review of International Studies* 34 (S1): 115–35. https://doi.org/10.1017/S0260210508007821.

Blenkarn, Patrick. 2016. 'On Failures'. *Performance Matters* 2 (1): 99–105.

Boal, Augusto. 1995. *The Rainbow of Desire: The Boal Method of Theatre and Therapy*. Edited by Adrian Jackson. Abingdon UK: Routledge.

———. 1998. *Legislative Theatre: Using Performance to Make Politics*. London, UK: Routledge.

———. 2002. *Games for Actors and Non-actors*. London, UK: Routledge.

———. 2006. *The Aesthetics of the Oppressed*. Edited by Adrian Jackson. London, UK: Routledge.

———. 2008. *Theatre of the Oppressed*. New edition. London, UK: Pluto Press.

Boal, Julian, and José Soeiro. 2021. 'Theatre of the Oppressed as a Dialectical Game?' in *The Routledge Companion to Theatre of the Oppressed*, edited by Kelly Howe, Julian Boal, and José Soeiro, 67–75. Abingdon, UK: Routledge.

Bode, Leticia, and Kajsa E. Dalrymple. 2016. 'Politics in 140 Characters or Less: Campaign Communication, Network Interaction, and Political Participation on Twitter'. *Journal of Political Marketing* 15 (4): 311–332.

Bødker, Henrik, and Chris Anderson. 2019. 'Populist Time: Mediating Immediacy and Delay in Liberal Democracy'. *International Journal of Communication* 13 (19): 5948–66.

Bogatyrev, Pyotr. 1999. 'Czech Puppet Theatre and Russian Folk Theatre'. *TDR/The Drama Review* 43 (3): 97–114.

Boiger, Michael, and Batja Mesquita. 2012. 'The Construction of Emotion in Interactions, Relationships, and Cultures'. *Emotion Review* 4 (3): 221–29. https://doi.org/10.1177/1754073912439765.

Bos, Linda, Wouter van der Brug, and Claes H. de Vreese. 2013. 'An Experimental Test of the Impact of Style and Rhetoric on the Perception of Right-Wing Populist and Mainstream Party Leaders'. *Acta Politica* 48 (2): 192–208. https://doi.org/10.1057/ap.2012.27.

Braggins, Sheila. 2012. *The Mystery Behind the Voice: A Biography of Alfred Wolfsohn*. Leicester, UK: Troubador Publishing.

Braidotti, Rosi. 2013. *The Posthuman*. Cambridge, UK: Polity Press.

———. 2017. 'Four Theses on Posthuman Feminism'. In *Anthropocene Feminism*, edited by Richard Gusin, 21–48. Minneapolis, MN: University of Minnesota Press.

Bread and Puppet Theatre. 1985. 'Cheap Art Manifesto No. 3'. Glover, VT: Bread and Puppet Press.

Brecht, Stefan. 1988. *Peter Schumann's Bread and Puppet Theatre*. Vol. 1. 2 vols. London, UK: Methuen; Routledge.

Brown, Helen, Jane Seitz, Peter Schumann, Kelly Morris, and Richard Schechner. 1968. 'With the Bread and Puppet Theatre: An Interview with Peter Schumann'. *TDR/The Drama Review* 12 (2): 62–73.

Browning, Christopher S. 2019. 'Brexit Populism and Fantasies of Fulfilment'. *Cambridge Review of International Affairs* 32 (3): 222–44. https://doi.org/10.1080/09557571.2019.1567461.

Brubaker, Rogers. 2017. 'Why Populism?' *Theory and Society* 46 (5): 357–85. https://doi.org/10.1007/s11186-017-9301-7.

Bucy, Erik P., Jordan M. Foley, Josephine Lukito, Larissa Doroshenko, Dhavan V. Shah, Jon C.W. Pevehouse, and Chris Wells. 2020. 'Performing Populism: Trump's Transgressive Debate Style and the Dynamics of Twitter Response'. *New Media & Society* 22 (4): 634–58. https://doi.org/10.1177/1461444819893984.

Burisch, Nicole. 2016. 'From Objects to Actions and Back Again: The Politics of Dematerialized Craft and Performance Documentation'. *TEXTILE* 14 (1): 54–73. https://doi.org/10.1080/14759756.2016.1142784.

Butler, Judith. 1996. *Bodies That Matter: On the Discursive Limits of 'Sex'*. Abingdon, UK: Routledge.

———. 2004. *Precarious Life: The Powers of Mourning and Violence*. London, UK; New York, NY: Verso.

———. 2015. *Notes toward a Performative Theory of Assembly*. Cambridge, MA: Harvard University Press.

Caleo, Susan Bamford. 2019. 'Many Doors: The Histories and Philosophies of Roy Hart Voice Work and Estill Voice Training'. *Voice and Speech Review* 13 (2): 188–200. https://doi.org/10.1080/23268263.2018.1534931.

Canovan, Margaret. 1999. 'Trust the People! Populism and the Two Faces of Democracy'. *Political Studies* 47 (1): 2–16. https://doi.org/10.1111/1467-9248.00184.

————. 2005. *The People*. Key Concepts. Cambridge, UK; Malden, MA: Polity.

Cappelletto, Chiara. 2011. 'The Puppet's Paradox: An Organic Prosthesis'. *Res: Anthropology and Aesthetics* 59–60 (March): 325–36. https://doi.org/10.1086/RESvn1ms23647798.

Carroll, John. 1996. 'Critical and Transformative Research in Drama Classrooms'. In *Researching Drama and Arts Education: Paradigms and Possibilities*, edited by Philip Taylor, 72–84. London: Falmer Press.

Casullo, Maria Esperanza. 2020. 'The Body Speaks before It Even Talks: Deliberation, Populism and Bodily Representation'. *Journal of Deliberative Democracy* 16 (1). https://doi.org/10.16997/jdd.380.

Cavarero, Adriana. 2005. *For More Than One Voice: Toward a Philosophy of Vocal Expression*. Stanford, CA: Stanford University Press.

Centre Artistique International Roy Hart. 2021. 'Roy Hart Theatre Legacy'. 3 December 2021. https://roy-hart-theatre.com/legacy/.

Ceron, Andrea, and Giovanna d'Adda. 2016. 'E-Campaigning on Twitter: The Effectiveness of Distributive Promises and Negative Campaign in the 2013 Italian Election'. *New Media & Society* 18 (9): 1935–55. https://doi.org/10.1177/1461444815571915.

Chadwick, Rachelle. 2020. 'Methodologies of Voice: Towards Posthuman Voice Analytics'. *Methods in Psychology* 2 (November): 100021. https://doi.org/10.1016/j.metip.2020.100021.

Chadwick, Andrew, Cristian Vaccari, and Ben O'Loughlin. 2018. 'Do Tabloids Poison the Well of Social Media? Explaining Democratically Dysfunctional News Sharing'. *New Media & Society* 20 (11): 4255–74. https://doi.org/10.1177/1461444818769689.

Chan, Stephen. 2003. 'The Performativity of Death: Yukio Mishima and a Fusion for International Relations'. *Borderlands* 2 (2).

Chari, Anita. 2020. *Somatic Voices in Performance Research and Beyond*. Edited by Christina Kapadocha. Routledge Voice Studies. London, UK; New York, NY: Routledge/Taylor & Francis Group.

Charrett, Catherine. 2019. 'Diplomacy in Drag and Queer IR Art: Reflections on the Performance, "Sipping Toffee with Hamas in Brussels"'. *Review of International Studies* 45 (2): 280–99. https://doi.org/10.1017/S0260210518000451.

Chatterje-Doody, Precious N., and Rhys Crilley. 2019. 'Populism and Contemporary Global Media: Populist Communication Logics and the Co-Construction of Trans-national Identities'. In *Populism and World Politics*, edited by Frank A. Stengel, David B. MacDonald, and Dirk Nabers, 73–99. Cham: Springer International Publishing. https://doi.org/10.1007/978-3-030-04621-7_4.

Chattopadhyay, Siddheswar. 2020. *Theatre in Ancient India*. New Delhi, India: Manohar Publishers.

Chou, Mark. 2014. *Greek Tragedy and Contemporary Democracy*. London, UK: Bloomsbury. https://doi.org/10.5040/9781501301469.

Chou, Mark, and Roland Bleiker. 2009. 'The Symbiosis of Democracy and Tragedy: Lost Lessons from Ancient Greece'. *Millennium: Journal of International Studies* 37 (3): 659–82. https://doi.org/10.1177/0305829809103238.

Chouliaraki, Lilie. 2006. *The Spectatorship of Suffering*. London, UK; Thousand Oaks, CA: Sage Publications.

Christensen, Julia F. 2017. 'Pleasure Junkies All around! Why It Matters and Why "the Arts" Might Be the Answer: A Biopsychological Perspective'. *Proceedings of the Royal Society B: Biological Sciences* 284 (1854): 20162837. https://doi.org/10.1098/rspb.2016.2837.

Clarke, Simon, Paul Hoggett, and Simon Thompson, eds. 2006. *Emotion, Politics and Society*. Basingstoke, UK: Palgrave Macmillan.

CNN. 2016. 'Trump: We're Going to Win so Much (2016)'. Albany, NY: CNN Politics. https://edition.cnn.com/videos/politics/2017/08/18/trump-albany-rally-winning-sot.cnn.

Cohen, Jean L. 2019. 'What's Wrong with the Normative Theory (and the Actual Practice) of Left Populism'. *Constellations* 26 (3): 391–407. https://doi.org/10.1111/1467-8675.12427.

Cohn, Carol. 1987. 'Sex and Death in the Rational World of Defense Intellectuals'. *Signs* 12 (4): 687–718.

Colleoni, Elanor, Alessandro Rozza, and Adam Arvidsson. 2014. 'Echo Chamber or Public Sphere? Predicting Political Orientation and Measuring Political Homophily in Twitter Using Big Data: Political Homophily on Twitter'. *Journal of Communication* 64 (2): 317–32. https://doi.org/10.1111/jcom.12084.

Committee on Standards in Public Life. 2017. *Intimidation in Public Life: A Review by the Committee on Standards in Public Life*. London, UK: UK Parliament.

Connolly, William E. 2002. Identity/Difference: Democratic Negotiations of Political Paradox. Minneapolis, MN: University of Minnesota Press.

———.. 2013. 'The "New Materialism" and the Fragility of Things'. *Millennium: Journal of International Studies* 41 (3): 399–412. https://doi.org/10.1177/0305829813486849.

Conquergood, Dwight. 2002. 'Performance Studies: Interventions and Radical Research'. *TDR/The Drama Review* 46 (2): 145–56.

Conway, Janet, and Jakeet Singh. 2011. 'Radical Democracy in Global Perspective: Notes from the Pluriverse'. *Third World Quarterly* 32 (4): 689–706.

Coole, Diana. 2007. 'Experiencing Discourse: Corporeal Communicators and the Embodiment of Power'. *The British Journal of Politics and International Relations* 9 (3): 413–33. https://doi.org/10.1111/j.1467-856x.2006.00258.x.

———. 2013. 'Agentic Capacities and Capacious Historical Materialism: Thinking with New Materialisms in the Political Sciences'. *Millennium: Journal of International Studies* 41 (3): 451–69. https://doi.org/10.1177/0305829813481006.

Coole, Diana, and Samantha Frost, eds. 2010. *New Materialisms: Ontology, Agency, and Politics*. Duke University Press. https://doi.org/10.1215/9780822392996.

Cossarini, Paolo, and Fernando Vallespín, eds. 2019. *Populism and Passions: Democratic Legitimacy after Austerity*. Routledge Advances in Democratic Theory. New York, NY: Routledge.

Crawford, Kevin, and Noah Pikes. 2019. 'Vocal Traditions: The Roy Hart Tradition'. *Voice and Speech Review* 13 (2): 237–48. https://doi.org/10.1080/23268263.2019.1576998.

Critchley, Simon. 2017. 'Tragedy's Philosophy'. In *Performing Antagonism: Theatre, Performance and Radical Democracy*, edited by Tony Fisher and Eve Katsouraki, 25–42. London, UK: Palgrave Macmillan.

Crouch, Colin. 2004. *Post-Democracy*. Themes for the 21st Century. Malden, MA: Polity Press.

Cunningham, Anne C. 2018. *Populism in the Digital Age*. New York, NY: Greenhaven Publishing.

Danchev, Alex, and Debbie Lisle. 2009. 'Introduction: Art, Politics, Purpose'. *Review of International Studies* 35 (4): 775–79.

Davenport, Thomas H., and John C. Beck. 2001. *The Attention Economy: Understanding the New Currency of Business*. Boston, MA: Harvard Business School Press.

Davis, Richard, and David Taras, eds. 2020. *Power Shift? Political Leadership and Social Media*. New York, NY: Routledge.

Davis, Susan. 2015. '*Perezhivanie* and the Experience of Drama, Metaxis and Meaning Making'. *NJ* 39 (1): 63–75. https://doi.org/10.1080/14452294.2015.1083138.

Dayan, Daniel. 2013. 'Conquering Visibility, Conferring Visibility: Visibility Seekers and Media Performance'. *International Journal of Communication* 7 (1): 137–53.

Debord, Guy. 1994. The Society of the Spectacle. New York, NY: Zone Books. (Original work published 1967).

Deleuze, Gilles. 1978. 'Continuous Variation: Seminar at the University of Paris 24 January 1978'. Translated by Timothy S. Murphy. https://deleuze.cla.purdue.edu/sites/default/files/pdf/lectures/en/Continuous%20Variation%2001%20%281969-11-30%29.pdf.

Demertzēs, Nikos, ed. 2013. *Emotions in Politics: The Affect Dimension in Political Tension.* Palgrave Studies in Political Psychology Series. New York, NY: Palgrave Macmillan.

Denzin, Norman K., Yvonna S. Lincoln, and Linda Tuhiwai Smith, eds. 2008. *Handbook of Critical and Indigenous Methodologies.* Los Angeles, CA: Sage.

Dhrodia, Azmina. 2017. 'Unsocial Media: Tracking Twitter Abuse against Women MPs'. *Amnesty Global Insights* (blog). 4 September 2017. https://medium.com/@AmnestyInsights/unsocial-media-tracking-twitter-abuse-against-women-mps-fc28aeca498a.

Dolan, Jill. 2005. *Utopia in Performance: Finding Hope at the Theater.* Ann Arbor, MI: University of Michigan Press.

Drylie-Carey, Lindsay, Sebastián Sánchez-Castillo, and Esteban Galán-Cubillo. 2020. 'European Leaders Unmasked: Covid-19 Communication Strategy through Twitter'. *El Profesional de La Información* (September): e290504. https://doi.org/10.3145/epi.2020.sep.04.

Duffy, Brook Erin, and Emily Hund. 2019. 'Gendered Visibility on Social Media: Navigating Instagram's Authenticity Bind'. *International Journal of Communication* 13: 4983–5002.

Duncombe, Constance. 2019. 'Digital Diplomacy: Emotion and Identity in the Public Realm'. *The Hague Journal of Diplomacy* 14 (1–2): 102–16. https://doi.org/10.1163/1871191X-14101016.

Dwyer, Paul. 2016. 'Peacebuilding Performances in the Aftermath of War: Lessons from Bougainville'. In *Critical Perspectives on Applied Theatre,* edited by Jenny Hughes and Helen Nicholson, 127–49. Cambridge, UK: Cambridge University Press. https://doi.org/10.1017/CBO9781107587977.007.

Eagleton, Terry. 1990. *The Ideology of the Aesthetic.* Oxford, UK; Cambridge, MA: Blackwell.

Eckersall, Peter, Helena Grehan, and Edward Scheer. 2017. *New Media Dramaturgy: Performance, Media and New-Materialism.* New Dramaturgies. London, UK: Palgrave Macmillan.

Eckersley, Mark. 2012. *Australian Indigenous Drama.* Altona, VIC: Tasman Press.

Edkins, Jenny, and Adrian Kear. 2013. *International Politics and Performance: Critical Aesthetics and Creative Practice.* Abingdon UK: Routledge.

Eidsheim, Nina Sun. 2011. 'Sensing Voice: Materiality and the Lived Body in Singing and Listening'. *The Senses and Society* 6 (2): 133–55. https://doi.org/10.2752/174589311X12961584845729.

Elund, Jude. 2015. 'Embodiment, Virtual Experience and the Body: Possibilities for Subversion?' In *Subversion, Sexuality and the Virtual Self,* edited by Jude Elund, 16–38. London, UK: Palgrave Macmillan. https://doi.org/10.1057/9781137468345_2.

Engesser, Sven, Nayla Fawzi, and Anders Olof Larsson. 2017. 'Populist Online Communication: Introduction to the Special Issue'. *Information, Communication & Society* 20 (9): 1279–92. https://doi.org/10.1080/1369118X.2017.1328525.

Enroth, Henrik. 2017. 'Fear as a Political Factor'. *International Political Sociology* 11 (March): 55–72. https://doi.org/10.1093/ips/olw033.

Esposito, Eleonora, and Sole Alba Zollo. 2021. '"How Dare You Call Her a Pig, I Know Several Pigs Who Would Be Upset If They Knew"*: A Multimodal Critical Discursive Approach to Online Misogyny against UK MPs on YouTube'. *Journal of Language Aggression and Conflict* 9 (1): 47–75.

Farhi, Paul. 2015. 'Why Does Bernie Sanders Dress Like That? Because He Can'. *The Washington Post*, 13 October, sec. Style. https://www.washingtonpost.com/lifestyle/style/why-does-bernie-sanders-dress-like-that-because-he-can/2015/10/12/55ca840e-6141-11e5-b38e-06883aacba64_story.html.

Featherstone, David, and Lazaros Karaliotas. 2019. 'Populism'. *Soundings* 72 (72): 31–47. https://doi.org/10.3898/SOUN.72.02.2019.

Fieschi, Catherine. 2004. 'Introduction'. *Journal of Political Ideologies* 9 (3): 235–40. https://doi.org/10.1080/1356931042000263492.

Fincham, Benjamin. 2016. *The Sociology of Fun*. London, UK: Palgrave Macmillan.

Fine, Gary Alan, and Michaela de Soucey. 2005. 'Joking Cultures: Humor Themes as Social Regulation in Group Life'. *Humor – International Journal of Humor Research* 18 (1): 1–22. https://doi.org/10.1515/humr.2005.18.1.1.

Fine, Gary Alan, and Ugo Corte. 2017. 'Group Pleasures: Collaborative Commitments, Shared Narrative, and the Sociology of Fun'. *Sociological Theory* 35 (1): 64–86. https://doi.org/10.1177/0735275117692836.

Finlay, Linda. 2005. '"Reflexive Embodied Empathy": A Phenomenology of Participant-Researcher Intersubjectivity'. *The Humanistic Psychologist* 33 (4): 271–92. https://doi.org/10.1207/s15473333thp3304_4.

Finlayson, Alan. 2020. 'YouTube and Political Ideologies: Technology, Populism and Rhetorical Form'. *Political Studies* (July): 003232172093463. https://doi.org/10.1177/0032321720934630.

Fischer-Lichte, Erika. 2002. *History of European Drama and Theatre*. London, UK; New York, NY: Routledge.

Fisher, Tony. 2011. 'Radical Democratic Theatre'. *Performance Research* 16 (4): 15–26. https://doi.org/10.1080/13528165.2011.606046.

———. 2017. 'Introduction: Performance and the Tragic Politics of the Agōn'. In *Performing Antagonism*, edited by Tony Fisher and Eve Katsouraki, 1–23. London, UK: Palgrave Macmillan. https://doi.org/10.1057/978-1-349-95100-0_1.

Forgette, Richard. 2004. *Congress, Parties, & Puzzles: Politics as a Team Sport*. Popular Politics & Governance in America, v. 7. New York, NY: Peter Lang.

Fortier, Mark. 2002. *Theory/Theatre: An Introduction*. 2nd ed. London, UK: Routledge.

Foucault, Michel. 1975. *Discipline and Punish: The Birth of the Prison*. New York, NY: Pantheon Books.

Foyn Bruun, Ellen. 2015. 'Listen Carefully'. *Dramatherapy* 37 (1): 3–14. https://doi.org/10.1080/02630672.2015.1076016.

Freeden, Michael. 2017. 'After the Brexit Referendum: Revisiting Populism as an Ideology'. *Journal of Political Ideologies* 22 (1): 1–11. https://doi.org/10.1080/13569317.2016.1260813.

Freeden, Michael, Lyman Tower Sargent, and Marc Stears, eds. 2013. *The Oxford Handbook of Political Ideologies*. 1st ed. Oxford Handbooks in Politics & International Relations. Oxford, UK: Oxford University Press.

Friedberg, Anne. 2009. *The Virtual Window: From Alberti to Microsoft*. 1st paperback ed. Cambridge, MA: MIT Press.

Gabbatt, Adam. 2015. 'Donald Trump's Tirade on Mexico's "Drugs and Rapists" Outrages US Latinos'. *The Guardian*, 16 June 2015, sec. US Elections 2016. https://www.theguardian.com/us-news/2015/jun/16/donald-trump-mexico-presidential-speech-latino-hispanic.

Gamble, Christopher N., Joshua S. Hanan, and Thomas Nail. 2019. 'What is New Materialism?' *Angelaki* 24 (6): 111–34. https://doi.org/10.1080/0969725X.2019.1684704.

Garber, Elizabeth. 2019. 'Objects and New Materialisms: A Journey across Making and Living with Objects'. *Studies in Art Education* 60 (1): 7–21. https://doi.org/10.1080/00393541.2018.1557454.

Garner, Stanton. 2019. *Bodied Spaces: Phenomenology and Performance in Contemporary Drama*. Ithaca, NY: Cornell University Press. https://doi.org/10.7591/9781501735370.

Gebhardt, Mareike. 2021. 'The Populist Moment: Affective Orders, Protest, and Politics of Belonging'. *Distinktion: Journal of Social Theory* 22 (2): 129–51. https://doi.org/10.1080/1600910X.2019.1653346.

Gerbaudo, Paolo. 2017. *The Mask and the Flag: Populism, Citizenism and Global Protest*. New York: Oxford University Press.

———. 2018. 'Social Media and Populism: An Elective Affinity?' *Media, Culture & Society* 40 (5): 745–53. https://doi.org/10.1177/0163443718772192.

Goffman, Erving. 1956. *The Presentation of Self in Everyday Life*. New York, NY: Knopf Doubleday Publishing Group.

Goktepe, Katherine. 2018. '"Sometimes I Mean Things so Much I *Have* to Act": Theatrical Acting and Democracy'. *Constellations* 25 (3): 373–87. https://doi.org/10.1111/1467-8675.12350.

Gomberg-Muñoz, Ruth. 2016. 'Hardship Politics: The Strategic Sharing of Migration Stories'. *Journal of Contemporary Ethnography* 45 (6): 741–64. https://doi.org/10.1177/0891241616652192.

Gonawela, A'ndre, Joyojeet Pal, Udit Thawani, Elmer van der Vlugt, Wim Out, and Priyank Chandra. 2018. 'Speaking Their Mind: Populist Style and Antagonistic Messaging in the Tweets of Donald Trump, Narendra Modi, Nigel Farage, and Geert Wilders'. *Computer Supported Cooperative Work (CSCW)* 27 (3–6): 293–326. https://doi.org/10.1007/s10606-018-9316-2.

Goodwin, Jeff, James M. Jasper, and Francesca Polletta, eds. 2001. *Passionate Politics: Emotions and Social Movements*. Chicago, IL: University of Chicago Press.

Graber, Naomi. 2017. 'Do You Hear the People Sing? Theater and Theatricality in the Trump Campaign'. *American Music* 35 (4): 435–45.

Grant, David. 2020. '"Objects with Objectives": Applied Puppetry from Practice into Theory'. *Applied Theatre Research* 8 (1): 13–29. https://doi.org/10.1386/atr_00023_1.

Green, Jeffrey E. 2010. *The Eyes of the People: Democracy in an Age of Spectatorship*. Oxford: Oxford University Press.

Gregg, Melissa, and Gregory J. Seigworth, eds. 2010. *The Affect Theory Reader*. Durham, NC: Duke University Press.

Gross, Justin H., and Kaylee T. Johnson. 2016. 'Twitter Taunts and Tirades: Negative Campaigning in the Age of Trump'. *PS: Political Science & Politics* 49 (04): 748–54. https://doi.org/10.1017/S1049096516001700.

Grosz, Elizabeth. 1987. 'Notes towards a Corporeal Feminism'. *Australian Feminist Studies* 2 (5): 1–16. https://doi.org/10.1080/08164649.1987.9961562.

———. 1994. *Volatile Bodies: Toward a Corporeal Feminism*. Theories of Representation and Difference. Bloomington, IN: Indiana University Press.

———. 1999. 'Darwin and Feminism: Preliminary Investigations for a Possible Alliance'. *Australian Feminist Studies* 14 (29): 31–45. https://doi.org/10.1080/08164649993317.

Gruzd, A., S. Doiron, and P. Mai. 2011. 'Is Happiness Contagious Online? A Case of Twitter and the 2010 Winter Olympics'. In *2011 44th Hawaii International Conference on System Sciences*, 1–9. Kauai, HI: IEEE. https://doi.org/10.1109/HICSS.2011.259.

Haans, Antal, and Wijnand IJsselsteijn. 2006. 'Mediated Social Touch: A Review of Current Research and Future Directions'. *Virtual Reality* 9 (2–3): 149–59. https://doi.org/10.1007/s10055-005-0014-2.

Habermas, Jürgen. 1979. *Communication and the Evolution of Society.* Boston, MA: Beacon Pr.

———. 1987. *The Theory of Communicative Action. A Critique of Functionalist Reason Volume 2 Lifeworld and System Volume 2 Lifeworld and System.* Translated by Thomas McCarthy. London: Polity Press.

Halberstam, Jack. 2011. *The Queer Art of Failure.* Durham NC: Duke University Press. https://doi.org/10.1215/9780822394358.

Hall, Kira, Donna M. Goldstein, and Matthew Bruce Ingram. 2016. 'The Hands of Donald Trump: Entertainment, Gesture, Spectacle'. *HAU: Journal of Ethnographic Theory* 6 (2): 71–100. https://doi.org/10.14318/hau6.2.009.

Hall, Todd H., and Andrew A.G. Ross. 2019. 'Rethinking Affective Experience and Popular Emotion: World War I and the Construction of Group Emotion in International Relations'. *Political Psychology* 40 (6): 1357–72. https://doi.org/10.1111/pops.12608.

Hameleers, Michael, Linda Bos, and Claes H. de Vreese. 2017. 'The Appeal of Media Populism: The Media Preferences of Citizens with Populist Attitudes'. *Mass Communication and Society* 20 (4): 481–504. https://doi.org/10.1080/15205436.2017.1291817.

Hannan, Jason. 2018. 'Trolling Ourselves to Death? Social Media and Post-Truth Politics'. *European Journal of Communication* 33 (2): 214–26. https://doi.org/10.1177/0267323118760323.

Haraway, Donna. 1991. *Simians, Cyborgs, and Women: The Reinvention of Nature.* Reprinted. Abingdon UK: Routledge.

Harding, James, and John Rouse, eds. 2006. *Not the Other Avant-Garde: The Transnational Foundations of Avant-Garde Performance.* Ann Arbor, MI: University of Michigan Press. https://doi.org/10.3998/mpub.166699.

Hardt, Michael, and Antonio Negri. 2005. *Multitude: War and Democracy in the Age of Empire.* New York, NY: Penguin Books.

Harris, Anne M., and Stacy Linn Holman Jones. 2019. *The Queer Life of Things: Performance, Affect, and the More-Than-Human.* Lanham, MD: Lexington Books.

Hart, Roy. 1967. 'How a Voice Gave Me a Conscience'.*Presented at the 7th International Congress of Psychotherapy*, Wiesbaden, August. http://www.roy-hart.com/hvgmc.htm.

Haseman, Brad, and Joe Winston. 2010. '"Why Be Interested?" Aesthetics, Applied Theatre and Drama Education'. *Research in Drama Education: The Journal of Applied Theatre and Performance* 15 (4): 465–75. https://doi.org/10.1080/13569783.2010.512182.

Hast, Susanna. 2018. *Sounds of War: Aesthetics, Emotions and Chechnya.* https://www.e-ir.info/publication/sounds-of-war-aesthetics-emotions-and-chechnya/.

Hastrup, Kirsten. 1995. *A Passage to Anthropology: Between Experience and Theory.* New York, NY: Routledge.

Heyes, Cecilia, and Caroline Catmur. 2022. 'What Happened to Mirror Neurons?'. *Perspectives on Psychological Science* 17 (1): 153–68. https://doi.org/10.1177/1745691621990638.

Hickey-Moody, Anna Catherine. 2020. 'New Materialism, Ethnography, and Socially Engaged Practice: Space-Time Folds and the Agency of Matter'. *Qualitative Inquiry* 26 (7): 724–32. https://doi.org/10.1177/1077800418810728.

Highmore, Ben, Melissa Gregg, and Gregory J. Seigworth. 2010. 'Bitter after Taste: Affect, Food, and Social Aesthetics'. In *The Affect Theory Reader*, 118–37. Durham, NC: Duke University Press.

Hoffmann, Christian R. 2018. 'Crooked Hillary and Dumb Trump: The Strategic Use and Effect of Negative Evaluations in US Election Campaign Tweets'. *Internet Pragmatics* 1 (1): 55–87. https://doi.org/10.1075/ip.00004.hof.

Hoggett, Paul, and Simon Thompson, eds. 2012. *Politics and the Emotions: The Affective Turn in Contemporary Political Studies*. New York, NY: Continuum.

Homolar, Alexandra, and Ronny Scholz. 2019. 'The Power of Trump-Speak: Populist Crisis Narratives and Ontological Security'. *Cambridge Review of International Affairs* 32 (3): 344–64. https://doi.org/10.1080/09557571.2019.1575796.

Honig, Bonnie. 2011. *Emergency Politics: Paradox, Law, Democracy*. Second printing and First paperback printing. Princeton, NJ: Princeton University Press.

Howe, Kelly. 2021. 'Constraints and Possibilities in the Flesh: the Body in Theatre of the Oppressed'. In The Routledge Companion to Theatre of the Oppressed, edited by Kelly Howe, Julian Boal and José Soeiro, 76–85. Abingdon, UK: Routledge.

Howe, Kelly, Julian Boal, and José Soeiro, eds. 2021. The Routledge Companion to Theatre of the Oppressed. Abingdon, UK: Routledge.

Hutchison, Emma. 2019. 'Emotions, Bodies, and the Un/Making of International Relations'. *Millennium: Journal of International Studies* 47 (2): 284–98. https://doi.org/10.1177/0305829818811243.

Hutchison, Emma, and Roland Bleiker. 2014. 'Theorizing Emotions in World Politics'. *International Theory* 6 (3): 491–514. https://doi.org/10.1017/S1752971914000232.

Ihde, Don. 2007. *Listening and Voice Phenomenologies of Sound*. Albany, NY: State University of New York Press. http://site.ebrary.com/id/10575797.

Irigaray, Luce. 1985. *This Sex Which Is Not One*. Ithaca, NY: Cornell University Press.

Jacobs, Jerry A. 2013. *In Defense of Disciplines: Interdisciplinarity and Specialization in the Research University*. Chicago, IL; London, UK: The University of Chicago Press.

Jäger, Anton, and Arthur Borriello. 2020. 'Left-Populism on Trial: Laclauian Politics in Theory and Practice'. *Theory & Event* 23 (3): 740–64.

Jannarone, Kimberly. 2001. 'Puppetry and Pataphysics: Populism and the Ubu Cycle'. *New Theatre Quarterly* 17 (3): 239–53. https://doi.org/10.1017/S0266464X00014755.

Jenkins, Laura. 2005. 'Corporeal Ontology: Beyond Mind-Body Dualism?'. *Politics* 25 (1): 1–11. https://doi.org/10.1111/j.1467-9256.2005.00223.x.

Jensen, Ole B., Sven Kesselring, and Mimi Sheller, eds. 2019. *Mobilities and Complexities*. 1st ed. Abingdon, Oxon; New York: Routledge.

Jessop, Bob, and Ngai-Ling Sum. 2001. 'Pre-Disciplinary and Post-Disciplinary Perspectives'. *New Political Economy* 6 (1): 89–101. https://doi.org/10.1080/13563460020027777.

Kalpokas, Ignas. 2019. 'Affective Encounters of the Algorithmic Kind: Post-Truth and Posthuman Pleasure'. *Social Media + Society* 5 (2): 205630511984567. https://doi.org/10.1177/2056305119845678.

Kaltwasser, Cristobal Rovira, Paul Taggart, Paulina Ochoa Espejo, and Pierre Ostiguy, eds. 2017. *The Oxford Handbook of Populism*. Oxford, UK: Oxford University Press.

Kant, Immanuel. 2005. *Critique of Judgement*. New York: Dover.

Karagiannis, Nathalie, and Peter Wagner. 2005. 'Towards a Theory of Synagonism⋆'. *Journal of Political Philosophy* 13 (3): 235–62. https://doi.org/10.1111/j.1467-9760.2005.00222.x.

———. 2008. 'Varieties of Agonism: Conflict, the Common Good, and the Need for Synagonism'. *Journal of Social Philosophy* 39 (3): 323–39. https://doi.org/10.1111/j.1467-9833.2008.00428.x.

Keller, Tobias R., and Ulrike Klinger. 2019. 'Social Bots in Election Campaigns: Theoretical, Empirical, and Methodological Implications'. *Political Communication* 36 (1): 171–89. https://doi.org/10.1080/10584609.2018.1526238.

Kenny, Michael. 2017. 'Back to the Populist Future?: Understanding Nostalgia in Contemporary Ideological Discourse'. *Journal of Political Ideologies* 22 (3): 256–73. https://doi.org/10.1080/13569317.2017.1346773.

Kershaw, Baz. 1992. *The Politics of Performance: Radical Theatre as Cultural Intervention.* London; New York: Routledge.

———. 1999. *The Radical in Performance: Between Brecht and Baudrillard.* London, UK; New York, NY: Routledge.

Kim, Youngmi. 2008. 'Digital Populism in South Korea? Internet Culture and the Trouble with Direct Participation'. *Korea Economic Institute Academic Paper Series* 3 (8): 113–26.

Kitchen, Jennifer. 2020. 'Theatre and Drama Education and Populism: The Ensemble "Family" as a Space for Dialogic Empathy and Civic Care'. *British Educational Research Journal* (July. https://doi.org/10.1002/berj.3668.

Klein, Julie Thompson. 2010. 'A Taxonomy of Interdisciplinarity'. In *Oxford Handbook of Interdisciplinarity,* edited by Julie Thompson Klein, Robert Frodeman, and Carl Mitchem, 15–30. Oxford, UK: Oxford University Press.

Klinger, Ulrike, and Jakob Svensson. 2015. 'The Emergence of Network Media Logic in Political Communication: A Theoretical Approach'. *New Media & Society* 17 (8): 1241–57. https://doi.org/10.1177/1461444814522952.

Koefoed Hansen, Lone. 2011. 'The Interface at the Skin'. In *Interface Criticism,* edited by Christian Ulrik Andersen and Soren Bro Pold, 63–90. Aarhus, Denmark: Aarhus University Press.

Kourilsky, Françoise. 1974. '*Peter Schumann's Bread and Puppet Theatre*: Dada and Circus'. *The Drama Review* 18 (1): 104–09. https://doi.org/10.2307/1144868.

Kringelbach, Morten L., and Kent C. Berridge. 2009. 'Towards a Functional Neuroanatomy of Pleasure and Happiness'. *Trends in Cognitive Sciences* 13 (11): 479–87. https://doi.org/10.1016/j.tics.2009.08.006.

Kurylo, Bohdana. 2020. 'The Discourse and Aesthetics of Populism as Securitisation Style'. *International Relations* (November): 004711782097307. https://doi.org/10.1177/0047117820973071.

Laclau, Ernesto. 2005. *On Populist Reason.* London, UK: Verso.

Laclau, Ernesto and Chantal Mouffe. 1985. *Hegemony and Socialist Strategy: Towards a Radical Democratic Politics.* 2nd ed. Radical Thinkers. London, UK: Verso.

Latour, Bruno. 2007. *Reassembling the Social: An Introduction to Actor-Network-Theory.* Oxford, UK: Oxford University Press.

Leder, Drew. 1990. *The Absent Body.* Chicago, IL: University of Chicago Press.

Lederman, Shmuel. 2014. 'Agonism and Deliberation in Arendt: Agonism and Deliberation in Arendt: Shmuel Lederman'. *Constellations* 21 (3): 327–37. https://doi.org/10.1111/1467-8675.12096.

Le Feuvre, Lisa. 2019. 'Extending Bodies'. *Tate Etc.* (blog). 2019. https://www.tate.org.uk/tate-etc/issue-36-spring-2016/extending-bodies.

Liddle, Roger. 2017. 'Some Lessons of the SDP for Labour's Present Predicament'. *The Political Quarterly* 88 (1): 76–86. https://doi.org/10.1111/1467-923X.12334.

Linds, Warren. 1998. 'A Journey in Metaxis: Theatre of the Oppressed as Enactivist Praxis'. *N.A.D.I.E. Journal* 22 (3): 71–86.

Linklater, Kristin. 1976. *Freeing the Natural Voice.* 1st ed. New York, NY: Drama Book Specialists.

Little, Adrian, and Moya Lloyd. 2009. *The Politics of Radical Democracy*. Edinburgh, UK: Edinburgh University Press.

Lyall, Catherine. 2019. *Being an Interdisciplinary Academic: How Institutions Shape University Careers*. Cham, Switzerland: Palgrave Pivot.

Macaulay, Marcia. 2019. 'Bernie and the Donald: A Comparison of Left- and Right-Wing Populist Discourse'. In *Populist Discourse*, edited by Marcia Macaulay, 165–95. Cham, Switzerland: Springer International Publishing. https://doi.org/10.1007/978-3-319-97388-3_6.

Machin, Amanda. 2014. 'Mouffe, Merleau-Ponty and Others: The View from Somewhere?' *Parallax* 20 (2): 73–87. https://doi.org/10.1080/13534645.2014.896553.

Magnat, Virginie. 2016. 'Decolonizing Performance Research'. *Études Anglaises* 69 (2): 135–48.

———. 2021. *The Performative Power of Vocality*. Abingdon, UK: Routledge.

Maly, Ico. 2020. 'Algorithmic Populism and the Datafication and Gamification of the People by Flemish Interest in Belgium'. *Trabalhos Em Linguística Aplicada* 59 (1): 444–68. https://doi.org/10.1590/010318136858816202000409.

Malzacher, Florian. 2020. 'Theatre as Assembly'. In *Why Theatre*, edited by Kaatje de Geest, Carmen Hornbostel, and Milo Rau, 170–73. Berlin, Germany: Verbrecher Verlag.

Manning, Erin. 2007. *Politics of Touch: Sense, Movement, Sovereignty*. Minneapolis, MN: University of Minnesota Press.

———. 2016. *The Minor Gesture*. Durham, NC: Duke University Press.

March, Luke. 2017. 'Left and Right Populism Compared: The British Case'. *The British Journal of Politics and International Relations* 19 (2): 282–303. https://doi.org/10.1177/1369148117701753.

Margetts, Helen. 2018. 'Social Media, Chaotic Pluralism, and Populism'. In *Populism in the Digital Age*, edited by Anne Cunningham, 61–68. New York, NY: Greenhaven Publishing.

———. 2019. '9. Rethinking Democracy with Social Media'. *The Political Quarterly* 90 (January): 107–23. https://doi.org/10.1111/1467-923X.12574.

Marino, Angela. 2018. *Populism and Performance in the Bolivarian Revolution of Venezuela*. Performance Works. Evanston, IL: Northwestern University Press.

Markowitz, Shane. 2019. 'The Global Rise of Populism as a Socio-Material Phenomenon: Matter, Discourse, and Genetically Modified Organisms in the European Union'. In *Populism and World Politics: Exploring Inter- and Transnational Dimensions*, edited by Frank A. Stengel, David B. MacDonald, and Dirk Nabers, 302–35. Cham, Switzerland: Palgrave Macmillan.

Massumi, Brian. 1993. *The Politics of Everyday Fear*. Minneapolis, MN: University of Minnesota Press.

Mazurek, Kevin A., and Marc H. Schieber. 2019. 'Mirror Neurons Precede Non-Mirror Neurons during Action Execution'. *Journal of Neurophysiology* 122 (6): 2630–35. https://doi.org/10.1152/jn.00653.2019.

Mazzoleni, Gianpietro. 2008. 'Populism and the Media'. In *Twenty-First Century Populism: The Spectre of Western European Democracy*, edited by Daniele Albertazzi and Duncan McDonnell, 49–64. Basingstoke, UK: Palgrave Macmillan.

Mcclintock, Anne. 2013. Imperial Leather: Race, Gender, and Sexuality in the Colonial Contest. Abingdon, UK: Routledge.

McDermott, Rose. 2014. 'The Body Doesn't Lie: A Somatic Approach to the Study of Emotions in World Politics'. *International Theory* 6 (3): 557–62. https://doi.org/10.1017/S1752971914000268.

McDonald, Michael, and John Curtis Samples. 2006. *The Marketplace of Democracy: Electoral Competition and American Politics*. Washington, DC: Cato Institute : Brookings Institution Press. http://site.ebrary.com/id/10149861.

McKenzie, Jon. 2006. 'Is Performance Studies Imperialist?. *TDR/The Drama Review* 50 (4): 5–8.

McLoughlin, Liam, and Rosalynd Southern. 2021. 'By Any Memes Necessary? Small Political Acts, Incidental Exposure and Memes during the 2017 UK General Election'. *The British Journal of Politics and International Relations* 23 (1): 60–84. https://doi.org/10.1177/1369148120930594.

McLuhan, Marshall. 2010. *Understanding Media: The Extensions of Man*. Repr. Routledge Classics. London, UK: Routledge.

McRobbie, Angela. 2020. *Feminism and the Politics Of 'Resilience' Essays on Gender, Media and the End of Welfare*. Cambridge UK: Polity Press.

McSmith, Andy. 2014. 'UKIP Spin Doctor Forced to Intervene as Farage Falters in Disastrous Radio Interview'. *The Independent*, 14 May 2014, sec. UK Politics. https://www.independent.co.uk/news/uk/politics/ukip-spin-doctor-forced-to-intervene-as-farage-falters-in-disastrous-radio-interview-9387776.html.

Mello, Alissa. 2016. 'Trans-Embodiment: Embodied Practice in Puppet and Material Performance'. *Performance Research* 21 (5): 49–58. https://doi.org/10.1080/13528165.2016.1223448.

Menon, Pratiksha, and Julia R. DeCook. 2021. 'The Dirtbag Left: Bernie Bros and the Persistence of Left-Wing Misogyny'. In *The Palgrave Handbook of Gendered Violence and Technology*, edited by Anastasia Powell, Asher Flynn, and Lisa Sugiura, 375–93. Cham, Switzerland: Springer International Publishing. https://doi.org/10.1007/978-3-030-83734-1_19.

Merleau-Ponty, Maurice, and Donald A. Landes. 2013. *Phenomenology of Perception*. Abingdon UK: Routledge.

Miller, Patrick R., and Pamela Johnston Conover. 2015. 'Red and Blue States of Mind: Partisan Hostility and Voting in the United States'. *Political Research Quarterly* 68 (2): 225–39. https://doi.org/10.1177/1065912915577208.

Moffitt, Benjamin. 2016. *The Global Rise of Populism: Performance, Political Style, and Representation*. Stanford, CA: Stanford University Press.

Moore, Andrew. 2019. 'Hedonism'. In *The Stanford Encyclopedia of Philosophy*, edited by Edward N. Zalta. https://plato.stanford.edu/archives/win2019/entries/hedonism/.

Moorhead, Rosy. 2012. 'Sheila Braggins Talks to Rosy Moorhead about Her Biography of Alfred Wolfsohn, the German Voice Coach and Philosopher'. *Times Series*, 10 May. https://www.times-series.co.uk/leisure/books/9699835.sheila-braggins-talks-to-rosy-moorhead-about-her-biography-of-alfred-wolfsohn-the-german-voice-coach-and-philosopher/

Moran, Joe. 2010. *Interdisciplinarity*. 2nd ed. London, UK: Routledge.

Morris, James. 2020. 'Simulacra in the Age of Social Media: Baudrillard as the Prophet of Fake News'. *Journal of Communication Inquiry* (December): 019685992097715. https://doi.org/10.1177/0196859920977154.

Mouffe, Chantal, ed. 1992. *Dimensions of Radical Democracy: Pluralism, Citizenship, Community*. Phronesis. London, UK: Verso.

———. 2000. *The Democratic Paradox*. London, UK: Verso.

———. 2005. *On the Political*. Thinking in Action. London, UK: Routledge.

———. 2007a. 'Art and Democracy: Art as an Agonistic Intervention in Public Space'. *Open! Platform for Art, Culture and the Public Domain* 14. https://onlineopen.org/art-and-democracy.

———.. 2007b. 'Artistic Activism and Agonistic Spaces'. *Art & Research* 1 (2): 1–5.

———.. 2014. 'Populism Is a Necessity'. *The European*, May. https://www.theeuropean. de/en/chantal-mouffe–4/8420-why-the-eu-needs-populism.

———. 2018. *For a Left Populism*. Paperback ed. London, UK: Verso.

———.. 2020. 'The Role of Theatre in the Struggle against Neoliberal Hegemony'. In *Why Theatre?* edited by Kaatje de Geest, Carmen Hornbostel, and Milo Rau,, 192–95. Berlin, Germany: Verbrecher Verlag.

Mouffe, Chantal and Elke Wagner. 2013. *Agonistics: Thinking the World Politically*. London, UK: Verso.

Mudde, Cas. 2009. Populist Radical Right Parties in Europe. Cambridge, UK: Cambridge University Press.

Mudde, Cas, and Cristóbal Rovira Kaltwasser. 2012. Populism in Europe and the Americas: Threat or Corrective for Democracy? Cambridge, UK: Cambridge University Press.

———. 2017. *Populism: A Very Short Introduction*. Very Short Introductions. New York, NY: Oxford University Press.

Müller, Jan-Werner. 2016. *What Is Populism?* Philadelphia, PA: University of Pennsylvania Press.

Munster, Anna. 2006. *Materializing New Media: Embodiment in Information Aesthetics*. 1st ed. Interfaces, Studies in Visual Culture. Hanover, NH: Dartmouth College Press, University Press of New England.

Neelands, Jonathan. 2016. 'Democratic and Participatory Theatre for Social Justice: There Has Never Been a Famine in a Democracy. But There Will Be'. In *Drama and Social Justice: Theory, Research and Practice in International Contexts*, edited by Kelly Freebody and Michael Finneran, 30–39. Abingdon, UK: Routledge.

Neumann, Annja. 2019. 'Wrestling with Marionettes: Entangled Embodiment and Posthuman Agency in Schnitzler's "Zum Großen Wurstel"'. *Austrian Studies* 27: 163. https://doi.org/10.5699/austrianstudies.27.2019.0163.

Newham, Paul. 1993. 'The Psychology of Voice and the Founding of the Roy Hart Theatre'. *New Theatre Quarterly* 9 (33): 59–65. https://doi.org/10.1017/S0266464X00007478.

———. 1994. *The Singing Cure: An Introduction to Voice Movement Therapy*. Boston, MA: Shambhala.

Nichols, Robert, and Jakeet Singh, eds. 2014. *Freedom and Democracy in an Imperial Context: Dialogues with James Tully*. Abingdon UK: Routledge. https://doi.org/10.4324/9780203491461.

Nicholson, Helen. 2013. 'The Poetics of Failure as Pedagogy'. *Research in Drama Education: The Journal of Applied Theatre and Performance* 18 (3): 213–15. https://doi.org/10.1080/13569783.2013.811960.

———. 2014. *Applied Drama: The Gift of Theatre*. 2nd ed. Theatre and Performance Practices. Basingstoke, UK: Palgrave Macmillan.

———. 2017. 'Being Happy'. *Research in Drama Education: The Journal of Applied Theatre and Performance* 22 (4): 461–64. https://doi.org/10.1080/13569783.2017.1376915.

Nowakowski, Adam. 2021. 'Do Unhappy Citizens Vote for Populism?' *European Journal of Political Economy* 68 (June): 101985. https://doi.org/10.1016/j.ejpoleco.2020.101985.

Obradovic-Wochnik, Jelena, and Gemma Bird. 2020. 'The Everyday at the Border: Examining Visual, Material and Spatial Intersections of International Politics along the "Balkan Route"'. *Cooperation and Conflict* 55 (1): 41–65. https://doi.org/10.1177/0010836719882475.

Ocasio-Cortez, Alexandria. 2020. *Congresswoman Alexandria Ocasio-Cortez on Self-Love, Fighting the Power, and Her Signature Red Lip*. Vogue: Beauty Secrets. https://www.vogue.com/video/watch/alexandria-ocasio-cortez-beauty-secrets?c=series.

Odysseos, Louiza. 2001. 'Laughing Matters: Peace, Democracy and the Challenge of the Comic Narrative'. *Millennium: Journal of International Studies* 30 (3): 709–32. https://doi.org/10.1177/03058298010300030501.

O'Grady, Alice, ed. 2017. *Risk, Participation, and Performance Practice: Critical Vulnerabilities in a Precarious World.* Cham, Switzerland: Palgrave Macmillan.

Okagbue, Osita. 2013. *African Theatres & Performances.* Abingdon, UK: Routledge.

Ortolani, Benito. 1995. *The Japanese Theatre: From Shamanistic Ritual to Contemporary Pluralism.* Rev. ed. Princeton, NJ: Princeton University Press.

Ostiguy, Pierre, Benjamin Moffitt, and Francisco Panizza, eds. 2021. *Populism in Global Perspective: A Performative and Discursive Approach.* Conceptualising Comparative Politics, vol. 13. New York, NY: Routledge.

Ott, Brian L. 2017. 'The Age of Twitter: Donald J. Trump and the Politics of Debasement'. *Critical Studies in Media Communication* 34 (1): 59–68. https://doi.org/10.1080/15295036.2016.1266686.

Oxford Languages. 2018. 'Word of the Year 2016'. 18 April 2018. https://languages.oup.com/word-of-the-year/2016/.

Pain, Paromita, and Gina Masullo Chen. 2019. 'The President Is in: Public Opinion and the Presidential Use of Twitter'. *Social Media + Society* 5 (2): 205630511985514. https://doi.org/10.1177/2056305119855143.

Parikka, Jussi. 2012. 'New Materialism as Media Theory: Medianatures and Dirty Matter'. *Communication and Critical/Cultural Studies* 9 (1): 95–100. https://doi.org/10.1080/14791420.2011.626252.

Parviainen, Jaana. 2010. 'Choreographing Resistances: Spatial–Kinaesthetic Intelligence and Bodily Knowledge as Political Tools in Activist Work'. *Mobilities* 5 (3): 311–29. https://doi.org/10.1080/17450101.2010.494838.

Penttinen, Elina. 2013. *Joy and International Relations: A New Methodology.* War, Politics and Experience. Abingdon, UK: Routledge.

Pickering, J. Brian, Vegard Engen, and Paul Walland. 2017. 'The Interplay between Human and Machine Agency'. In *Human-Computer Interaction. User Interface Design, Development and Multimodality*, edited by Masaaki Kurosu, 10271:47–59. Lecture Notes in Computer Science. Cham, Switzerland: Springer International Publishing. https://doi.org/10.1007/978-3-319-58071-5_4.

Plastow, Jane. 2015. 'Embodiment, Intellect, and Emotion: Thinking about Possible Impacts of Theatre for Development in Three Projects in Africa'. In *Anthropology, Theatre, and Development*, edited by Alex Flynn and Jonas Tinius, 107–26. London, UK: Palgrave Macmillan UK. https://doi.org/10.1057/9781137350602_5.

Plato. 2007. *The Republic.* Translated by Desmond Lee. London, UK: Penguin Books Ltd.

Pollak, Sally. 2017. 'Talking Rye with Bread and Puppet's Peter Schumann'. *Seven Days*, 13 September 2017. https://www.sevendaysvt.com/vermont/talking-rye-with-bread-and-puppets-peter-schumann/Content?oid=8058721.

Pooley, Jeff. 2010. 'The Consuming Self: From Flappers to Facebook'. In *Blowing up the Brand: Critical Perspectives on Promotional Culture*, edited by Melissa Aronczyk and Devon Powers, 71–89. New York, NY: Peter Lang.

Postman, Neil. 2006. *Amusing Ourselves to Death: Public Discourse in the Age of Show Business.* 20th anniversary ed. New York, NY: Penguin Books.

Power, Cormac. 2010. 'Performing to Fail: Perspectives on Failure in Performance and Philosophy'. In *Ethical Encounters: Boundaries of Theatre, Performance and Philosophy*, edited by Daniel Watt and Daniel Meyer-Dinkgräfe, 125–34. Newcastle upon Tyne, UK: Cambridge Scholars.

Prendergast, Monica, and Juliana Saxton. 2016. *Applied Theatre: International Case Studies and Challenges for Practice*. Bristol, UK: Intellect.

Press, Clare, Geoffrey Bird, Rüdiger Flach, and Cecilia Heyes. 2005. 'Robotic Movement Elicits Automatic Imitation'. *Cognitive Brain Research* 25 (3): 632–40. https://doi.org/10.1016/j.cogbrainres.2005.08.020.

Preston, Sheila. 2016. *Applied Theatre: Facilitation: Pedagogies, Practices, Resilience*. Applied Theatre. London, UK: Bloomsbury Methuen Drama.

Prior, Hélder. 2021. 'Digital Populism and Disinformation in "post-Truth" Times'. *Communication & Society* 34 (4): 49–64. https://doi.org/10.15581/003.34.4.49-64.

Rai, Shirin M. 2010. 'Analysing Ceremony and Ritual in Parliament'. *The Journal of Legislative Studies* 16 (3): 284–97. https://doi.org/10.1080/13572334.2010.498098.

———. 2015. 'Political Performance: A Framework for Analysing Democratic Politics'. *Political Studies* 63 (5): 1179–97. https://doi.org/10.1111/1467-9248.12154.

Rai, Shirin, and Janelle G. Reinelt, eds. 2016. *The Grammar of Politics and Performance*. Interventions. London, UK: Routledge.

Rancière, Jacques. 1995. *On the Shores of Politics*. Radical Thinkers 21. London, UK: Verso.

———. 1999. *Disagreement: Politics and Philosophy*. Translated by Julie Rose. Minneapolis, MN: University of Minnesota Press.

———. 2010. *Dissensus: on Politics and Aesthetics*. Translated by Steve Corcoran. London, UK; New York, NY: Continuum. http://site.ebrary.com/id/10427317.

———. 2011. *The Emancipated Spectator*. London, UK: Verso.

Reichert, Ramón, and Annika Richterich. 2015. 'Introduction: Digital Materialism'. *Digital Culture & Society* 1 (1): 5–18. https://doi.org/10.14361/dcs-2015-0102.

Reinelt, Janelle. 2007. 'TDR Comment: Is Performance Studies Imperialist? Part 2'. *TDR/The Drama Review* 51 (3): 7–16.

———. 2019. 'Politics Populism Performance'. *Performance Research* 24 (8): 59–68. https://doi.org/10.1080/13528165.2019.1718432.

Repko, Allen F., Rick Szostak, and Michelle Phillips Buchberger. 2020. *Introduction to Interdisciplinary Studies*. 3rd ed. Los Angeles, CA: Sage.

Richardson, Ingrid, and Larissa Hjorth. 2019. 'Haptic Play: Rethinking Media Cultures and Practices'. *Convergence: The International Journal of Research into New Media Technologies* 25 (1): 3–5. https://doi.org/10.1177/1354856518815275.

Rico, Guillem, Marc Guinjoan, and Eva Anduiza. 2017. 'The Emotional Underpinnings of Populism: How Anger and Fear Affect Populist Attitudes'. *Swiss Political Science Review* 23 (4): 444–61. https://doi.org/10.1111/spsr.12261.

Rimini Protokoll. n.d. 'State 1–4'. *Rimini Protokoll* (blog). https://www.rimini-protokoll.de/website/en/project/staat-1-4.

Ringmar, Erik. 2018. 'Eugene Gendlin and the Feel of International Politics'. In *Researching Emotions in International Relations*, edited by Maéva Clément and Eric Sangar, 33–50. Cham, Switzerland: Springer International Publishing. https://doi.org/10.1007/978-3-319-65575-8_2.

Roberts-Miller, Patricia. 2002. 'Fighting without Hatred: Hannah Arendt's Agonistic Rhetoric'. *JAC* 22 (3): 585–601.

Rösch, Felix. 2018. 'The Power of Dance: Teaching International Relations through Contact Improvisation'. *International Studies Perspectives* 19 (1): 67–82. https://doi.org/10.1093/isp/ekx002.

———. 2021. 'Affect, Practice, and Change: Dancing World Politics at the Congress of Vienna'. *Cooperation and Conflict* 56 (2): 123–40. https://doi.org/10.1177/0010836720954467.

Rowe, Cami. 2009. 'That Whole Gender Paradigm: Iraq War Veterans Redefining Security'. Paper presented at International Studies Association Annual Convention. New York.

———. 2010. 'Performance Studies as IR Methodology: Using Performance Studies to Evaluate Dialogic Norm Construction'. *Paper presented at Millennium Annual Conference.* London School of Economics. London.

Rowell, Leslie. 2016. *Oral History Interview with Elka Schumann.* Vermont 1970s Counterculture Project. Glover, Vermont. 1970s-37. Vermont Historical Society. https://www.digitalvermont.org/vt70s/AudioFile1970s-37.

Ryan, Holly Eva, and Matthew Flinders. 2018. 'From Senseless to Sensory Democracy: Insights from Applied and Participatory Theatre'. *Politics* 38 (2): 133–47. https://doi.org/10.1177/0263395717700155.

Ryder, Andrew. 1995. 'Peter Schumann: Puppets, Bread and Art'. *The Puppetry Home Page.* http://www.sagecraft.com/puppetry/papers/Schumann.html.

Sakki, Inari, and Jari Martikainen. 2021. 'Mobilizing Collective Hatred through Humour: Affective–Discursive Production and Reception of Populist Rhetoric'. *British Journal of Social Psychology* 60 (2): 610–34. https://doi.org/10.1111/bjso.12419.

Sakki, Inari, and Katarina Pettersson. 2016. 'Discursive Constructions of Otherness in Populist Radical Right Political Blogs: Discursive Constructions of Otherness'. *European Journal of Social Psychology* 46 (2): 156–70. https://doi.org/10.1002/ejsp.2142.

Salmela, Mikko, and Christian von Scheve. 2017. 'Emotional Roots of Right-Wing Political Populism'. *Social Science Information* 56 (4): 567–95. https://doi.org/10.1177/0539018417734419.

———. 2018. 'Emotional Dynamics of Right- and Left-Wing Political Populism'. *Humanity & Society* 42 (4): 434–54. https://doi.org/10.1177/0160597618802521.

Salverson, Julie. 2008. 'Taking Liberties: A Theatre Class of Foolish Witnesses'. *Research in Drama Education: The Journal of Applied Theatre and Performance* 13 (2): 245–55. https://doi.org/10.1080/13569780802054943.

Sanders, Bernie. 2020. 'Press Conference by Bernie Sanders'. March 4. https://www.rev.com/blog/transcripts/bernie-sanders-speech-transcript-sanders-reacts-to-super-tuesday-results.

Sangar, Eric, and Maéva Clément, eds. 2018. *Researching Emotions in International Relations: Methodological Perspectives on the Emotional Turn.* Palgrave Studies in International Relations. Cham, Switzerland: Palgrave Macmillan.

Sayer, Andrew. 2018. 'Post-Disciplinary Encounters between Lancaster and the Rest of the World'. In *Mobilities and Complexities*, edited by Ole B. Jensen, Sven Kesselring, and Mimi Sheller, 26–32. London, UK: Routledge.

Scarry, Elaine. 2010. *On Beauty and Being Just.* Nachdr. Princeton Paperbacks. Princeton, NJ: Princeton University Press.

Schechner, Richard. 1977. *Essays on Performance Theory, 1970–1976.* 1st ed. New York, NY: Drama Book Specialists.

———. 2002. *Performance Studies: An Introduction.* London, UK: Routledge.

Schlichter, Annette. 2014. 'Un/Voicing the Self: Vocal Pedagogy and the Discourse-Practices of Subjectivation'. *Postmodern Culture* 24 (3). https://doi.org/10.1353/pmc.2014.0011.

Schmitt, Carl. 1996. *The Concept of the Political.* Chicago, IL: University of Chicago Press.

Schneider, Rebecca. 2015. 'New Materialisms and Performance Studies'. *TDR/The Drama Review* 59 (4): 7–17. https://doi.org/10.1162/DRAM_a_00493.

Schroeder, Ralph. 2018. *Social Theory after the Internet: Media, Technology, and Globalization*. London, UK: UCL Press.

Schumann, Max. 2021. 'Elka Schumann in Memoriam'. 2021. https://breadandpuppet. org/elka-schumann-in-memoriam.

Schumann, Peter. 2018. *Concordia Honorary Doctorate*. 2018. YouTube video. Montreal, QC. https://www.youtube.com/watch?v=18jYMP5iYPg.

Sedgwick, Eve Kosofsky. 2003. *Touching Feeling: Affect, Pedagogy, Performativity*. Series Q. Durham, NC: Duke University Press.

Serres, Michel. 2016. *The Five Senses: A Philosophy of Mingled Bodies*. London, UK: Bloomsbury Academic.

Shane, Tommy. 2018. 'The Semiotics of Authenticity: Indexicality in Donald Trump's Tweets'. *Social Media + Society* 4 (3): 205630511880031. https://doi.org/10.1177/ 2056305118800315.

Shapiro, Michael J. 2013. *Studies in Trans-Disciplinary Method: After the Aesthetic Turn*. Interventions. London, UK: Routledge.

Shaw, Eric. 2021. '"This Really Has the Potential to Destroy Us": Jeremy Corbyn's Management of the Problem of Anti-Semitism in the Labour Party 1'. *The Political Quarterly* 92 (2): 211–19. https://doi.org/10.1111/1467-923X.12994.

Shilliam, Robbie. 2021. *Decolonizing Politics: An Introduction*. Decolonizing the Curriculum. Cambridge, UK: Polity.

Shilling, Chris. 2012. *The Body and Social Theory*. 3rd ed. Theory, Culture & Society. Los Angeles, CA: Sage.

Silva, Filipe Carreira da, and Mónica Brito Vieira. 2018. 'Populism and the Politics of Redemption'. *Thesis Eleven* 149 (1): 10–30. https://doi.org/10.1177/0725513618813374.

Skoric, Marko M., Qinfeng Zhu, Debbie Goh, and Natalie Pang. 2016. 'Social Media and Citizen Engagement: A Meta-Analytic Review'. *New Media & Society* 18 (9): 1817–39. https://doi.org/10.1177/1461444815616221.

Sloan, Cathy. 2018. 'Understanding Spaces of Potentiality in Applied Theatre'. *Research in Drama Education: The Journal of Applied Theatre and Performance* 23 (4): 582–97.

Smith, Anthony H. 1973. *Orghast at Persepolis: An International Experiment in Theatre Directed by Peter Brook and Written by Ted Hughes*. New York, NY: Viking Press.

Smith, Matt. 2015. 'The Practice of Applied Puppetry: Antecedents and Tropes'. *Research in Drama Education: The Journal of Applied Theatre and Performance* 20 (4): 531–36. https://doi.org/10.1080/13569783.2015.1073581.

Sotiris, Panagiotis. 2019. 'Is a "Left Populism" Possible?'. *Historical Materialism* 27 (2): 3–39. https://doi.org/10.1163/1569206X-00001832.

Spitta, S.D. 2009. 'Revisiting the Sixties and Refusing Trash: Preamble to and Interview with Peter Schumann of Bread and Puppet Theater'. *Boundary 2* 36 (1): 105–25. https://doi.org/10.1215/01903659-2008-026.

Stanlake, Christy. 2009. *Native American Drama: A Critical Perspective*. Cambridge, UK: Cambridge University Press.

Staufer, Simon Julian. 2021. 'Donald Trump, Bernie Sanders and the Question of Populism'. *Journal of Political Ideologies* 26 (2): 220–38. https://doi.org/10.1080/13569317. 2020.1855777.

Stavrakakis, Yannis, Giorgos Katsambekis, Nikos Nikisianis, Alexandros Kioupkiolis, and Thomas Siomos. 2017. 'Extreme Right-Wing Populism in Europe: Revisiting a Reified Association'. *Critical Discourse Studies* 14 (4): 420–39. https://doi.org/10.1080/ 17405904.2017.1309325.

Steele, Brent J., and Alexandra Homolar. 2019. 'Ontological Insecurities and the Politics of Contemporary Populism'. *Cambridge Review of International Affairs* 32 (3): 214–21. https://doi.org/10.1080/09557571.2019.1596612.

Stehr, Nico, and Peter Weingart, eds. 2000. *Practising Interdisciplinarity.* Toronto, Canada: University of Toronto Press.

Stengel, Frank A., David B. MacDonald, and Dirk Nabers, eds. 2019. *Populism and World Politics: Exploring Inter- and Transnational Dimensions.* Cham, Switzerland: Springer International Publishing. https://doi.org/10.1007/978-3-030-04621-7.

Stephen, Lynn. 2013. *We Are the Face of Oaxaca: Testimony and Social Movements.* Durham, NC: Duke University Press.

Stern, Tom. 2014. *Philosophy and Theatre: An Introduction.* London, UK: Routledge.

Stocking, Galen, and Nami Sumida. 2018. 'Social Media Bots Draw Public's Attention and Concerns'. Pew Research Centre. https://www.pewresearch.org/journalism/wp-content/uploads/sites/8/2018/10/PJ_2018.10.15_social-media-bots_FINAL.pdf.

Sutherland, Meghan. 2012. 'Populism and Spectacle'. *Cultural Studies* 26 (2–3): 330–45. https://doi.org/10.1080/09502386.2011.647646.

Sylvester, Christine. 2003a. 'Dramaturgies of Violence in International Relations'. *Borderlands* 2 (2). https://webarchive.nla.gov.au/awa/20040815195140/http://www.borderlandsejournal.adelaide.edu.au/vol2no2_2003/sylvester_editorial.htm.

———. 2003b. 'Global "Development" Dramaturgies/Gender Stagings'. *Borderlands* 2 (2). https://webarchive.nla.gov.au/awa/20040803015430/http://www.borderlandsejournal.adelaide.edu.au/vol2no2_2003/sylvester_global.htm.

———. 2005. 'The Art of War/the War Question in (Feminist) IR'. *Millennium: Journal of International Studies* 33 (3): 855–78. https://doi.org/10.1177/03058298050330030801.

———. 2013. *War as Experience: Contributions from International Relations and Feminist Analysis.* London, UK: Routledge.

Taggart, Paul A. 2000. *Populism.* Concepts in the Social Sciences. Buckingham, UK: Open University Press.

Tambakaki, Paulina. 2017. 'Agonism Reloaded: Potentia, Renewal and Radical Democracy'. *Political Studies Review* 15 (4): 577–88. https://doi.org/10.1177/1478929916635882.

Tambornino, John. 2002. *The Corporeal Turn: Passion, Necessity, Politics.* Lanham, MD: Rowman & Littlefield Publishers.

Tate, Shirley Anne. 2018. *The Governmentality of Black Beauty Shame Discourse, Iconicity and Resistance.* London, UK: Palgrave Macmillan :Imprint: Palgrave Pivot.

Taussig, Michael, Richard Schechner, and Augusto Boal. 1990. 'Boal in Brazil, France, the USA: An Interview with Augusto Boal'. *TDR (1988-)* 34 (3): 50. https://doi.org/10.2307/1146069.

Taylor, Astra, ed. 2011. *Occupy! Scenes from Occupied America.* London, UK: Verso.

Taylor, Christopher. 2015. '"This Is What Democracy Looks Like!": Occupy and the Local Touch of the Political'. In *What Comes after Occupy?: The Regional Politics of Resistance,* edited by Todd A. Comer, 2–21. Newcastle upon Tyne, UK: Cambridge Scholars.

Taylor, Diana. 2003. *The Archive and the Repertoire: Performing Cultural Memory in the Americas.* Durham, NC: Duke University Press.

———. 2020. *¡Presente! The Politics of Presence.* Dissident Acts. Durham, NC: Duke University Press.

Tesich, Steve. 1992. 'A Government of Lies'. *The Nation,* 6 January 1992.

Tesich, Steve. 1997. *Arts and Leisure.* New York, NY: Samuel French.

Thatcher, Gavin, and Daniel Galbreath. 2019. 'Singing Bodies: Reconsidering and Retraining the Corporeal Voice'. *Theatre, Dance and Performance Training* 10 (3): 349–64. https://doi.org/10.1080/19443927.2019.1637370.

Thompson, James. 2011. *Performance Affects: Applied Theatre and the End of Effect.* Paperback ed. Basingstoke, UK: Palgrave Macmillan.

Tillis, Steve. 1992. *Toward an Aesthetics of the Puppet: Puppetry as a Theatrical Art.* Contributions in Drama and Theatre Studies, no. 47. New York, NY: Greenwood Press.

Tomlin, Liz. 2016. *Acts and Apparitions: Discourses on the Real in Performance Practice and Theory, 1990–2010.* Manchester, UK: Manchester University Press.

Torre, Carlos de la. 2015. *The Promise and Perils of Populism: Global Perspectives.* Lexington, KY: University Press of Kentucky.

Torre, Carlos de la. 2019. 'Is Left Populism the Radical Democratic Answer?'. *Irish Journal of Sociology* 27 (1): 64–71. https://doi.org/10.1177/0791603519827225.

Trump, Donald. 2017. 'Despite the Negative Press Covfefe'. Twitter.

Trump, Donald J., and Tony Schwartz. 1987. *Trump: The Art of the Deal.* New York, NY: Random House.

Tully, James. 1995. *Strange Multiplicity: Constitutionalism in an Age of Diversity.* 1st ed. Cambridge UK: Cambridge University Press

———. 2014. *On Global Citizenship: James Tully in Dialogue.* 1st ed. London, UK: Bloomsbury Publishing Plc.

Tumasjan, Andranik, Timm Sprenger, Philipp Sandner and Isabell Welpe. 2010. 'Predicting Elections with Twitter: What 140 Characters Reveals About Political Sentiment'. *Proceedings of the International AAAI Conference on Web and Social Media* 4 (1): 178–185.

Turner, Jonathan H. 2007. 'Self, Emotions, and Extreme Violence: Extending Symbolic Interactionist Theorizing'. *Symbolic Interaction* 30 (4): 501–30. https://doi.org/10.1525/si.2007.30.4.501.

Van Den Abbeele, Georges. 2019. 'Challenges for a Left Populism: A Response to Chantal Mouffe'. *Global Discourse* 9 (2): 439–43. https://doi.org/10.1332/204378919X15583524285793.

Van Dijck, José. 2013. *The Culture of Connectivity: A Critical History of Social Media.* Oxford, UK: Oxford University Press.

Van Doorn, Niels. 2011. 'Digital Spaces, Material Traces: How Matter Comes to Matter in Online Performances of Gender, Sexuality and Embodiment'. *Media, Culture & Society* 33 (4): 531–47. https://doi.org/10.1177/0163443711398692.

Varga, Darrell. 2013. *Bread and Puppet Theatre.* https://vimeo.com/87924957#_=_.

Varol, Onur, Emilio Ferrara, Clayton A. Davis, Filippo Menczer, and Alessandro Flammini. 2017. 'Online Human-Bot Interactions: Detection, Estimation, and Characterization'. ICWSM Conference. https://doi.org/10.48550/ARXIV.1703.03107.

Vazquez-Arroyo, Antonio Y. 2014. 'At the Edges of Civic Freedom: Violence, Power, Enmity'. In *Freedom and Democracy in An Imperial Context: Dialogues With James Tully,* edited by Nichols Robert and Singh Jakeet, 48–70. London, UK: Routledge.

Vettraino, Elinor, Warren Linds, and Divya Jindal-Snape. 2017. 'Embodied Voices: Using Applied Theatre for Co-Creation with Marginalised Youth'. *Emotional and Behavioural Difficulties* 22 (1): 79–95. https://doi.org/10.1080/13632752.2017.1287348.

Vittoria, Paolo. 2019. 'Paulo Freire and Augusto Boal: Praxis, Poetry, and Utopia'. In *The Routledge Companion to Theatre of the Oppressed,* edited by Kelly Howe, Julian Boal, and José Soeiro, 58–65. Abingdon, UK: Routledge.

Vivienne, Jabri. 2003. 'Pinter, Radical Critique, and Politics'. *Borderlands* 2 (2). https://web.archive.org.au/awa/20040815195109mp_/http://www.borderlandsejournal.adelaide.edu.au/vol2no2_2003/jabri_pinter.htm.

Voelz, Johannes. 2018. 'Toward an Aesthetics of Populism, Part I: The Populist Space of Appearance'. *Yearbook of Research in English and American Literature (REAL)* 34: 203–28.

Vuuren, Petro Janse van, and Christian F. Freisleben. 2020. 'How to Catch a Flying Pig: Facilitating Embodiment Work in Online Rooms'. *Research in Drama Education: The Journal of Applied Theatre and Performance* 25 (2): 268–85. https://doi.org/10.1080/13569783.2020.1730169.

Waitt, Gordon, Ella Ryan, and Carol Farbotko. 2014. 'A Visceral Politics of Sound'. *Antipode* 46 (1): 283–300. https://doi.org/10.1111/anti.12032.

Watts, Jake, and Tim Bale. 2019. 'Populism as an Intra-Party Phenomenon: The British Labour Party under Jeremy Corbyn'. *The British Journal of Politics and International Relations* 21 (1): 99–115. https://doi.org/10.1177/1369148118806115.

Weber, Cynthia. 2006. *Imagining America at War: Morality, Politics and Film*. London, UK: Routledge.

Wenman, Mark. 2013. *Agonistic Democracy: Constituent Power in the Era of Globalisation*. Cambridge, UK: Cambridge University Press. https://doi.org/10.1017/CBO9780511777158.

Weyland, Kurt. 2017. *Populism*. Edited by Cristóbal Rovira Kaltwasser, Paul Taggart, Paulina Ochoa Espejo, and Pierre Ostiguy. Vol. 1. Oxford UK: Oxford University Press. https://doi.org/10.1093/oxfordhb/9780198803560.013.2.

———. 2021. 'Populism as a Political Strategy: An Approach's Enduring – and Increasing – Advantages'. *Political Studies* 69 (2): 185–9. https://doi.org/10.1177/00323217211002669.

White, Gareth, ed. 2015. *Applied Theatre: Aesthetics*. Applied Theatre. London, UK: Bloomsbury Methuen Drama.

Wilcox, Lauren B. 2015. *Bodies of Violence: Theorizing Embodied Subjects in International Relations*. Oxford Studies in Gender and International Relations. Oxford, UK: Oxford University Press.

Wingenbach, Ed, ed. 2011. *Institutionalizing Agonistic Democracy: Post-Foundationalism and Political Liberalism*. Abingdon, UK: Routledge.

Winter, Rachel. 2020. 'Fanon Bernie Sanders: Political Real Person Fan Fiction and the Construction of a Candidate'. *Transformative Works and Cultures* 32 (March). https://doi.org/10.3983/twc.2020.1679.

Wirz, Dominique. 2018. 'Persuasion Through Emotion? An Experimental Test of the Emotion-Eliciting Nature of Populist Communication'. *International Journal of Communication* 12: 1114–38.

Wise, Linda. 2007. 'Essay Voice and Soul – The Alfred Wolfsohn/Roy Hart Legacy'. *Voice and Speech Review* 5 (1): 43–52. https://doi.org/10.1080/23268263.2007.10769740.

Wodak, Ruth. 2015. *The Politics of Fear: What Right-Wing Populist Discourses Mean*. London, UK: Sage.

Wolfsohn, Alfred. 2007. *The Human Voice*. CD. Roy Hart Theatre Archives. Malérargues, France. www.roy-hart.com.

———. 2012. *Orpheus, or the Way to a Mask*. Edited by Jay Livernois. Translated by Marita Günther and Sheila Braggins. Woodstock, CT: Abraxas Publishing.

Wood, Matthew, Jack Corbett, and Matthew Flinders. 2016. 'Just Like Us: Everyday Celebrity Politicians and the Pursuit of Popularity in an Age of Anti-Politics'. *The British Journal of Politics and International Relations* 18 (3): 581–98. https://doi.org/10.1177/1369148116632182.

Woolley, Samuel C. 2016. 'Automating Power: Social Bot Interference in Global Politics'. *First Monday* (March).https://doi.org/10.5210/fm.v21i4.6161.

Writers for the 99%. 2012. *Occupying Wall Street: The Inside Story of an Action That Changed America*. Chicago, IL: Haymarket books.

Young, Iris Marion. 2002. *Inclusion and Democracy*. Repr. Oxford Political Theory. Oxford, UK: Oxford University Press.

Zarrilli, Phillip B. 2004. 'Toward a Phenomenological Model of the Actor's Embodied Modes of Experience'. *Theatre Journal* 56 (4): 653–66. https://doi.org/10.1353/tj.2004.0189.

Zasúlich Pérez Ariza, Vera, and Mauricio Santís-Chaves. 2016. 'Haptic Interfaces: Kinesthetic vs. Tactile Systems'. *Revista EIA* 13 (26): 13–29.

Zembylas, Michalinos. 2020. 'The Affective Modes of Right-Wing Populism: Trump Pedagogy and Lessons for Democratic Education'. *Studies in Philosophy and Education* 39 (2): 151–66. https://doi.org/10.1007/s11217-019-09691-y.

Zienkowski, Jan, and Ruth Breeze, eds. 2019. *Imagining the Peoples of Europe: Populist Discourses across the Political Spectrum*. Discourse Approaches to Politics, Society, and Culture (DAPSAC), volume 83. Amsterdam, The Netherlands: John Benjamins Publishing Company.

Zummo, Marianna Lya. 2020. 'Performing Authenticity on a Digital Political Stage Politainment as Interactive Practice and (Populist?) Performance'. *Iperstoria* (June, No 15, 2020): Populism and Its Languages. https://doi.org/10.13136/2281-4582/2020.I15.589.

INDEX